Rethinking Media Literacy

COUNTERPOINTS

Studies in the Postmodern Theory of Education

Joe L. Kincheloe and Shirley R. Steinberg
General Editors

Vol. 4

PETER LANG
New York • Washington, D.C./Baltimore • San Francisco
Bern • Frankfurt am Main • Berlin • Vienna • Paris

Peter McLaren
Rhonda Hammer
David Sholle
Susan Smith Reilly

Rethinking Media Literacy

A Critical Pedagogy of Representation

PETER LANG
New York • Washington, D.C./Baltimore • San Francisco
Bern • Frankfurt am Main • Berlin • Vienna • Paris

Library of Congress Cataloging-in-Publication Data

Rethinking media literacy: a critical pedagogy of representation/ by Peter McLaren... (et al...).
p. cm. — (Counterpoints; vol. 4)
Includes bibliographical references.
1. Mass media—Study and teaching. I. McLaren, Peter
II Series: Counterpoints (New York, N.Y.); vol. 4.
P91.3 R49 302.23'07—dc20 94-40539
ISBN 0-8204-1802-1 (Pbk.)
ISSN 1058-1634

Die Deutsche Bibliothek-CIP Einheitsaufnahme

Rethinking media literacy: a critical pedagogy of representation /Peter McLaren.. - New York; Washington, D.C./Baltimore; San Francisco; Bern; Frankfurt am Main; Berlin; Vienna; Paris: Lang.
(Counterpoints vol. 4)
ISBN 0-8204-1802-1
NE: McLaren, Peter; GT

Cover design by George Lallas.

The paper in this book meets the guidelines for permanence and durability of the Committee on Production Guidelines for Book Longevity of the Council on Library Resources.

Printed in the United States of America.

Contents

Acknowledgments

We would like to thank Stan Denski, Ron Scott, and Lisa Mclaughlin for their significant contributions to portions of this book. Thanks to Joe Kincheloe, Shirley Steinberg and Michael Flamini for their encouragement in taking on this project. Much appreciation to Doug Kellner for his suggestions and comments. Thanks and love to Laura McLaren-Layera for the cover photo.

The chapters appearing in this volume have appeared elsewhere in modified form:

Chapter I originally appeared in slightly altered form as David Sholle and Stan Denski, "Reading and writing the media: Critical media literacy and postmodernism," in C. Lankshear & P. McLaren (eds.), *Critical Literacy: Politics, Praxis, and the Postmodern* (Albany, NY: SUNY Press, 1993), 297-321.

Chapter II an earlier version originally appeared in *Educational Theory,* Winter 1991, Vol.41, No.1

Chapter III originally appeared in *Strategies*, no. 7, 1994, pp.98-131.

Slightly altered versions of this paper will appear in Christine Sleeter and Peter McLaren (eds.) *Multiculturalism and Critical Pedagogy,* Albany, New York: State University of New York Press, and Peter McLaren, *Critical Pedagogy and Predatory Culture,* London; Routledge.

Some sections of this paper have appeared in Peter McLaren, "Multiculturalism and the Postmodern Critique: Towards a Pedagogy of Resistance and Transformation." *Cultural Studies,* vol. 7, no. 1, 1993, 118-146 and Peter McLaren, "Critical Pedagogy, Multiculturalism, and the Politics of Risk and Resistance:

A Response to Kelly and Portelli," *Journal of Education*, vol. 173, no. 3, 1991, pp. 29-59.

Chapter IV originally appeared in substantially altered form as "Drug abuse, race relations, and the prime time news program," (*co-authored with Ron Scott*) in J. Schwoch, M. White & S. Reilly, *Media Knowledge: Readings in Popular Culture, Pedagogy, and Critical Citizenship* (Albany, NY: SUNY Press, 1992), 63-80.

Chapter V appeared in a altered form as David Sholle, "Buy our news: Tabloid television and commodification," *Journal of Communication Inquiry*, volume 17, number 1, winter 1993, 56-72.

Chapter VI orignally appeared in *The Journal of Urban and Cultural Studies* and *Journal of Curriculum Theorizing*. And an earlier version appeared in *Polygraph* and *Anthropologie et Sociétés*.

Chapter VII appears in a different form in David L. Paletz (Editor), *Political Communication Research: Approaches, Studies, Assessments*. Ablex Publishers, Norwood, N.J. (1994).

Notes on Contributors

Stan Denski is Director of Telecommunications and Assistant Professor of Communication and Theatre at Indiana University at Indianapolis. He teaches in the area of media theory and video production. His articles have appeared in *Popular Music & Society, Tracking: Popular Music Studies, Journal of Film and Video* and in various edited collections. He has just completed a book, *Critical Media Pedagogy,* co-authored with David Sholle.

Rhonda Hammer is an Associate of the University of Toronto Media Centre and an Assistant Professor of Communications at the University of Windsor. She has been involved in the production of educational video programs for over 20 years and has conducted media literacy and video production workshops for a number of communicty groups and grass-roots organizations. Her latest video productions include *Adjust Your Set; The Static is Real* (a video on sexual harassment in the university) 1994 (co-proudction: York University, University of Toronto media Centre and the University of Windsor) and *From Zine to Zone: On Media Fandom* (1993). She tied for first palce for the Zalampas Multimedia Award for best Media production of 1991 for her video *PCA 90—'The Video'*.

She has authored articles and chapters on communciations and feminist theory, media literacy and critical pedagogy, and is completing a study of the colonization of women.

Joe Kincheloe teaches Cultural Studies and Education at Penn State University. He is the author of *Getting Beyond the Facts: Teaching Social Studies in the Late Twentieth Century* (Lang: 1989), *Curriculum as Social Psychoanalysis: Essays on the Significance of Place* (with William F. Pinar, SUNY: 1991), *Teachers as Researchers: Qualitative Paths to Empowerment* (Falmer, 1991), *The Stigma of Genius: Einstein and Education* (with Shirley R.

Steinberg and Deborah J. Tippins, Hollowbrook: 1992), *Toward a Critical Politics of Teacher Thinking: Mapping the Postmodern* (Bergin and Garvey: 1993), and *Toil and Trouble: Good Work, Smart Workers and the Integration of Academic and Vocational Education* (Lang: 1995).

Doug Kellner is professor of philosophy at the University of Texas-Austin. He is the author of many books and essays, including *Herbert Marcuse and the Crisis of Marxism; Jean Baudrillard; Critical Theory, Marxism, and Modernity; and Television and the Crisis of Democracy; The Persian Gulf War;* and *Media Culture.*

Peter McLaren is formerly Renewed Scholar-in-Residence, Miami University of Ohio and Director, Center for Education and Cultural Studies. He is currently Associate Professor, Graduate School of Education, University of California, Los Angeles. His essays have appeared in such journals as *The Harvard Educational Review, Educational Theory, The American Journal of Semiotics, Polygraph, Curriculum Inquiry, Philosophy and Social Criticism, Journal of Education, Cultural Studies, Strategies, Journal of Curriculum Theorizing, and College Literature.* Co-edited books include *Paulo Freire: A Critical Encounter* (with Peter Leonard), *Politics of Liberation* (with Colin Lankshear), *Critical Literacy* (with Colin Lankshear), *Critical Pedagogy, the State and Cultural Struggle* (with Henry Giroux) and *Between Borders* (with Henry Giroux). He is the author of the award-winning *Life in Schools* and the highly acclaimed ethnography, *Schooling as a Ritual Performance.*

Susan Reilly is Professor of Mass Communication at Miami University, Oxford, Ohio. She is the co-author of *Media Knowledge: Readings in Popular Culture, Pedagogy and Critical Citizenship,* and *Writing for the Computer Screen: A Guide for Videotex Writers;* and writer/producer of the award-winning television documentaries "The Fear Inside: Alternatives for Rural Battered Women" and "Hometown in Peril: A Case Study of a Hazardous Waste Dump Site." She is currently working "Transcending the Boundaries: the Bessie Coleman Story."

Ron Scott is Associate Professor of Mass Communication at Miami University. He is interested in non-majority images in the media and is author of chapters in *The Madonna Connection: Representations, Politics, Subcultural identities and Cultural Theory* and *Media Knowledge: Readings in Popular Culture, Pedagogy and Critical Citizenship*. He is presently working on a book titled *Color Bars: The Myth of Diversity on American Television.*

David Sholle is Director of the Mass Communication Graduate Program and Assistant Professor of Communication at Miami University, Oxford, Ohio. His papers on media studies, popular culture and critical pedagogy have appeared in *Cultural Studies, Journal of Urban and Cultural Studies, Journal of Education, Critical Studies in Mass Communication, Journal of Communication Inquiry* and *Journal of Film and Video*. He has just finished a book with Stan Denski on media education and critical pedagogy.

Shirley Steinberg developed the "In-Process Collective" which employs dialogue and social drama in a constantly evolving format. She is the co-editor (with Joe L. Kincheloe) of the new Peter Lang Series, *Counterpoints* and is author of *The Stigma of Genius; Einstein and Education* (with Joe L. Kincheloe and Deborah Tippins, Hollowbrook; 1992). She is the general managing editor of *Taboo: The Journal for Cultural Studies and Education* (Lang: Volume 1, No. 1, 1995). An educational consultant and lecturer, Steinberg is the author (with Joe L. Kincheloe) of *Kinderculture: Exploring Cults of Childhood* (Westview: 1995).

Preface

Douglas Kellner

A media culture has emerged in which sounds, and spectacles which help produce the fabric of our everyday life. Radio, television, film, and the other products of the cultural industries provide the materials out of which we forge our very identities, our sense of selfhood, our notion of what it means to be male or female, of sexuality, our sense of class, of ethnicity and race, of nationality, of "us" and "them." Media images help shape our view of the world and our deepest values: what we consider good or bad, positive or negative, moral or evil. Media stories provide the symbols and resources through which we constitute a common culture and through the appropriation of which we insert ourselves into this culture. Media spectacles demonstrate who has power and who is powerless, who is allowed to exercise force and violence, and who is not. They dramatize and legitimate the power of the forces that be and show the powerless that they must stay in their places or be destroyed.

We are immersed from cradle to grave in a media and consumer society and thus it is important to learn how to understand, interpret, and criticize its meanings and messages. The media are a profound and often misperceived source of cultural pedagogy: they contribute to educating us how to behave and what to think, feel, believe, fear, and desire—and what not to. Consequently, the gaining of critical media literacy is an important resource for individuals and citizens in learning how to cope with a media environment and how to resist media manipulation and to empower oneself in relation to our media and culture.

The articles in this collection practice critical media pedagogy, stressing the importance of developing critical and reflexive approaches to the study of mass-mediated culture and communication, as well as the production of alternative media and culture. The articles embody the importance of combining theory with practice both in the sense that, first, theory can help in the critical analysis of media texts, while the practice of critical media pedagogy can produce new theoretical insights. But, secondly, there is also an activist orientation in some of the studies where critical media pedagogy is employed in the practice of producing alternative media and in teaching others how to engage in media activism.

Such an approach that combines theory and practice is important because all too many of the more influential forms of contemporary critical theory neglect these topics. The Frankfurt School, for instance, developed a powerful critique of the cultural industries and the ways that they manipulate individuals into conforming to the beliefs, values, and practices of the existing society, but the critical theorists lack theories of how one can resist media manipulation, how one can come to see through its ruses and seductions, how one can read against the grain to derive critical insights into self and society through the media, and how one can produce alternative forms of media and culture.

Many of the traditions of cultural studies have produced excellent instruments for readings of texts, research into the audience and the use of media, and analysis of how culture reproduces society, but many of these traditions neglect the issue of critical pedagogy and media literacy. In the light of the evasions of these concerns, it is refreshing to see studies that confront the issues of critical pedagogy in its many ramifications, ranging from criticism of forms of television news and entertainment to developing strategies for the production of alternative media.

The authors attempt to develop a concept of critical media literacy that is distinguished from functional literacy and cultural literacy. Functional literacy refers to the acquisition of the rudimentary skills of reading and writing, while cultural literacy refers to acquisition of basic knowledge concerning one's culture, society, and polity. These are the concerns of standard pedagogy. Critical literacy, by contrast, refers to the gaining of skills necessary to analyze and critically dissect all the forms of culture with which individuals interact, ranging from books to the artifacts of film, television, radio, and the other products of the cultural industries. Critical literacy gives individuals power over their culture and thus empowers them, enabling people to create their own meanings, identities, and to shape and transform the material and social conditions of their culture and society.

The issue of critical media literacy is thus part of a process of critical pedagogy that teaches individuals how their culture, society, and polity are structured and work. Critical media pedagogy involves teaching how to activate students and citizens so that they can learn to more actively create their own meanings, lives, and society. The media themselves are forms of pedagogy so critical media pedagogy needs to counter media pedagogy by teaching individuals how to read and criticize the media and how to produce alternative media and culture.

The authors of the following studies deploy a variety of methods and theories to produce a pedagogy of representation and to engage the crucial task of rethinking media literacy. These approaches range from the critical theories of the Frankfurt School, British cultural studies, critical forms of postmodern theory, social semiotics, Marxian dialectics, feminism, and other forms of critical media, cultural, and social analysis. But the movement of critical pedagogy underlies all of the various studies collected here. All of the authors are concerned with the transformation of education, with producing new forms of pedagogy that will empower individuals and revitalize our decaying democracy. These goals are articulated with particular clarity in the concluding interviews in which the authors speak of their own teaching practices, their own attempts to produce critical media literacy.

The studies collected here address various key topics within the myriad forms of our media society. These topics include presentation of a critical epistemological framework for media pedagogy, dissection of TV news and information, entertainment and advertising in our consumer society, and the production of political spectacle to sell public policy and manufacture consent to specific policies. Indeed, the eruption of the Gulf war provides an excellent case study to demonstrate the powerful effects of media spectacles and the ways that they mobilize support for public policy and produce new ideals and values. After the 1960s, the military fell into disfavor in U.S. society and the end of the Cold War threatened the military with huge budget cuts and possible displacement to the margins of society. The Gulf war enabled the U.S. military to demonstrate its prowess and in turn propagated images of the wonders of U.S. military technology, the power of the U.S. military, and warrior citizens who reveled in the U.S. military intervention, as if it were a sports event.

Concern for critical media literacy and discerning the massive effects of the media in our contemporary society raise the issue of public policy and media politics, and the creation of alternative media. A democratic society involves the active participation of its citizens, which in turn requires that the citizens be informed so that they can intelligently participate in the events and issues of the day. This requires a media that actually informs its citizens and citizens who apply their knowledge to active social participation. The decline of democracy in the United States is partially a result of a media spectator society where individuals passively consume media spectacles and fail to actively participate in their social life.

Overcoming the crisis of democracy thus requires, first, media institutions committed to democratic debate, articulation of a variety of views and voices, and access to a wide range of citizens.[1] But genuine democracy also requires that citizens actively seek out information and apply it in the process of democratic participation in their social and political life. In the current situation of commercial-controlled media, reform of the media system and the creation of alternative media are necessary. Yet it is difficult, if not impossible, for the average citizen to transform the existing media system. However, the new technologies of video camcorders, home computers, short-wave radio—as well as the institutions of public access television,

---

[1] For my own views on these topics, see *Television and the Crisis of Democracy* (Boulder, Col.: Westview Press, 1990); *The Persian Gulf TV War* (Boulder, Col.: Westview Press, 1992) and *Media Culture* (New York and London: Routledge, 1995).

community radio, computer networks, and community media centers—make possible the creation of alternative media.

The new media technologies provide both new challenges and dangers. There is the danger that a new media technopoly (Neil Postman) will further colonize everyday life, as consumers passively absorb 500 plus channels of the same old cultural forms. Yet the new technologies also provide individuals with weapons to produce new forms of culture and to program their own cultural environment. Portable video camcorders and public access television makes it possible for individuals to produce their own television. Computer bulletin boards makes possible a new exchange of information and ideas. Low power radio would make possible more citizens communication via broadcast technologies. Community information and media centers could bring people together to use and discuss media and to empower citizens to seek their own information and to produce their own media.

Thus the new media technologies provide new opportunities for producing alternative media practices and strategies. As the studies that follow argue, critical pedagogy ultimately requires the restructuring of the media, schooling, and everyday life. Contemporary societies are producing wondrous new technologies and immense social wealth, but it is unequally distributed and often used as forms of domination and destruction, rather than to promote human betterment. A critical media pedagogy must intervene in this challenging and threatening situation and struggle to overcome the worst features of existing societies and cultures by striving to create better ones. Critical media pedagogy thus inevitably intersects with progressive politics and the project of radical social transformation. To the extent that these studies contribute to this project, they are advancing both our theory and politics in the present ambiguous political moment.

Introduction

Shirley R. Steinberg
and Joe L. Kincheloe

Critical teacher educators periodically bring up the need for media studies in North American schools, for teachers to develop a critical understanding of the role of media in the formation of the state as well as the production of their own and their students' subjectivity. Such ideas are not typically met with great enthusiasm by the educational establishment; indeed, some of the responses are disturbingly hostile. In *A Critical Pedagogy of Representation: Rethinking Media Literacy,* Peter McLaren, Rhonda Hammer, David Sholle, and Susan Reilly take up the challenge of studying the media in educational settings that fail to encourage such analysis. The authors are committed to the idea that educators must understand the multiple contexts that shape the identifications and desires of students, including the shared experiences they bring to the classrooms. One of the most important factors in the manufacturing of student experience, and the ideological production we call "learning" is media, TV in particular. Both the editors and the authors of this book are dismayed by how little educators make pedagogical use of media experience outside of the analysis of written texts.

The literature within the field of critical pedagogy has dramatically developed in the last ten years. In addition to its conversation with the work of the Frankfurt School, it has grown in its "frank and productive" negotiations with feminist and poststructuralist theory in the Great Hall of postmodernism (McLaren, 1994; 1993; Kincheloe, 1993). The authors recognize the natural union of critical pedagogy with critical media studies, as they focus on ideological critique and confrontation with various social texts such as music videos, news programs and debates surrounding multiculturalism. As critical teachers/researchers, the authors assume the figurative role of psychoanalysts in an attempt to treat the social schizophrenia induced by the simulations of hyperreality. In doing so, they recognize that the disease is not lodged in the patient but is embedded in the structural relationship between patient and the overdeterminations of the late capitalist hegemony. Before treatment begins, however, media critique has to advance; it has to transcend the traditional practice of locating textual meaning as an isolated and decontextualized object of interpretation. No textual meaning can be understood outside of the orbit of the codes of the discourses and the ideological interests that shadow all texts. Without an understanding of how the same cultural texts may be constructed differently by individuals in different situations, or how individuals are simultaneously constructed by those texts, the impact of media will always be reduced to a simplistic cause-effect relationship between producer and receiver. The authors of this book have escaped the shackles of reductionistic "transmission" models of mass communications.

But what does it mean to transcend and escape the Cartesian-Newtonian ways of seeing? Here is where the authors display their talents and political commitments. Understanding that contemporary media helps shape a consciousness that blends uncritically into prevailing social conditions, the authors argue that a critical media literacy requires that students not simply develop the ability to interpret media meanings but also the ways they themselves consume and affectively invest in the media. Such a project encourages students to explore their own sense of historical agency as they come to realize that everyday decisions and choices are not simply "free," nor are they a product of rational decisions alone. Rather, they are semiotically inscribed by emotional and bodily commitments relating to the production of desire and mood, all of which leads, in Chomsky's famous phrase, to the "manufacture of consent." Students, teachers, and cultural workers can utilize such knowledge to help them resist their unwitting consent to adjust social practices by organizing alliances and constructing forms of empowerment that allows them to address the regressive and undemocratic outcomes of postmodern institutions. While effective organizations committed to critical and inclusive conceptions of community certainly exist, their influence still pales in comparison to right-wing alliances. Critical media literacy is necessary in the struggle to construct counter-hegemonic practices that are grounded in a recognition of the complex workings of power in a "democratic" state.

Teachers at all levels need to appreciate the manufacture of consent via the control of images and information. An understanding of the relationship among subjectivity formation, image and information production, and the radicalization of discourse is an important but neglected feature of critical pedagogy. In our classes, we empathize with our students' earnest attempts to understand the dynamics of consciousness construction and the concept of subjectivity. To many of our students, reality has been formulated through corporate sponsorship in a way that misrepresents their own ideological relationship to the material conditions of existence and the creation of a democratic public space. Indeed, what our students designate as knowledge emerges from a media-saturated cultural landscape. If educators and cultural workers are interested in who students are and how their subjectivities are formed, they must address the complex politics of media representation.

The narrowness of political life and the implosion of political vision cannot be separated from the prevailing media illiteracy. Without either an understanding of the historical struggles for social change or an appreciation of alternative perspectives on existing social and educational realities, students are often baffled by their initial encounters with the critical conversation. This is why a critical media literacy is so important to students. As John Dewey realized during the modernist industrialization of America, a new education was necessary for new social conditions. The critical media literacy that concerns us is not designed for the children of Dewey's age but for the children of hyperreality; it addresses their experiences in a manner that serves to bring them into the postmodern educational conversation. The postmodern condition demands a new angle of approach, a new grammar of subjectivity and political agency to produce critical encounters and pedagogical engagement. Indeed, critical media literacy may be the shortest path to an understanding of the humanization of inhumanity and the destructiveness of post-industrial western civilizations.

Of course, it is the western post-industrial version of existence that is privileged by the logic of capital that underlies the media curriculum. With the cost of entering the media market measured in the hundreds of millions of dollars, only the conglomerates can enter the fray. Those groups without such wealth cannot challenge such economic power. When their voice is heard, it is reshaped and bent to the contours of the dominant ideologies. Racism, sexism, and economic inequality are often discussed in such contexts, but not in a manner that connects them to the lived experience of individuals. Here rests the role of a critical pedagogy of media: to take these various forms of oppression and connect them to the real life experiences of students. But critical media literacy is not to be confused with a bourgeois pedagogy that privileges experience at the expense of developing a critical language that interrogates the meanings produced in the name of experience. As particular video clips are analyzed in light of everyday lived experiences, students come to understand the connection between hegemonic social relationships, manifestations of power, and the production of our individual ways of seeing. When students analyze the "talking heads" of TV news shows, for example, they witness the same views articulated over and over again.

Depictions of life in the social margins as told by those who live it are not common media fare. The tendency of the "experts" who regularly appear on the network news programs to blame the victims of injustice is only one of a plethora of TV manifestations of dominant cultural hegemony. George Will, Ted Koppel, Morton Kondrake, David Broder, Sam Donaldson, David Brinkley and other [white boys] of the media establishment have little understanding of oppression and less appreciation of media hegemony. Nevertheless, they continue to appear week in and week out with their pseudo-profundities about American politics and American culture. In their white and upper-middle class-centered assessments of the world, they consistently ignore the social, political, and economic conditions that produce hopelessness among the dispossessed and its accompanying pathologies. In order to develop the ability to demystify such ideological dynamics and to understand the ways they shape their consciousness, students must become critical readers of the media and its relationship to the hegemonic articulation of everyday life. Around this project, *A Critical Pedagogy of Representation: Rethinking Media Literacy* develops its cohesion. The authors strive to develop a transformative alternative practice replete with counterrepresentations and countermemories.

As the authors uncover the ideological positionality of allegedly objective media productions, they also lay bare the politics of representation. To sustain their privilege, dominant groups must control representation, they must encode the world in forms that support their own power and ensure a decoding that remains mystified in its motivated social amnesia. But such an attempt, the authors tell us, is not as easy as many analysts have led us to believe. Indeed, we misconstrue reality when we assume that power groups simply impose their meanings on the symbols and codes of a culture. Systems and language systems are always multi-accentual,which means that lodged within dominant cultural codes are the preconditions for oppositional interpretations. At this point, the critical chasm opens, allowing those dissatisfied with the manipulations of power to expose the oppressive nature of accepted representations. From this vantage point within the chasm emerge oppositional pedagogies of representation that are empowered to trace and to challenge the nature of consciousness construction, the production of knowledge, and the formation of subject positions in the political arena.

The utility of a critical pedagogy of media studies begins to materialize at this point. As oppositional pedagogies of representation expose the hidden processes of social meaning and manipulation, possibilities of empowerment emerge—possibilities of what we have elsewhere referred to as post-formal ways of seeing. In the multiaccentual spaces opened by oppositional readings, languages of criticism emerge that allow students and teachers to move beyond common sense readings of daily life. It is at this point that autobiography and personal experience take a dramatic turn. As hidden social processes are integrated into post-formal ways of seeing, the analysis of student and teacher lives becomes an emancipatory confrontation. Oppression is unmasked at structural and personal levels, as patriarchy, scientism, the logic of capital, and white supremacy are robbed of their Klingon cloaking devices.

Such actions directly address the crisis of meaning faced by the children and adults of hyperreality. As they leave school with little understanding of that which most concerns them, critical pedagogy alerts them to the ways society works, ways success is achieved through good citizenship practices, and the interests served by prevailing definitions of "refined taste," "proper deportment," and "good manners." The mainstream educational purpose of *adjusting* students to the status quo cannot withstand the attempt of a critical lived world in the name of social justice, to develop a public philosophy of difference. Such a philosophy takes multiculturalism seriously, as it redefines the nature of community. In this context hope is rekindled and possibility is reborn. The struggle to transform education into something that matters in the lives of students has begun.

We are proud to be associated with authors of this volume who share the vision and commitment to a radical democracy. As always, we thank Michael Flamini, our editor at Peter Lang without whom this book series, *Counterpoints*, would not have been possible. Michael's courage and social imagination serve as an inspiration to all of us who participate in the fight against oppression and for democratic, inclusive, and emancipatory social institutions. We also want to thank Jenny McLaren for her devotion to this project and for her tireless energy in preparing the finished manuscript.

Chapter I

Critical Media Literacy: Reading, Remapping, Rewriting

David Sholle
and Stan Denski

> "I believe that the system of meanings and values which a capitalist society has generated has to be defeated in general and in detail by the most sustained kinds of intellectual and educational work."
>
> Raymond Williams (1989, p. xxi)

As media teachers/practitioners/critics we hope to offer a vision of a critical media practice linking the shared concerns of critical pedagogy, critical literacy and media studies. Like critical pedagogy, a critical literacy of *media* must focus its energies toward the opening up of new spaces from within which traditionally marginalized and excluded voices may speak. Our approach to both the contemporary mass media and media education is straightforward; the structures of media production, and the corresponding educational structures within which the creators of media products are trained, may be approached as sets of complex social practices which (to varying degrees) either serve to reproduce existing social inequalities or serve to overcome these inequalities in support of an emancipatory democracy. Our task here is to map those areas within the practices of contemporary media and media education which work either toward the continued exclusion of voices which challenge the status quo, or to offer possibilities for empowerment and the potential defeat of the dominant hegemony; the chance and fleeting glimpse of a *promisse de bonheure.*[1]

The media (including its structures of production, distribution, economics, policy, technologies, etc.), media education at all levels, and critical literacy, each exists as a site of struggle across the terrain of contemporary cultural politics in the United States. Further, each contributes pieces toward what we will offer as a new theorization of critical media literacy, offered in the context of the accumulation of media in the postmodern condition. This particular historical moment of postmodern late capitalism is embroiled in various sets of hegemonic practices in which the media plays a central and complex part in everyday life.

PEDAGOGY, SCHIZOPHRENIA AND PRACTICE

Schizophrenia and Media Education

Contemporary media education is characterized by a condition most closely resembling that of schizophrenia. Media educators, trained not as educators but as theorists, live categorically distinct separate lives. These are lives led at desks and in libraries, as producers of media theory; lives engaged in the analysis and criticism of the mechanisms of mass mediated hegemony, describing the intricacies of processes through which dominant cultural values are reproduced, maintained, supported and resisted; lives led envisioning an "other" future, not simply the extension of present conditions. And lives led at the lectern in the media production classroom; lives, at least partially, engaged in the reproduction of dominant culture and dominant practice.

This metaphor of schizophrenia is particularly useful in examining the "split personality" character of the contemporary media educator, a phenomenon engendered by the various *distancing dichotomies* caught up in the practice of "teaching the media." These dichotomies are "distancing," both in impeding

[1] A vision of a future "utopia," not in the sense of the imaginary but in Marcuse's sense of a future society of transformed social relations realizable through political action.

the project of cultural democracy and in creating a rupture, an unbridgeable gap between theories and practices which may actually be alligned. These dichotomies appear and reappear throughout the various structures and processes of contemporary education, and our lives as educators sometimes seem to be lived out in the tensions generated between these various oppositional poles of teaching versus research, teacher versus scholar, teacher versus student, the library (where knowledge is produced) versus the lectern (where knowledge is reproduced), "the ivory tower" versus "the real world," and, what seems to us to be the root of all of these; *theory versus practice.*

These dichotomies, however, have become increasingly problematized by both critical education theory's focused and expansive theorization of pedagogy, and by various aspects of the postmodern condition. This is why it seems to us also, from our positions as media educators/schizophrenics, that the most important contribution of critical pedagogical theory to media studies lies in its potential role as figurative psychoanalyst in the treatment of our metaphorical schizophrenia. That is; the power of a properly theorized pedagogy is in its capacity to disrupt the operations of the distancing dichotomies which lurk at center of our disease.

This metaphor of schizophrenia is also multi-leveled. Henry S. Kariel (1989) suggests this notion of an underlying psychological disorder in commenting:

> Making us aware of our distinctive interests, the knowledge of our impending end alerts us to the way we are needlessly submissive, pathologically distracted and preoccupied. It alerts us to the imposition of autonomous abstractions such as Success, of indispensable ideals and ontologies. It is this knowledge of our finitude which moves me to decenter the optimism and rationalism of the Enlightenment by installing a counter-progressive structure, a map for coping under contemporary conditions (p. *xiii*).

This is the second level of our schizophrenia—the postmodern condition; the uneasy alliance (or, perhaps, split personality) of modernity and postmodernity. Centering on questions of authority and loss of authority in the project of critique within the public sphere, postmodernism seems to ask: From what position do we speak? What is our project? Indeed, can we have a project in modernism's sense—can we speak with authority without silencing others? And so on. Finally, we are faced with the question: How can we construct a non-totalizing politics based in postmodernism's concerns for difference and the other, without altogether erasing the possibility of a vital political project?

The first manifestation of our schizophrenia in the practice of media education and its reappearance in the practice of post-modern cultural politics are part and parcel of a third level of schizophrenia—that of late capitalism and the work of hegemony. In the postmodern, hegemony is won not simply through the transmission of ideas and the control of the population through centralization and homogenization—it operates also through the *abundance of choice,* and the resultant increased fragmentation of the populace.

In capitalist representation, signs are not part of a central code that unifies their meaning and connects them with expression. Rather, as Deleuze and Guattari have described it, the deterritorialized flows of content/expression escape the rigid circuits of capitalist production at which point they become "schizophrenic flux-signs of desire" (Bogue, 1989, p. 102). Put another way; meaning and affect no longer connect through a system of values unified in a coherent narrative (such as a theology or national myth). Instead, redundant and asignifying images mobolize affect without the need for ideological commitment.[2]

---

[2] The Right has been particularly successful in achieving a voice of authority by its management of affective committments through electronic mass media, think tanks, the state educational apparatus, and quasi-public interest groups (Accuracy in Media, etc.). The right's particular "politics of truth" is thus implemented through pedagogical strategies, that is, strategies of maintaining and motivating the appropriation of discourses. This pedagogical dimension was evident in the recent events in the gulf. The war was (is) horrific enough in itself, but even more horrifying is the 91% approval rating of George Bush, itself a reflection of the success of the discursive (pedagogical) campaign of the war in the mobolization of the affective committment of the populace through the deployment of empty signifiers such as "freedom, "the American way of life," etc. The greatest loss for the left in this war, may be the right's success in cementing its control of the direction of committment (even though that committment may be directionless, it is certainly not traveling in the direction of social change). Bush's

Again, another set of distancing dichotomies is evidenced in these schizophrenic moments: modern versus postmodern, centralization versus fragmentation, meaning versus affect, content versus expression, etc. Overcoming these dichotomies will depend on the formation of a pedagogical practice that can link the critical project of modernity to possibilities opened up by the new theoretical ground of postmodernity.

Praxis and Agency

At the center of critical pedagogy is the reconstruction of media theory and practice into media *praxis*: the praxis of media education. Critical pedagogy's disruption of the theory/practice dichotomy leads us toward this emerging notion of media praxis. We believe that any meaningful conceptualization of critical media literacy can only exist within a properly theorized notion of praxis.

Praxis, in the sense which adds most to this discussion, refers to self-creative activity through which men and women create (make, produce) and change (shape) the historical, human world and themselves. Praxis includes an element of critique of existing historical conditions and an element of possibility for reworking those conditions. In addition, the concept of praxis attempts to link or loop together theory and practice—in its strongest sense of "*practice as action.*" The notion of a loop or circuit in rotation is crucial in describing the relationship between theory and practice. In the loop, theory and practice are in a transductive relationship, circulating back upon each other without cancelling each other out. This is not a simple unity of theory and practice, but neither are theory and practice separate activities that merely connect or attach to each other at certain chosen moments.

It is in this sense then that praxis expresses human potentialities, something different both from what simply is, and what merely ought to be. Media praxis suggests, in this specific context, a curricular approach directed at possiblities contained

---

demise is not necessarily an overturning of this direction, as is evident in Clinton's affirmation of Bush's position (despite his campaign strategy of standing for "Change").

within the mass media. Possibilities to counter the soporific and alienating results of both a traditional focus on technology, and a fundamental misrepresentation of the inexorable bond between theory and practice. In the context of a critical media pedagogy, it is through a pedagogy of praxis (one of critique and possibility) that the debilitating effects of distancing dichotomies and a schizophrenic existence are broken down. In the circuit of theory and practice the stance of *professional* and *theorist* as two separate positions can no longer make sense. At the same time, the dichotomy of reading and writing so central to theoritizations of literacy projects is itself *transformed* as existing notions of what it is to read and what it is to write are released from the sterile sphere of technical skills.

Context and Practice

Any pedagogical practice must be formulated in the context of its specific historical location. Media must be examined in the context of their accumulation in the postmodern condition; in terms of the saturation of everyday life by the hegemonic practices of late capitalism and its subsumption of practice under the rubric of *consumerism*; in the situation of the erasure of the marginal and exclusion of the other; and in the light of the place of media in the everyday lives of students who bring this background to every pedagogical encounter. We want to examine the goals of a critical media literacy project in these terms. In its greater location within the projects of critical theory and critical pedagogy, it must seek out silenced voices, address the terror and terrorism of the other, and employ practices directed at the opening of new space for new voices. Where does all this lead? What are the specific elements which inscribe a coherent theorization of a critical media literacy?

PAST MODELS OF MEDIA LITERACY

In looking at past models of media literacy, reinforced is the idea that the distancing dichotomy of the theoretical versus the practical (resulting, in part, from the desparate undertheorization of pedagogy) has set up structures within which current existing approaches to critical media literacy operate. Once these inadequacies in present approaches are uncovered other theoretizations of critical media literacy become possible in the spaces opened up by the disruption of these distancing dichotomies—A disruption resulting from critical pedagogy's interrogations, and postmodern culture's assault upon the grand narratives.

Any adequate approach to media literacy must work within and against these disruptions, particulary in coming to terms with the recent historical conjuncture named and re-named by a number of diverse theorists as "The Postmodern." We will rely on a broad definition of the postmodern, "as among other things, the rupturing of the unitary fixity and homogenizing logic of the grand narratives of Western European thought" (Mclaren and Hammer, 1989, p. 30). For our purposes, this condition includes: the related phenomenon of the dissolution of the opposition of *high art* to *popular culture* ; the construction of subjectivities through consumer myths and images; the construction of lifestyles as affective conditions; and the deintensifying of media production of ideology in favor of the production of difference for difference's sake. We want to explore what media literacy means today in light of these phenomena, but also in light of that other side of the postmodern—its theoretical work in deliniating the politics of difference and identity.

First, we must be clear about what media literacy is not. Early versions of media literacy were constructed on a model of the media acting as a creator of messages that imposed meaning on the audience. These programs of media literacy simply cannot account for the phenomenon of contemporary postmodernism. The simpliest version of media literacy recommends a process of parents monitoring their children's viewing and discussing programs with them. An extension of this view proposes the development of "critical viewing skills"—understanding the grammar of television, the types of genres, the "meanings" that it produces. These approaches are limited by their reliance on a theory of the media-audience link as one of activity-passivity, and on their assumption of familial relationships as nurturing/ authoritarian. These approaches face the further limitation imposed by liberal undertheorizations of "critical thinking" in which all politics are removed from the concept of "critical," reducing it to the level of the banal and unproblematic discussion of "cognitive thinking skills."[3]

A second and similar attempt at a media literacy program is based in the notion of "visual literacy." Again; this is a skills-based approach rooted in developing visual competence: an understanding of spatial construction, movement, film grammar, and so on. All of these approaches also rely on a notion of *descrimination,* that is; media literacy involves judging what is *good* and *bad* in media content. This descrimination may pertain to judging the political correctness of media or its status as "art." Such judgements are foreordained by a preselected canon of standards.

Critical approaches to media literacy differ from these other approaches by focusing on the production/consumption of media in the context of their existence as ideological texts. However, this text-based approach again relies on a communication model of encoding/decoding. Grossberg (1988) explains why the difference between encoding (production) and decoding (consumption) must be abandoned or at least severely amended. This dichotomy between encoding and decoding "divides interpretation into the search for intended or preferred meanings and received or effective meanings" (p. 169). But if one considers the context of communication, these two moments are never wholly seperable. "Encoding is a continuous force and decoding is already active in the efforts to decode" (p. 169).

Accordingly, the notion that ideology functions as an imposition of meaning (often hidden from decoders) upon a passive receptacle ignores the fact that meaning is produced on both sides of the communication situation. Further placing the practice of ideological production within the context of the post-

---

[3] As Peter McLaren (1989, p. 161) notes, "In their discussion of "critical thinking" the new conservatives and liberals have neutralized the term *critical* by repeated and imprecise usage, removing its political and cultural dimensions and laundering its analytic potency to mean "thinking skills...By defining academic success almost exclusively in terms of creating compliant, productive, and patriotic workers, the new conservative agenda for a 'resurgent America' dodges any concern for nurturing critical and committed citizens."

modern calls into question the notion that the primary and only effectivity of modern communication media is in the production of "meanings" as discrete knowledges. If there is any validity to the shift to a postmodern condition—a condition in which signifiers float, in which stable "truths" no longer function as foundations, and in which meaning and affect are separated—then any media literacy program focused upon ideological demystification must be rearticulated.

It is not that the production of meaning in the broad sense of ideology does not exist; rather, it is that *no adequate theory of media literacy can remain simply at this level.* In this chapter we will argue that media literacy must be theorized through and within the context of postmodernism. But how seriously need we take the propostion that postmodernism has fundamentally changed the conditions of media production and consumption? Most important, however, is the question of whether we must abandon the entire ideology project of modernist theory. And, if we do so, do we risk abandoning politics altogether? The chapters in this volume address these concerns *in* a variety of contexts and *through* a variety of approaches—feminist, neomarxist, postmodernist, postcolonialist.

MEDIA LITERACY AND A CRITICAL POSTMODERNISM

Postmodernism, as a form of cultural criticism and as an historical condition, directly challenges the project of modernism. We believe it rightly questions modernism's reliance on the notion of the autonomous individual, the emphasis on the linearity of thought, the aesthetic of rationality and order, the rationality of science in the process of progress, the preeminence of Western European thought, and history as the process of the progress of Western culture. However, we cannot accept the postmodernist stance without question, we cannot simply accept its critique of modernism as total and final, nor can we simply meld the various "Posts" together into a sweeping theory.[4]

---

[4] See, Hebdige, 1988, p. 181.

Postmodern theory makes us aware of how our subjectivity and experiences are constructed, how the meaning we attempt to grasp slips away in our failure to affectively commit to it, how our institutions and discursive formations lead us to erase difference and stand against the "other," and how the production of information and symbols has weakened the link between images and reality. While such a breaking down of our present condition can lead us to question that condition and resist it, there is also the very real potential within postmodern theory for it to lead to *fatal strategies*, wherein resistance is replaced by refusal, and critique by play.

This regressive postmodernism is most evident in Baudrillard's (1988) burned out space of hyper-conformity, and the further aestheticization of his position by Kroker (1988), in which the masses celebrate their own extermination in the black hole of television. Lost in this regressive version of postmodernism is any sense of how people struggle with the images and codes that confront them. Likewise, the affirmation of difference is disconnected from any account of how cultural, political and economic constraints position various groups in asymmetrical power relations. In short, a postmodernism that endlessly plays with literary texts, or maps out a world of simulations in which there is no place from which to speak, erases any critical sense of history or politics (Giroux, 1988, p. 24). Media literacy cannot exist under this view of the postmodern, for within the Baudrillardian space of the electronic simulation of reality the only strategy left for the subject is self-parody.

The bleak nihilism of postmodernist deconstruction must be connected to critical pedagogy's project of reconstruction (from out of the ashes looking back at the end of the world). The pessimism and despair which characterizes the postmodernism of Jameson, Lyotard, and Baudrillard must be understood as emanating from the context of their own individual subject positions. For those whose lives have benefited through the occupation of a position of privilege within these various "grand narratives," the collapse of these structures, the unmasking of the once absolute and eternal as now arbitrary and transient; the retransformation of the natural back into the cultural; the collapse of the mythic back into the arena of the human and the political; all of this will most certainly find their response in words like *crisis, the end of meaning, the end of history,* and so on. However, from the subject positions of those who have been excluded by these narratives, whose own voices have been silenced and marginalized, *such a collapse may be experienced as liberatory and empowering* (McClary, 1989/90). In other words; the response to these "collapses" may range from despair to celebration depending upon your location within a given set of asymmetrical power relations.[5] And this opens up the possibility of a *critical postmodernism.*

It is in this sense that Hebdige (1989) has argued that theories of the "post" have *"no intrinsic political belonging in themselves"* (p. 51). While for Baudrillard, postmodernity is characterized by the utter annihilation of difference and the end of history and politics, a *critical postmodernism* is "identified with diversity and difference, a politics of contestation and change" (p. 52). We must seek to connect postmodernism's notions of culture, difference and subjectivity with the modernist concerns for the language of public life, thus reaffirming "a public philosophy" that broadens and deepens individual liberties and rights through rather than against a radical notion of democracy. By drawing upon this politicized notion of the postmodern, the practice of media literacy can be seen to still offer "vital strategies."

If media literacy is to be advanced within a critical pedagogy, it must be conceived as a political, social and cultural practice. Thus, a critical theory of media literacy must propose it as an arena of practices that still offers strategies that can be taken seriously as "vital." It is crucial then to distinguish between those postmodern positions that lead either to an aestheticiza-

---

[5] These regressive and nihilistic theorizations of the postmodern condition hold within them the danger of the gradual descent into an intellectual cynicism. While political apathy in the face of the intricate workings of the cultural hegemony of late-capitalism is one in an array of possible responses, a celebration of difference and a willingness to work for a future you know full well in advance that you will never live to see is another, preferable response. This is a willingness to participate in what Raymond Williams calls, the "long revolution."

tion of politics or to a cultural pessimism, and that of a critical postmodernism offered by Giroux (1988):

> At its best, a critical postmodernism wants to redraw the map of modernism so as to effect a shift in power from the privileged and the powerful to those groups struggling to gain a measure of control over their lives in what is increasingly becoming a world marked by a logic of disintegration. (p. 162)

As such, a critical postmodernism integrates the elements of the modernist political project with the resistant strategies of postmodernism. As theoretical projects, both modernism and postmodernism are flawed in certain respects, and each needs to be examined for its strengths and weaknesses. In particular, the elements of modernism which link memory, agency and reason to the construction of a democratic public sphere need to be retained in the construction of a theory of media literacy for the present conditions of the postmodern world (Giroux, 1988, pp. 6-7).

THE CONTEXT OF CRITICAL MEDIA LITERACY

Given the above discussion how can a critical media literacy be developed? The location of these matters within the terrain of postmodern cultural theory may help to further flesh out the character of our media literacy theory. In postmodern late capitalist America, our efforts to describe a critical theory of media literacy are caught up in an initial paradox. On the one hand, the increasing development of science and technology provides the possibility of freeing humans from dehumanizing and backbreaking labor. In turn, this freedom offers humanity new opportunities for the development of, and access to, a culture that promotes a more critical and discriminatory sensibility in all modes of communication and experience. On the other hand, the development of technology and science, constructed according to the laws of capitalist rationality, has ushered in forms of domination and control that appear to thwart rather than extend the possibilities of human emanicipation.

Given the existing social formation, the modes of communication are operated predominantly in the interests of oppression. This is not a simple mechanical operation but is tied to the hegemonic conjunture of market, military and political interests. Within this grouping of interests the media serve to construct consensus and dissensus, to reconfigure the relationship of meaning and affect in the construction of a narrative of nation, to surveill the population and in so doing create systems of normalization and subjectification. However, this operation of the media is not a seamless operation closing off all possiblities of alternative use. The media then is a leaky system that is struggled over in its production and reception.

Popular Culture as Background

Our discussion is grounded in the assertion that *educational theory must engage with the popular as the background that informs students' engagement with any pedagogical encounter* . In this, however, the distancing dichotomy of "high" culture versus "low" culture must be avoided. This is not simply a matter of either criticizing popular culture for the purpose of devalorizing student experience, or obversely celebrating the popular in an acritical acceptance.[6] Rather, as Giroux and Simon (1989) suggest, we must consider popular culture as the background of knowledge forms and affective instruments which ground student "voice" (p. 243).[7]

Attending to the popular in student experiences involves not simply valorizing that experience, but working with (and on) that experience. Such a pedagogy must allow students to speak from their own experience at the same time that it encourages them to identify and unravel the codes of popular culture that may work to construct subject relations that serve to silence and disempower them. Popular culture must be viewed as a complex and contradictory sphere in which dominant culture attempts to structure experience through the production of meaning, and which at the same time may provide possibilities for more open democratic formations.

---

[6] Not to be confused with the undertheorized notion of "resistance" as in the recent works of Fiske, Jenkins, etc.(see Sholle, 1990).

[7] See also, Giroux & McLaren, 1989, p. xxiv

Student Knowledge
It has long struck us as odd that the vast majority of students leave school from age 16 on with extremely hazy levels of knowledge about matters which will concern them most in their lives. We am referring to their "knowledge" of: 1) personal health, nutrition and medical matters; 2) social and sexual interaction between individuals and groups; 3) the structure and operation of the state, political organizations, local government, welfare benefits, housing, etc., in short, the economic and institutional underpinning of society (Alvarado, 1990, p. 2).

Currently, however, the popular media works more toward both the erasure of these knowledge forms, and in support of the regressive postmodern definition of "freedom" as the broad choice of consumption objects. The contemporary popular media fragments, creates dissensus, threatens/erases the practical base of knowledge that marginal or powerless groups need in order to take hold of their everyday lives and work toward changing their historical conditions. And the state of media education within the contemporary U.S. university tends to function more as an acritical training ground complicit (at the very least) in an ongoing program of mediated cultural reproduction rather than toward the kind of linking and bridging within a critical pedagogy of media praxis imagined by Alvarado:

> For our purposes today, such distinctions [as those drawn between "theoretical" and "practical"] don't help our understanding of "The Place and Purpose of Media Education . . . What I am indicating here is that, at its best, Media Education involves work on the *symbolic*, media *content*, and *practical work*, together with work on areas which I initially identified as being important, i.e., work on the personal, the social, the economic, the political, the institutional and the contemporary (1990, p. 3).

We are again confronted with the operations of the distancing dichotomy of theory versus practice and the concomitant undertheorization of pedagogy. What other understandings of critical media literacy become possible in the new spaces opened up by the disruption of these dichotomies? What new imaginings of a media pedagogy within a critical theory of the postmodern emerge from these spaces?

The Media Schoolhouse

In the light of these concerns, television can be looked at as a *pedagogical machine*, constructing discourses that function primarily in the locus of a mode of transmission where "culture becomes defined solely by markets for culture" (Wexler, 1989, p. 98). If we are to educate students to become media literate, we must attend to the multiple references and codes that position them. This means paying attention to the manner in which popular culture texts are constructed by and construct various discursive codes, but also how such texts express various contradictory ideological interests and how these texts might be taken up in a way that creates possibilities for different constructions of cultural and political life.

CRITICAL MEDIA LITERACY: THREE COUNTER-HEGEMONIC PRACTICES

One: Re-reading the Media

Contemporary media are themselves pedagogical in function; they contribute to constructions of knowledge and the subject of knowledge. Thus, a first step in a critical media literacy program involves the practice of ideology critique in a confrontation with the text. In the context of postmodernism, this means educating students to become media literate in a world of changing representations. This entails reworking the traditional practice of ideology critique, which tends to locate meaning in the text as an *isolated object* of interpretation. Instead, the practice of critique must involve a number of considerations: 1) The critical reading of how cultural texts are regulated by various discursive codes; 2) How such texts express and represent different ideological interests; 3) How they might be taken up differently by various subjects in different contexts.

In this process of literacy acquisition, ideological criticism is an important first stage in the initial task of taking apart or breaking down the "natural" and "eternal," and its replacement with the *cultural* and the *historical*. It is here also where *hegemony* as the mechanism of ideology is introduced. It is in this introduction to media hegemony that a full array of rupturing practices, processes of demythologizing, and denaturalizing—that is, the processes of *making the invisible visible*—are undertaken. And it is here also where the contributions of contemporary structuralist and poststructuralist literary theory can be examined through the power of its critique in the disintegration of the traditional source centered "transmission" models of mass communication. And it is here where we might begin to consider critical pedagogy's corresponding disruption of "transmission" models of education and examine the collapse of the distancing dichotomies of (among others) "reader/writer" and "teacher/student" necessary for the potential of both media and media education to be realized.

Media as a pedagogical machine is not simply a producer of meanings (an encoding of truths to be appropriated by the "minds" of the audience); it also produces "subjectivity." Certainly, students need to engage media representations as constructive of meanings which discursively set the boundaries of how reality may be approached, but they need to also look at how these meanings are mobolized in everyday life, how they hook up with emotional (affective) commitments that are historically situated. Mark Poster succinctly characterizes these processes of the media in contemporary conditions in a manner worth quoting at length:

> For the subject in electronically mediated communication, the object tends to become not the material world as represented in language but the flow of signifiers itself. In the mode of information it becomes increasingly difficult, or even pointless, for the subject to distinquish a "real" existing "behind" the flow of signifiers, and as a consequence social life in part becomes a practice of positioning subjects to receive and interpret messages. . . . Media language—contextless, monologic, self-referential—invites the recipient to play with the process of self-constitution, continuously to remake the self in "conversation" with differing modes of discourse. . . . The subject has no defined identity as a pole of a conversation (1990. p.14, 46).

At the level of critique the project of media literacy is to break down this practice by reconstituting the context of media communication and the material identity and agency of the reader/writer. Ideology critique is not disconnected from institutional, legal, cultural, political, and economic factors. The *contexts* of the text are both crucial to the reading of its historical construction and as the gateway to the further questions: Who produces images? For whose consumption? For what purposes? What alternative images are thereby excluded?

Most important to this project of a postmodern critical media literacy, this context *must* include the relationship of the reader to the text and the manner in which multiple-identities are produced and reworked in the reader/text relationship through diverse modes of address, closure, identification and re-inscription. Literacy (in its traditional form of learning a language) is a bi-polar practice, one involving developing skills of reading the language as well as speaking it. Media literacy has been treated differently, typically seen as simply the abililty to read or decode media messages. This separation of reading from writing, unwittingly or not, buys into models of communication that foreclose the *very possibility* of an active media literacy.

In terms of a a critical media literacy, it is also significant that this source centered paradigm informed not only early mass communication research, but also the emergence of television itself into its current form. We have known no other norm for the operation of the TV industries in the United States. However, an important facet of media illiteracy lies in the popular affective "common sense" understanding of the way television is as somehow normal and natural (how could it be other than this?). Emerging as a source centered medium and industry, television cares little for the reactions of its audiences, other than in the form of quantifiable data which may be used as a basis for advertising rates.

Revised and expansive conceptualizations of *reading* and *authorship* offered by literary theory, seem an important component in describing a basis for critical reading of mediated messages. In, for example, Barthes' notions of the oppositional relationship between two kinds of pleasure, *plaisir* and *jouissance,* we find this distinction between reading-as-*reading* and reading-as-*writing*. In a more concrete politics of reading, Friere has also proposed such a reconceptualization of literacy: "Reading is re-writing what we are reading. Reading is to discover the connections between the text and the context of the text, and also how to connect the text/context with my context, the context of the reader" (1987:10-11). A practice of reading as writing must address the material context of everyday life in both of these dimensions—Friere's concern with moral and political agency, and Barthes' concern with the politics of pleasure (affective commitment).

The media must be "deconstructed where it hurts," i.e., we need to connect this critique to everyday life and those areas of student experience to which they are actively committed. Ideology critique is counterproductive at best when it simply draws upon an academic jargon to find various myths. Instead, we must question naturalized knowledge, pinpoint areas of ideology that students connect to and that make a difference in their lives. We must take seriously the experiences through which students constitute their identities and draw upon it as means for criticizing the dominant culture (Giroux, 1988, p. 175). This leads us to consider the second area of counterhegemonic practice in critical media literacy.

Two: Affective Reflexivity; remapping Subject Positions

Denaturalizing the text is not an isolated practice. If we know and can see that MTV is sexist in its representation, what implications follow? Do we then still watch MTV? The idea is not to batter and condemn popular forms (the lesson is not; "Ok, now don't watch television."). Instead, we must attend to the *affective investments* that students bring to the text—why do they watch what they watch, who do they watch it with, and what do they do with it?. Again, we must question the communication model of examining the media. As Heath (1990) has adeptly pointed out:

> We need to understand the institution (of television) in respect of its fundamental universalizing function, universalizing not in the sense of the creation of some one coherent subject, some representative reason for its orders, but in that, more basically, of the universalization of the function of reception. The hierarchy of message and medium on which notions of communication habitually depend here shifts: what is transmitted is important, but it is the realization and maintenance of the function of reception that is all-important. (p. 270)

Examining the reception of texts does not simply consist in cataloging the plurality of responses to the media, as if "audiences making meaning" assures an activity of producing critical or resistant readings. The reading as resistance approach leaves untouched television's role in constructing the reality in which readings are offered (Heath, 1990, p. 285). The point is not that readers do not on occasion make critical readings, but that an approach which simply valorizes the reader as resistant is still trapped in the active/passive dichotomy.

Ideology does not directly create action or belief or investment. In fact, perhaps one of the conditions of postmodern representation and appropriation is that we see the meaning, we don't believe it, but we go on watching it anyway. We must attend to the possibility that media construct identity and social position not by centralization and homogenization, but through fragmenting viewpoints, creating a condition where *difference can make no difference*, creating the postmodern condition. We still need to attend to how it is that current forms of media representation invite acquiescence to subject positions defined within prevailing social conditions, and how it is that media knowledge limits the range of possible interpretations of social relations. Students need then to be media literate not just in the sense of being able to decipher the meanings offered by the media, but also by attending to their own modes of affective investment and consumption of the media.

Grossberg's notion of affect is crucial here—that is, in everyday life we base our decisions not just on rational meanings, but through *emotional and bodily* committments, committments understood as falling between "libidinal economies of desire and affective economies of mood as two different planes on which psychic energy is always dispersed" (Grossberg, 1988, p. 285). In late capitalism these affective dimensions may be used for tactics that mobolize affective alliances through displacement, naturalization, normalization, etc. They may also, however, be reclaimed by audiences for the purposes of constructing different forms of empowerment that cut through these tactics. The question is how can we become different kinds of consumers? Perhaps more elaborately, this asks: Is there the potential for a meaningfully conceptualized *counter-hegemonic consumption* within a properly theorized postmodern critical media literacy?

Perhaps the means toward a counterhegemonic consumption lies in the increased effort to integrate notions of affect within the context of critical discourse (which has been historically hostile to them). While Jameson (1984) locates his own melancholy, in part, in "the waning of affect" in postmodern culture, we might be much more inclined to agree with Woodward's (1990-91) response that "the emotions are not dead, they are simply not present in academic discourse" (p. 4). It may be that two things (sub-projects, if you will) need to be done as part of this project of critical media literacy. Both have to do with the idea that any understanding of a "counterhegemonic consumption" must be structured in such a manner that directly confronts notions of *desire* , and desire's problematic relationship with both "comsumption" and "agency" in the context of postmodern culture. It seems that we need to both expand the discourse, that is, increase the ways in which we talk about the politics of consumption and desire; and, as part of this expansion of existing discursive locations, open up new discursive territories in which a language of the emotions might take root.

Critical media literacy must offer a practice of dialogue with students in order that commitments, styles of consumption and investments in the media be foregrounded, questioned and understood. Students must question the text and what "they" do with the text. Teachers must take seriously students commitments to and affective investments in various forms of popular culture in order to both critically interrogate self-production and to draw out student "activity" that opens up possibilities for counterhegemonic practices. Media literacy must draw out these responses in the context of the historically bounded meanings available in media production, the interpretive assets available to the reader and the reading formations that readers bring to acts of reception.

This literacy of reading and re-writing involves asking "who I am when I see this?" Here, the theoretical contribution of postmodern theory in tracing how the subject is constituted in multiple subjectivities is crucial in cutting through the banal theory of the individual framed by liberal pluralism. Television, particulary in advertisments, depends, first of all, on creating a dependent spectator; it constitutes the subject as consumer at the same that it constitutes the subject as judge and validator of the meaning of the ad (Poster, 1990:67). The monologic framing of the subject as consumer depends at the same time on the fragmentation of individual subjects into meaning producers who validate the ad and their own "freedom" in relation to it, by regarding themselves as free-floating self-"constituters." In asking students to examine their multiple subjectivity in relation to media constructions, media literacy must turn the focus back onto the specificity of subject positions generated in media reading.

The media function by fragmenting the subject in order to produce a "knowing, cynical, self-constituing" viewer who nevertheless goes on consuming works by actually eliminating self-reflection. The practice of media literacy needs to retrieve the moment of self-reflexivity by encouraging the student to directly attend to their own identifications and investments in the act of consumption. In Shor and Friere's terms this is a reinvigoration of the act of critical consciousness as "gaining reflective distance on one's own thoughts, actions and social community" (1987, p. 167).

Finally, being media literate means both having a voice, and giving the other a voice—seeing one's subjectivity in the threat of the other and then overcoming that threat in the recognition of the partiality of one's own perspective. Media literacy is not a practice that takes place in isolation. In order to understand the media, one's self, one's relation to it, one must be able to speak (with a voice) and be able to recognize who is speaking in the media and who is not speaking. By recognizing the other, the difference that exists in a positive sense, we break down the dichotomies that structure captialist hegemony—core/ periphery, majority/minority, First World/Third World, etc. Knowledge must be reinvented and reconstructed by inviting students to be *border crossers* (Giroux, 1990, p. 124). Such a pedagogy defines itself as a project of educating students to take the stand of the other, to practice an analysis of their own conditions, and to believe that they can make a difference.

Three: Re-writing and the vital strategy of authorship

Finally, a critical media literacy produces a transformative alternative practice. A mode of problematizing, this course of action produces, "against the grain," an alternative attack and creation of representation. Students need to be encouraged to invent counterrepresentations and counterforms of organization and evaluation. First of all, active reading should itself be seen as a form of production, a form of countermemory that produces a reinscription that counters our present forms of truth and justice.

Add to this an active writing—an alternative practice—a direct handling of the tools and processes of media practice. In this way the concepts of reader/writer within the emergence of a critical media literacy are connected to notions of *audience and producer*. To return to our initial paradox: given the technologies available and their potential for the democratization of the media, how can the oppositional potential of these media be so easily thwarted? Further, and more specific to our purposes here, how can these new technologies be used in the creation of a counter hegemony in support of the *long revolution* ?

Both television (or, in its expanded sense, "video,") and the classroom possess a potential to represent two democratic public spheres. As such, they also represent two crucial sites in the formation of subjectivities. Access to both (by "access" we refer to all levels of operations, programming and ownership) are fundamental aspects of the ongoing struggle over the sociocultural status quo, and all which that entails. Both the classroom, and the contemporary entertainment and news media are sites of struggle over the creation, recreation and maintenance of our individual understanding of the values and relations which arise from our collective understanding of past, present and future—the way things are and the way things could be and struggles over the celebration of difference and voices critical of the way things are, or their continued exclusion and supression.

Recent theory, and recent practice, have suggested a variety of approaches which erase the distance between these various dichotomized concepts and open up new space for new voices. In a manner which simultaneously suggests the contributions and problematics of literary theory, Gregory Ulmer (1989) offers a vision of a "pedagogy of invention" in his notion of the "mystory" and "mystorical" writing, in which the traditional categories of theory and practice, the expert, the popular and the personal, all collapse into a poststructuralist language play of autobiography and theory.

The recent exhibition, "Teaching TV," at New York City's Artists Space featured 40 video tapes made by or with young people. Critical educators have, in light of dominant structures, always faced problems of isolation and the related lack of mechanisms for support and communication. This meeting represents one example of the kind of gathering for the purposes of sharing and consolidation, a strategy crucial to a critical pedagogy of media praxis. As David Trend (1991:12) observes:

> The [political] right's program would disencourage the multiplicity of opinions so necessary to a functioning democracy by asserting an essential stratification of discourses. As a counterargument to such regressive logic, "Teaching TV" emphasized the resistant and antihierarchical aspects of youth culture. Rather than promoting the "functionalist" view of learning (currently favored by conservatives) that obliges students to adapt to existing social mandates, "Teaching TV" presented works that afford students an active role in making and remaking their world.

These experiments also illustrate the progressive potential of the video medium opened up in the spaces created in the dissolution of the dichotomies of reader/writer, source/receiver. Contained within these practices is the possibility of reversing media's current role in contemporary culture and politics: from a source of alienation and silence to a source for collective voice and agency. And, these new approaches reveal "a strategic point for developing theories of critical pedagogy. It suggests that technology and media are *less determinative of ideology than are the circumstances in which they are applied*" (emphasis added, Trend, 1991:14).

As theory and practice collapse upon each other into a reformation of a critical media praxis, the transformations of consciousness necessary for a meaningful project of critical media literacy become imaginable. Also imaginable is the growth of media education curricula and the increased role of critical media educators beyond the confines of the classroom and into new interrelations with the various new technologies of LPTV, public access, community radio, etc., and with the various community action, environmental, labor, reproductive rights, gay and lesbian groups who currently use these new media technologies.

As this occurs, notions of media literacy extend beyond critical viewing and into the creation of new media forms—forms of media practice—vital components in the counter-hegemony. To further connect this to Freire's groundbreaking *Pedagogy of the Oppressed*, media educators, in their own privileged positions in terms of race, class, and gender, must (as, in Freire's terms; oppressors at least in terms of their untransformed consciousness) undergo their own transformations of consciousness. And their pedagogy must result inevitably in the continued education of the oppressed by the oppressed. Critical media literacy must work to achieve

> modes of presentation, imaging, entertainment and argument that are realizations of collective desires, group aspirations, common projects, shared experience, at the same time that they refuse all ideas—all expression—of standing in for and subsuming the heterogeneous individual-sociality/social-individuality of the actual lives of actual men and women (Heath, 1990:298).

Conclusion

To call for a new media literacy is to call for new relations to representation and new possiblities for reading/writing. It is to call for self-constituting practice in which a critical language is used to enable us to "both identify ourselves and recreate ourselves as active subjects in history (Mclaren & Hammer, 1989, p. 49). It is call for imagination. This is the possibility to go beyond tomorrow without being naively idealistic. This is utopianism as a dialectical relationship between denouncing the present and announcing the future. To anticipate tomorrow by dreaming today.

REFERENCES

Alvarado, Manuel (1990) The place and purpose of media education, Introductory Plenary Presentation 8 April 1990, BFI Education Easter School—Liverpool pp. 2, 3.
Bogue, Ronald (1989). *Deleuze and Guattari*. New York: Routledge.
Giroux, Henry (1983). *Theory and Resistance in Education.* Granby, MA: Bergin & Garvey.

Giroux, Henry (1988). "Border pedagogy in the age of postmodernism." *Journal of Education*, *170*, 162-181.
Giroux, Henry (1988a). "Postmodernism and the discourse of educational criticism." *Journal of Education*, *170*, 5-30.
Giroux, Henry (1988b). *Teachers as Intellectuals.* Granby, MA: Bergin & Garvey.
Giroux, Henry (1988c). *Schooling and the Struggle for Public Life.* Minneapolis: University of Minnesota Press.
Giroux, Henry & Mclaren, Peter (1989). *Critical Pedagogy, the State, and Cultural Struggle.* Albany, NY: SUNY.
Giroux, Henry and Simon, Roger (1989). *Popular Culture, Schooling and Everyday Life.* Granby, MA: Bergin & Garvey.
Giroux, Henry (1990). "Liberal arts education and the struggle for public life: dreaming about democracy." *South Atlantic Quarterly*, *89*, 114-138.
Grossberg, Lawrence (1988). "Putting the pop back into postmodernism," In Andrew Ross (ed.), *Universal Abandon* (pp. 167-190). Minneapolis: University of Minnesota Press.
Heath, Stephen (1990). "Representing television," In P. Mellencamp (ed.), *Logics of Television* (pp. 267-302). Bloomington, IN: Indiana University Press.
Hebdige, Dick (1988). *Hiding in the Light.* NY: Routledge.
________ (1989). After the masses. *Marxism Today* . (January), pp. 48-53.
Jameson, Frederick (1984). "Postmodernism, or the cultural logic of Late Capitalism." *New Left Review*, *146*, 53-92.
Kariel, Henry S (1989). *The Desparate Politics of Postmodernism.* Amherst, MA: University of Massachusetts Press.
McClarey, Susan (1989/90). "This is not a story my people tell: musical time and space according to Laurie Anderson." *Discourse*, *12/1*, 104-128.
McLaren, Peter. (1989). *Life in Schools.* NY: Longman.
McLaren, Peter and Hammer, Rhonda (1989). "Critical pedagogy and the postmodern challenge." *Educational Foundations* , 29-62.
Poster, Mark (1990). *The Mode of Information.* Chicago: University of Chicago Press.
Sholle, David. (1990). "Resistance: pinning down a wandering concept in cultural studies discourse." *Journal of Urban and Cultural Studies*, *1*, pp. 87-07.
Shor, Ira and Freire, Paulo (1987). *A Pedagogy For Liberation.* Granby, MA: Bergin & Garvey.
Sullivan, Edmund V. (1987). "Critical pedagogy and television," In David Livingstone (ed.), *Critical Pedagogy and Cultural Power* (pp. 57-76). Granby, MA: Bergin & Garvey.
Trend, David. (1991). "To tell the truth: strategies for a critical media literacy." literacy." *After Image* (March), pp. 12-14.
Ulmer, Gregory. (1989). *Teletheory.* NY: Routledge.
Wexler, Philip (1989). "Curriculum in the closed society," In Giroux & Mclaren (Eds.), *Critical Pedagogy, the State, and Cultural Struggle* (pp. 92-104). Albany, NY: SUNY.
Williams, Raymond. (1961). *The Long Revolution.* New York: Columbia University Press.
Woodward, Kathleen (1990-1991). "Introduction." *Discourse*, *13*, *1*, pp. 3-11.

Chapter II

Rethinking the Dialectic: A Critical Semiotic Meta-Theoretical Approach for the Pedagogy of Media Literacy

Rhonda Hammer

> . . . it's also true that public intellectuals are accustomed to using words, and words are barely being used now, not even in soundbites—they've been replaced by visual slices. And intellectuals have not really learned to communicate in that language. Because it isn't just a different form of speech. It's a completely different form of speech. It's a completely different mode of communication.
>
> Patricia Williams. In: "Who's The Boss" by Joe Wood VLS, Oct. 92: 13

MEDIA LITERACY[1]

Terry Ramsaye begins his elegant history of the motion picture, *A Million and One Nights*, published in 1926, with a remark as true today as it was in the golden age of the silent film:

> In the public mind and in the consciousness of many of its students the motion picture seems a magic thing, born yesterday and full of growth this morning. But magic and miracles always fade in the light of information. It is the vastness of what we do not know which creates the great astonishments (p. xxxvii).

---

[1] For an expansion of this argument, in the relation to the treatment of women in film, please see: Rhonda Hammer and Anthony Wilden, "Women in Production: The Chorus Line," in: *The Rules Are No Game: The Strategy of Communication*, ed. A. Wilden.

It is not astonishing that most people are highly literate in the many kinds of non-verbal communication used by the iconic media, whether by that we mean the movies, magazines, picture books, or television. What is astonishing is the extent to which this literacy in the social media is unconscious, inarticulate, and unrecognized.

Gregory Bateson (perhaps one of the most iridescent and underrated contemporary semiotic scholars) defines communications as all behaviour,[2] and asserts that no communication can be understood without situating it within its socio-political economic context. The key word here is *context.* In other words, all communication takes place in relation. With respect to media literacy which is in fact a metacommunciation, this relates, in particular, to how media produces and reproduces social relations. An understanding of a theory informed by media literacy, therefore, assists students to decode their own environment. Moreover, as a metacommunicative theory it is necessarily a meta-theory in that it is contextual and dialectical, and is, thus, "a communication about communication." To be effective teachers, in this domain, we have to first and foremost understand students' particular contexts in the form of shared experience: and one of the primary factors in student learning today is media—especially T.V. Yet, it is astonishing how little teachers or university professors make use of this shared experience. Watching television is something that most people do—especially students—and thus provides for a common ground for addressing issues. A pedagogy of media literacy, therefore, allows for the provocation of our unconscious literacy to the conscious realm.

Television is playing the role of educator in the home. Society is encouraging parents to rely on T.V. as baby-sitter, teacher, moral educator and companion. In a society where 42% of adults claim they watch too much television, where there are an average of 5 acts of violence an hour in prime-time, 18 acts an

---

[2] As Bateson puts it: ". . . all perception and all response . . . all learning and all genetics, all neurophysiology and all endocrinology, all organization and all evolution-one entire subject-must be regarded as communicational in nature . . . (1972:282).

hour in children's time programs, "half of all the prime-time characters are victimized (two-thirds of those on children's time)" and the average 21-year-old has consumed more than 350,000 commercials, the necessity for teaching media literacy (and for producing quality educational video programming) is compulsory (Gerbner, 1989:12). In this sense, parents, teachers and/or academicians, have a responsibility to participate in the activity of tv-watching and to become more critical about the types of messages which are being purveyed. A critical metatheoretical semiotic approach, dialectical in nature, thus becomes necessary within this context. According to Wilden, [this kind of epistemology] "employs an ecological perspective grounded in the natural humanistic, and social sciences, including anthropology, politics and history" (1981:1).

It is common knowledge that young children are highly skilled at recognizing patterns in the media, notably those concerned with the condition of women in society, the authoritarianism of adults, the role of the police and the treatment of marginal peoples. But what they aren't being taught is how to reflect critically on social media. We as educators and communications scholars have a responsibility to adapt this type of critical pedagogy.

Much of today's teaching fails to stress the importance of understanding relationships rather than things. In his criticism of the teaching of grammar in the schools, for instance, Bateson notes that "children in school are still taught nonsense. They are told that a 'noun' is the 'name of a person, place, or thing,' and a 'verb' is an 'action word' and so on. That is, they are taught at a tender age that the way to define something is in itself, not in its relation to other things" (1979:18).

In this traditional hegemonic view, a word has a meaning independent of its' context (or environment). A decontexualized approach is precisely the manner in which we should *not* be teaching. Indeed, we should not be devoting one hour to one subject, hermetically sealed from others, and then followed by another hour on another subject, apparently unrelated to the first. We should be stressing the relationship of one subject to another, and the relationship of subjects to everyday life. This is especially true within the pedagogy of media literacy.

The contribution of this type of metatheory becomes evident in light of the difference between a critical dialectical epistemology and a "Newtonian" (reductionist) perspective which is "primarily that the Newtonian world ascribed reality to objects, excluding the context of the context—all metarelationships—while communication theory examines metarelationships to the exclusion of objects" (Wilder, 1978:13). What Steve Best calls "a tyranny of the specific" (Leach, 1992:13). For, as Bateson warns us: "if you break the pattern which connects the items of learning, you necessarily destroy all quality" (1979:8). The introduction of critical studies of media revolutionizes the student's perception of reality and sparks a new interest (a 'gestalt') in learning.

Most adults and children know about socio-political and economic practice; they know about class relations and their position in it; they know about bigotry and inequality. What they don't know is how to talk about them. But, when you talk about iconic media, and point out the relationships depicted, the dominant kinds of values it perpetuates—racism, sexism and violence (notably against women and children) and other dominant/subordinate relationships of class, race, gender and sexuality—the critical semiotic metatheoretical viewpoint opens the subject to real life. Media literacy teachers, therefore, need to assist students to understand dominant value patterns and power relationships (and metarelationships) in a dialectical contextual manner.

Basically, we need to learn, along with our students, how to understand the complex codes of television, while analyzing and questioning pathological kinds of behaviour like the glorification of violence (and the absence of ethics) communicated by the programming. Once students are able to enjoy a program, while still being analytical, they can begin to translate these critical insights into other kinds of learning and expression (and eventually, we hope, into their own counter-hegemonic media productions). Through this process they come to learn not to be deceived by 'absolute' answers nor by absolute relativity; they recognize the importance of constantly asking questions. As Bateson proposes, quoting e.e. cummings: "Always the more beautiful answer who asks the more difficult question"

(1979:235). Or, in other words, forever criticizing what we think we know.

Therefore, teaching media literacy requires becoming media literate ourselves; and the first step towards reaching this goal is to recognize that no media form is value-free. Indeed, all communication is informed by its context and thus cannot be perceived to be "objective." As Donaldo Macedo reminds us, "objectivity is, in fact, an ideological act. Objectivity always contains within it a dimension of subjectivity; thus it is dialectical" (1991: vii). Once again we are faced with the controversial and complex nature of dialectics, and its seminal position in the development and appropriate application of a critical semiotic metatheoretical approach, in relation to media literacy. This type of emergent epistemology is then, by nature, a metacommunication (a metatheory) as it recognizes levels of contextual constraint which necessarily includes an acceptance of how failures to distinguish between levels of abstraction leads to confusions of logical types.[3] Moreover, as Mary Daly explains it, the prefix *'meta'* is defined as being of "a higher logical type—in nouns formed from names of disciplines and designating new but related disciplines such as can deal critically with the nature, structure, or behaviour of the original ones" (1978:12). Hence it is dialectical, as only a dialectical approach both embraces and attempts to resolve the notions and realities of paradox and contradiction.

In his tracing of the evolution of dialectical method, Raymond Williams emphasizes the extension of the notion of contradiction "in the course of discussion or dispute to a notion of *contradictions in reality*" (1976:107, emphasis mine). He goes on to argue for this type of perspective in that it allows for the surpassing of contradictions, "both in thought and in the world history which was its objective character, in a higher and

[3] Simply put, the theory of logical types states "that there is a qualitative difference between items of information of different logical types that, if ignored, leads to serious confusion [or contradiction or paradox]. Logical types involve levels of generalization. . . . Logical typing becomes a way of understanding how a context (of a higher logical type) controls or constrains communication and behaviour within its domain (of a lower logical type)" (Nichols, 1981:72).

unified truth: the dialectical process [is] then the continual unification of opposites, in the complex relation of parts to a whole" (ibid.). Indeed, we could not ask for a better description of the paradoxical complexities which characterize contemporary iconic media and, consequently, the utility of such an epistemological method for the analysis of this iconoclastic (substantive) form. For as Schwock, White and Reilly describe it:

> The study of media culture often means an abandonment of the search for some sort of singular, overarching, "truth" or "correct reading" in favour of multiple and competing interpretations. This is a positive attribute in the study of popular media culture, because it allows for experience in the practice of reasonable documentation, the respectful differing of opinions, and the value of debate. There is often a sort of uncomfortableness on the part of students and teachers when a single, clear-cut answer does not emerge. Yet students and teachers should appreciate the evidence of ambiguity (1992: 121-122).

Although it would be impossible to provide for a complete and/or absolute definition of the dialectical process, I offer the reader in this chapter an historical overview of this fascinating and eclectic system of relations. In the following chapter, this dialectical approach will then be applied to television, in general, and to particular political-media scandals and the Gulf War to demonstrate the necessity of an epistemology which takes into account media literacy.

THE MADNESS OF METHODS

> "Would you tell me, please, which way I ought to go from here?"
> "That depends a good deal on where you want to get to," said the Cat.
> Lewis Carroll, *Alice's Adventures in Wonderland (1865)*

If the above quotation is in any way indicative of the plight of many contemporary social scientists, educational researchers, and teachers, it is not so much that they don't know where they are going, but that they lack a critical perspective (or approach, methodology, or epistemology) that can provide sufficient direction in understanding the complex and contradictory characteristics of the communication of everyday life.

This interest in the dialectic is inspired by its conceptual richness as a heuristic device that can enable teachers, researchers, and students to interrogate and transform the often illegitimate hierarchies of relations dealing with issues of class, race, gender and sexuality. With this consideration in mind, we have attempted to rethink various commonplace formulations of the dialectic from the perspective of what we are calling a critical semiotic meta-theoretical approach. By employing the work of communicational semioticians, critical theorists, and [meta] radical feminist[4] to re-examine conventional understandings of the dialectic, and placing under theoretical stress its regnant formulations in social-science usage, we will be able to put into crisis much of the political complacency at present reflected in dominant research methodologies, policy analysis, and pedagogical classroom approaches that haunt this present age of so-called educational reform. Such an approach, we argue, is able to force the status quo by providing a contextual and meta-communicational understanding of everyday practical experience and the politics of representation and power that informs it. More specifically, we are hoping that this problematization of the concept of "dialectics" and its historical usage will not only point to the complex and multi-leveled nature of communication, but also furnish teachers with a way to begin to understand and discuss the complexities of social life in what we have termed hierarchies of relations. As critical educators, we work with the conviction that an interrogation of the dialectic as a form of communication will enable teachers to rethink social problems in a more contextual and critical way, and thus employ an affective pedagogy of media literacy. This concern with re-examining the concept of the dialectic has very much to do with the development of a metacommunicative process that we feel has important potential both as an explanatory model as well as model of social change and thus a pedagogy of media

---

[4] Although there is no brief and/or precise description of this feminist approach, its' essence is captured by Daly who states: "It is women's own Gyn/Ecology that can break the brokenness of the 'fields,' deriding their borders and boundaries, changing the nouns of knowledge into verbs of knowing" (1978:11).

literacy for educators (cf. Hammer and Wilden, 1987; McLaren, 1989; McLaren and Hammer, 1989).

Thus, first part of the chapter necessarily deals with an historical survey of the dialectic, with an emphasis on the work of Hegel, Marx, and Engels. This is an attempt to show a similarity between the works of these early theorists of the dialectic and what is known as a critical semiotic meta-theoretical approach to understanding social phenomena. This is followed by a critique of some of the current misperceptions of the concept, which in turn is followed by an analysis of the so-called "laws of dialectics." The overall analysis is framed by a semiotic and "communicational" reading of the dialectic by Anthony Wilden and Richard Coe; one that is largely informed by the work of Gregory Bateson. The final section confronts educators with some current social antagonisms and ways in which a revisited dialectic might be used to engage such antagonisms in order to further the project of social and educational reform.

THE DIALECTIC

> To think dialectically is to decree the obsolescence of cherished concepts which explain even one's recent past. One of the marks of a true dialectician, however, is the ability to 'move beyond' the past without repudiating it in the names of new levels of critical consciousness presently enjoyed.
>
> Denis Goulet, "Introduction" to Paulo Freire's *Education: the Practice of Freedom* (1974)

The term 'dialectic'[5] has a long history of development by writers attempting to study the social and historical constitution of everyday life. This makes it all the more surprising that what is generally implied by the use of the term "dialectical" is rarely defined. In fact, the complexity of the idea is so important for explaining all aspects of communication that it does, I argue, warrant special attention. In this chapter I attempt to reconstruct some of the major conceptualization of the dialectic and

[5] The term dialectic finds its etymological foundations in the Greek dialektikos—dia meaning "through" or "between," lektikos which is derived from the verb lego, meaning "I say" or "I choose". In entirety, dialektikos pertains to discourse or discussion (Oxford English Dictionary).

conclude that certain Marxian conceptions of the dialectic best illustrate the critical semiotic meta-theoretical approach to social life that we are advocating. An understanding of the dialectical process[6] proves essential for explaining the multi-dimensional nature of communicational phenomena which Bateson (1972) saw reflected in all behaviour.[7]

THE ORIGINS OF THE CONCEPT

There does not seem to be a universally agreed upon consensus on when the term dialectic was first employed. Some historians contend that the notion of the dialectic is as ancient as the fifth century B.C.E., and that Aristotle (384-322 B.C.E.) recognized Zeno of Elea (490-430 B.C.E.) as being the inventor of the term. The notion of the "dialectic" can be traced at least as far back as Classical Greece (5th century) where a technique known as *eristic* was employed in the schools. This technique involved the presentation of a thesis by one student, followed by a series of questions initiated by another student which were designed to lead the first student to contradict himself and thus see the error of his argument. This was the main method used by Socrates (Coe, 1981).

Aristotle's conception was more complex. He believed that certain truths could be known definitely, while other types of truth could be known only probably. For Aristotle, dialectics was the method of reaching this second kind of truth. This was in keeping with the Socratic tradition that this kind of truth could be realized through the art of discussion, wherein speak-

---

[6] Here a critical semiotic meta-theoretical approach is being identified with metapunctuation, partially because of the way in which it punctuates experience in that it embraces a "both/and" logic which necessarily subsumes and translates from (repunctuates) "either/or" analytical logic. This "both/and" idea can now begin to be clarified as it analogous with what is meant by dialectical. (Clarification of the meaning of "punctuation" is provided for in footnotes 9 and 13).

[7] "Dialectics" is a highly complex and multidimensional notion. In discussing the evolution of this idea, and its essential nature—in both theory and praxis—we have drawn on a variety of sources, some of which include Acton 1967, Adorno 1973, Aiken 1957, Caute 1967, Coe and Wilden 1978, Coe 1981, Engels 1892, Giroux 1981, Godelier 1972, Hall 1967, Rius 1976, Wilden 1976, 1977a, 1980, 1987, Williams 1976 and Wilson 1972.

ers would represent different perspectives on the subject. For Socrates, it was through this art of discussion that speakers and listeners began to approach a fuller and more accurate truth. For what occurred in this dialectical process was the *recognition of contradiction between ideas*. Both Aristotle and Socrates asserted that it was through the awareness of contradictions that new knowledge could be achieved. The notion that two or more people discussing an idea will conceive something new can serve as the original model for dialectics (Coe 1981). The underlying understanding of the term is, then, that the dialectic is a meta-communicative *exchange of views*.[8]

It is interesting to note that a resemblance between this ancient notion of dialectics and certain characteristics of contemporary critical semiotic theory are already evident. Specifically, we refer to the Greek idea that different realities can be discovered through interaction. This resembles the communicational perspective of "punctuating" and "repunctuating" levels (and metalevels) of reality.[9]

The interpretation of the dialectic as described by the Greek philosophers was, however, idealistic.[10] It was not until the 19th century that a theoretical system of dialectics was fully realized. This was primarily the responsibility of the philosopher Georg Wilhelm Friedrich Hegel (1770-1831).[11]

---

8 Although Aristotle is perceived as being one of the earliest philosophers to employ the dialectical method, his approach was a more rigid application than was that of Socrates.

9 "Punctuation" is a term which Bateson borrowed from schoolbook grammar to characterize how one organizes the "flow of experience so that it takes on a sense of coherence" (Wilder 1978: 62). In other words, for the world to have any meaning at all, we must be able to consciously and unconsciously "impose an order" on the sequences of experience surrounding and involving living beings (Watzlawick 1967: 62).

10 Idealism refers to "any theoretical or practical view emphasizing mind, soul, spirit, life, or what is characteristically or what is characteristically of preeminent value or significance to it" (Runes 1960: 136).

11 G. W. F. Hegel was raised a Lutheran Christian and received his education in a theological seminary. After graduation he was a resident tutor for aristocratic families in both Bern and Frankfurt for seven years, after which he received a post as a teacher in Jena at the age of thirty-six. It was at Jena that he completed his first major work, The Phenomenology of the Mind (or Spirit) (Geist), while Napoleonic troops marched into the conquered city. From 1806-1808 Hegel served as editor to a daily

THE HEGELIAN DIALECTIC

Hegel's work has influenced almost every important philosophical movement of the twentieth century. It is indicative of the complexity and wealth of ideas examined by Hegel that not only has his work been associated with certain aspects of Marxism-and concurrently socialism-but that Hegel has also been seen as a forerunner of Fascism (as a result of his ideas concerning the State).

Unlike some early philosophers who viewed the world as static—i.e., in terms of fixed laws or classifications to explain certain phenomenon, Hegel viewed all concepts, all ideas, and all problems in *historical terms*. While most of his earlier peers discussed the world in terms of abstractions and universals (i.e., metaphysics), Hegel chose to view the world in a way which many of his contemporaries considered to be "inside out." By this expression, We are referring to Hegel's emphasis on looking at *a particular*. Not only does an idea in Hegel's view have a "fixed meaning" or "unchanging validity" but no particular can exist unless it is viewed in relation to its environment, or *context* (Aiken 1957: 72-3). Therefore, when a critical semiotic metatheoretical approach is taken in order to understand a particular phenomena, then nothing can be viewed as an isolated "thing" or "entity," but rather as a continuously changing process of events. For this reason, it is the 'historical consciousness' which alone grasps reality as it is; that is to say, as *"a process of becoming"* (ibid.; emphasis mine).

Hegel's radical departure from earlier philosophical notions, of abstracting thought from certain aspects of the "real" world, bears many similarities to certain characteristics of what is being called a critical semiotic meta-theoretical approach. Specifically, the emphasis on the relationship between parts, on the "pattern" which connects, on context, on levels of communication and, of course, on the definition of this emergent epistemology as being necessarily aesthetic and transdisciplinary.

---

newspaper and then headmaster of a school in Nuremberg. Having achieved recognition through further publications, Hegel was appointed Professor of Philosophy at Heidelberg (Acton 1967: 435; Aiken 1957: 82).

For Hegel's basic philosophy (like that of Bateson *et al.*, 1976) is a philosophy of change.

Hegel's philosophy of history argues that historical processes are always new. What he is suggesting here is that history does not repeat itself in accordance with causal laws, but that every stage or "moment", as Hegel calls it, must be viewed in the immediate context of its past, future, and present (ibid.). It is here that an understanding of Hegel's interpretation of dialectical opposition becomes necessary in clarifying his theory of historical development.

Unlike other philosophers who did not adequately deal with the idea or reality of contradiction, Hegel not only accepted such contradictions but embraced them as guides to a higher level of understanding, resolution, and consequently "philosophical truth." For example, in *Science of Logic*, Hegel wrote that:

> . . . 'all things are in themselves contradictory,' that movement is existing contradiction itself,' and that 'only insofar as something has contradiction in itself does it move, have impulse or activity' (cited in Acton 1967: 449).

Hegel, following Kant, saw every thesis as generating a contradictory antithesis; however, he regarded the thesis/antithesis contradiction as true only if both were "understood in a new light, as imperfect expressions of a higher, more inclusive proposition which contains what is significant in both of them" (ibid.). This proposition was what Hegel defined as "synthesis."[12]

If the contradiction of "A" is always treated just as "not-A," then "not-A" becomes, as Hegel reminds us, "a bare abstraction which is indistinguishable from nothing at all" (cited in Acton 1967: 449). The antithesis within a contradiction, therefore, must have a "positive" meaning; in other words, *it must have a charac-*

---

[12] "The originator of the terms thesis, antithesis, and synthesis was Johann Fichte (1762-1814), who regarded knowing as an act of creation, rather than discovery, and who, like Hegel, considered the dialectic to be a teleological process leading to a predesigned and necessary end, such as 'God', the 'Absolute', the 'Divine Idea', and so on" (Wilden, 1987: 246-247).

ter of its own. Hegel called this "the negation of the negation" (Wilson 1972: 224). In Hegel's dialectic, the "not-A" becomes a "B"; however, in conceiving it this way, the contradiction is removed and transformed to a higher level of meaning. This is the synthesis; a triadic movement "from a thesis, 'A', to its antithesis, 'not-A', which in turns gives way to a synthesis which transforms our conceptions of both 'A' and 'not-A'" (Acton 1967: 436).

For Hegel, then, "A" is a particular, "not-A" is the rest of the universe. Therefore, "not-A" cannot be placed as an opposite of "A", for it exists at a higher and more complex level. (This is one way in which the communicational rudiments of the critical semiotic meta-theoretical approach, with its emphasis on hierarchies of levels—e.g., the notion of metacommunication and meta-theory, as well as the translation of the theory of logical types—resembles the Hegelian dialectic). The dialectic does not, however, end here. On the contrary, it is only the beginning, for the synthesis must generate a new antithesis which can be removed only through a still higher synthesis; "it is a multi-levelled and continuous process" (Aiken 1957: 74).

This explanation of the dialectic proves essential for clarifying ideas involved in developing a critical semiotic meta-theoretical approach to understanding social life. Indeed, the notion of *levels of communication* comes immediately to mind. For not only does the notion of dialectics embody the notions of levels and/or logical types, but also necessarily involves the notion of metacommunication. Indeed, the "generation" of syntheses which, in turn, generate higher levels of theses and antitheses, and so on, resembles the idea of communication about communication and of higher levels of communication (in other words, meta-communication and/or meta-theory).

The notion of "punctuation"[13] can also be easily identified with this dialectical process if we look at it in the context of an

---

[13] The "general set of rules" which punctuation, in a communicational sense, represent are defined by the very context that they organize. It, therefore, becomes apparent that these ordering devices cannot be as specific, or as easily discernible, as is the punctuation of written language; nevertheless, their structural resemblance cannot be ignored. Within the context of Western society, for example, there are rules of governing (*Continues*)

the way in which we punctuate certain behaviors. Moreover, the same behaviors are punctuated differently when displayed by peoples whose status is differently defined by the constraints of the dominant value systems. The punctuation of human behavior is interrelated with the realities of relationship and context, Bateson reminds us:

> "In the punctuation of human interaction the critical reader will have observed that the adjectives . . . which purport to describe individual character are really not strictly applicable to the individual but rather describe transactions between the individual and his material and human environment. No man is "resourceful" or "dependent" or "fatalistic" in a vacuum. His characteristic, whatever it be, is not his but is rather a characteristic of what goes on between him and something (or somebody) else" (1972:298).

The choice of the label "punctuation" for describing the complexities involved in "ordering reality" was far from arbitrary. The nature of the term is consistent with the behaviors it endeavors to organize. Examples employed to illustrate this concept have been drawn, primarily, from written, verbal and/or nonverbal communication. These types of phenomena, however, serve only as an indication of the wide variety of metapatterns of relations encompassing communication as such. For the essence of communication is further revealed by this notion in that "communication is a semiotic and not a linguistic concept: it refers to the transmission of signals, signs, signifiers, and symbols in any communications system whatsoever. This may include interorganismic or intraorganismic communication, communication in biological systems, communications between animals and between human beings, psychological or socioeconomic communication. As such a term has the Marxian sense of Verkehr. 'Communion' is the product of all . . . communication" (Wilden 1972: 111).

Indeed, this "communion", as Wilden calls it, can only take place through the involvement of punctuation. And since it is being used to explain phenomena which are "semiotic", then the decision to call this notion "punctuation" evokes particular meaning (particular to both the kinds of "semiotic" relations it aids in describing—all communicational phenomena—and particular to the nature of the overall perspective in which it plays a vital role: a critical semiotic meta-theoretical approach).

> "The reason for using the term punctuation rather than syntax, is that syntax is either a strictly linguistic term or else it refers to the modes and rules of articulation within a given system (language for instance). Punctuation, however, may refer to the interface of another system within the given system. Thus gestures, facial expression, intonation, and so forth punctuate a spoken discourse; the logistics of print and paging punctuate a written discourse; death punctuates life" (ibid.: 112).

The idea that a critical semiotic meta-theoretical approach is a particular kind of punctuation takes on new meaning in light of this multidimensional explanation of what is meant by both the term punctuation and the kinds of relations it classifies.

argument between two people where each member punctuates the patterns differently. The first punctuation can now be seen as the "thesis," while the second punctuation (if it is a response, either verbal or non-verbal) can be seen as the "antithesis." Resolution of this argument can only take place if the participants *metacommunicate* about the relationship, recognizing how they are punctuating (or mispunctuating) the communication and agree to *repunctuate.* The repunctuation can then be immediately perceived as existing at a higher level and thus being the "synthesis."

However, one must beware of embracing the Hegelian dialectic wholeheartedly, for we must always remember its idealistic rudiments. For example, although the Hegelian "universe" is always interrelated—which, as previously expressed, was a radical and necessary concept for any understanding of phenomena—"it is a universe of ideal concepts, *not* our familiar material or social universe" (Sherman 1976: 57). In discussing contradictions, Hegel chooses to use such metaphysical examples as "Being" and "Nothing." Although his contention that an entity only achieves reality in relation to its "opposite" and the inevitable synthesis was important, some of Hegel's critics point out that to even place such concepts in opposition signifies that they are *identical.* This can be a very dangerous notion, in that the synthesis can assume the unification of concepts which are *not* equal. (In the case of "Being" and "Nothing," for example, the synthesis is one of "Becoming").

Hegel believed that philosophers must perceive the contradiction as a challenge in order to create a new synthesis which leads to a more "contextual" representation of the original notion. "The dialectic, as he conceives it, is at once a law of thought and a law of being" (Aiken 1957: 75). What at first appears real to us is, in Hegel's view, only an abstraction or a "bare particular" of the *real* existing relations, so that anything becomes real only when it ceases to be "a bare particular."

It is interesting to note what Hegel does with the notion of bare particular with respect to his definition of "human," which is essentially a criticism of the myth of individualism. Hegel uses his metaphor of the "bare particular" to describe how a human being can only become human (or a person) if he or she gives up his or her claim "to individual uniqueness and is content to be regarded as an aspect of the large social whole to which he belongs" (Aiken 1957: 75). (Although this is only the "tip of the iceberg" in the very complex and necessary argument surrounding individualism, Hegel's analysis must be recognized as contributing significant insight to the understanding of a dispute, which is vehemently argued to this day—i.e., the idea of individualism and its' role in perpetuating the dominant ideology.)[14]

There is, however, a concrete, real entity which, for Hegel, exists, and it is here than one can both identify his idealism and also see how his theological background and beliefs influence his view. The entity is called "the Absolute." It is Hegel's contention that the Absolute represents the matrix of the dialectic and that all syntheses are hierarchical, in that attaining the level of Absolute is their ultimate goal. Thus, every occurrence or event is merely a "moment" in the "unenvisageable totality" of the Absolute (ibid.). The Absolute—fully rational—is the ultimate ideal of reason for which "the dialectical consciousness of man can grasp only as a goal endlessly to be striven for, yet never reached or even comprehended . . ." (ibid.: 76). It is omnipotent and unattainable.

The Absolute serves a fundamental purpose with respect to Hegel's explanation of historical change and the dialectic of history. For each triadic process—thesis, antithesis, synthesis—represents a higher stage towards the development of the Absolute (ibid.). Thus, if in Hegel's development of "logic," no proposition is wholly denied, then the same proves true for his dialectic of history. Hegel believed that each successive generation in history must preserve and inherit aspects of its past, even though the current generation might consciously negate its antecedent.[15] Therefore, expressions of past culture must neces-

---

[14] As Wilden reminds us, "ideologies, like reality, involve levels of relation . . ." (1980: xxii).

[15] This complex process is aided by the German expression Aufhebung.

> "The German expression used to describe this kind of change is *Aufhebung*. Since this term embodies contradictory significations, it describes dialectical transformations rather well. On the one hand, it signifies: 'canceling, abolishing, ending, suspending neutralizing, removing, and counteracting.' On the

sarily exist in our culture today (Aiken 1957: 75; cf. Acton 1967: 445). When this is recognized, a more comprehensive social reality becomes evident. However, there is an ultimate "plan" in this societal transformation—that of both a dialectical and spiritual nature—the "dialectical unfolding or self-development of that which is completely unconditioned, namely, the absolute itself . . ." (Aiken 1957: 77).[16] This constant striving to achieve the unachievable is how Hegel perceives historical change. He interprets this as constituting a struggle towards the spiritual freedom of humankind (ibid.). Hegel's notion of freedom is thus autonomy (the ultimate freedom being embodied, of course, in the spirit of the absolute). Hegel recognizes "stages" of development in his envisagement of historical change, whereby each state is "higher" than the preceding stage.[17] Therefore, "Hegel himself treated all contradictions as dialectical moments in the life of absolute spirit, unified in a single comprehensive system of philosophy" (Acton 1967: 451).

The spirit, then, takes priority over the cultural history for "the description of any culture ... is merely incidental to its *spiritual significance* for the present age" (Aiken 1957: 78). Furthermore, according to Hegel, historical change cannot be studied by examining past events, but "only by reflection upon that record when it is conceived dialectically under the form of spirit . . ." (ibid.). What he is saying, then, is that we must see historical events, contradictions, and syntheses as having an ultimate direction or goal, i.e., the absolute; this "spiritual" mediator is essential to Hegel's interpretation of human freedom and the role of the state.

---

other, it also means: 'lifting, storing up, going beyond, preserving or retaining, and conserving'" (Coe and Wilden 1978: 47).

16 This is a good illustration of the dialectical both/and nature of a critical semiotic meta-theoretical approach. For within this Hegelian notion we can see the existence of both analytical either-or logic, the Absolute, and the dialectical both/and logic, the multi-leveled nature of the ever-changing ("unfolding") patterns of metacommunicational relationships involved in the Hegelian dialectic.

17 Note here the similarities of Hegel's idea of "historical change"—minus the idealism—and a critical semiotic meta-theoretical approach's emphasis on, and punctuation of, contextual and thus metacommunicational hierarchical levels of patterns of relationship, necessarily involved in all communicational phenomena.

It is difficult to understand Hegel's definition of freedom since it implies that no concept can be understood until it transcends its "non-existent" opposite (Aiken 1957: 79). Freedom for Hegel was the power to realize one's self and to achieve autonomy (ibid.). The self was a concrete personality which was invested with characteristics derived from education, training, and social values inscribed by society. It is interesting to note how closely Hegel's interpretation is to what we today know as socialization.

> The first step toward self-knowledge and self culture, therefore, is the recognition of one's membership within a historically-evolving community. Thus only does one find oneself as an integral human being. The free person is able to identify himself with the duties and responsibilities invested in him by the State, which, for Hegel, is the highest of all social institutions (ibid.)[18]

Hegel repeatedly stressed the importance of societal institutions as carriers of culture (ibid.: 77) and that these institutions and laws were only superseded by the state as manifestations of the absolute spirit. As Hegel put it:

> The State . . . is the idea of spirit in the external manifestation of human will and its freedom (cited in Aiken 1957: 80).

Thus we can observe the conservatism and idealism which permeates the Hegelian dialectic in its strictest sense. Furthermore, Wilden (1987: 247) notes that Hegel's "supposedly inherent binary opposition between positive and negative is simply a mechanical or electromagnetic metaphor, with no relevance to living nature or human history". Wilden goes on to comment that there is no general "dialectics of nature" but that we may find dialectical process wherever we find information at work in nature or society. Wilden also points out (p. 250) that negation is a linguistic operation not found in nature or history or communication between organisms. Similarly, Hegel's interpre-

---

[18] As Rius so straightforwardly translates this Hegelian notion:

> "Hegel's advice to any worker exploited by his boss would be: Don't worry yourself about material oppression, but only about the 'spiritual' kind. By obeying the state (God's representative on earth) you will find happiness and freedom (of the spirit). . ." (1976: 72).

tation of binary opposites deal only with matter-energy and take no account of information. In fact, the basic assumptions of Hegel's entire philosophy are imaginary since he makes reason into its own context (Wilden, 1987, p. 86).

Although Hegel's universe was what communication theorists would describe as a "closed system,"[19] we cannot ignore the significant contributions of Hegel's notion of the dialectic. For Hegel's concept of the dialectic is essentially what Marx embodied in his dialectical materialist methodology. As Lenin perceived it:

> The sum total, the last word and essence of Hegel's logic is the *dialectical method*-this is extremely noteworthy. And one thing more: in this most *idealistic* of Hegel's works there is the least idealism and the most materialism. 'contradictory,' but a fact (cited in Holland 1977: 235).

Moreover, the transdisciplinary (both/and) nature of a critical semiotic meta-theoretical approach is thus revealed in that it affords scholars with the opportunity to translate from this notion of dialectics, partially through an identification of problematics inherent in Hegel's dialectical process. Within this context, it should be noted that certain feminist critiques of Hegel are perceived as identifying limitations of the Hegelian concept of dialectic, *especially in the way that it translates into a form of male consciousness*. As Hartsock (1987) notes:

> Hegel's analysis makes clear the problematic social relations available to the self which maintains itself by opposition; [*sic*] each of the two subjects struggling for recognition risks its own death in the struggle to kill the other, but if the other is killed the subject is once again alone. In theory the male experience when replicated as epistemology leads to a world conceived as, and (in fact) inhabited by, a number of fundamentally hostile others whom one comes to know by means of opposition (even death struggle) and yet with whom one must construct a social relation in order to survive (170).[20]

---

19 "Simply stated, a closed system is one for which its context is effectively irrelevant or defined as such (e.g. the solar system, the cosmos as a whole); an open system, in contrast, is one that depends on its environment for its continuing existence and survival (e.g. an organism, a population, a society)" (Wilden 1980: xxxi).

20 It must be emphasized that a translation of the Hegelian dialectic (and, to a lesser degree, that offered by Marx and Engels) is an essential aspect of a critical semiotic meta-theoretical approach, which necessarily encom-

Furthermore, according to Wilden (1987: 250), dialectical logic does not have anything essential to do with 'not', 'negation', or (Hegel's) stalled 'third law of dialectics: the 'negation' of the negation'. Negation is, Wilden reminds us, a linguistic operation not found in nature or history or communication between organisms. The other two laws, 'the transformation of quantity into quality (and vice versa)' and the 'interpretation of (binary) opposites', deal only with matter-energy and take no account of information.

MARX AND ENGELS TRANSFORM THE DIALECTIC

The works of Karl Marx[21] (1818-1883) and Friedrich Engels[22] (1820-1895) have been recognized by many as being some of the most important writings to have emerged from the nineteenth century. Refusing to be constrained by rigid schools of thought, their writings today are associated with philosophy, sociology, political science, economics, and to some degree, anthropology, and psychology.[23] The works of Marx and his successors, espe-

---

passes meta-critical feminist theory. For as Mary O'Brien argues materialist feminism works in a dialectical fashion in that:

> We seek to uncover contradictions in traditional thought: to root these contradictions in the realities of male experience; to point out that they have been valid in specific historical circumstances; to say why they are no longer valid; to conserve what is valuable and to transcend what is not; to create something new which is none the less continuous with history and creative of a future.

O'Brien's explanation provides for a complementary framework for Harstock's criticisms.

21 Karl Marx, born in Trier, Germany, came from a long succession of rabbis. His father, however, broke with family tradition and studied law, due to the influence of the French Revolution which relaxed some of the restrictions on Jews. When it became illegal, once again, for Jews to hold office, Hirschel Marx had his entire family baptized as Christians, in order to retain his position (Wilson, 1972: 131).

22 Friedrich Engels was the son of a wealthy factory owner. He shared many of the beliefs and convictions of the young Marx and became his closest friend and collaborator after meeting with him in 1844 in Paris. Together Marx and Engels undertook a lifetime commitment to understanding the real social world, questioning its structure, and attempting to offer solutions for change.

23 Or as Rius so humorously puts it, "Marx has something to say to everybody. There is not a major change in the last hundred years which doesn't owe something to Comrade Charlie's influence" (1976: 14).

cially, has contributed to the development of what has come to be known as critical pedagogy. The concern of Marx and Engels for understanding the patterns of relationship involved in the communication of everyday life, is probably one of the most appropriate representations of the necessity and worth of a pedagogy of media literacy.

This section sets out to briefly examine the treatment and applications of the notion of dialectics put forward by Marx and Engels. Moreover, as the real qualities and complexities of what is meant by dialectics is revealed, many characteristics of what is being called a "critical semiotic meta-theoretical approach" should become more fully realized.

The notion of the dialectic played an essential role in the analyses put forward by Marx and Engels.

> In Marx's investigation of capitalism, the mechanical mode of analysis of systems is subordinate to a new kind of deduction . . . developed out of, and in critique of, Hegel's dialectic (Therborn 1976: 46).[24]

Although Marx never wrote a full-length treatise on dialectics, his work nevertheless constitutes the most outstanding examples of its applications (Sherman 1976: 57). In explanation, the Marxian dialectic substitutes "matter" for the Hegelian "spirit" (Hall 1967: 389). This replacement of matter for spirit formed the basis of what Marx and Engels called "historical materialism."

HISTORICAL MATERIALISM

We have seen that Hegel's philosophy was idealist in nature, yet what was revolutionary in Hegel was his conception of historical change (Aronowitz 1981; Wilson 1972: 167; Aiken 1957: 188-89). Marx felt that "philosophers have only *interpreted* the world, in various ways; the point is to *change* it" (1845, cited in Rius 1976: 65). Rather than dealing with abstractions, Marx

---

[24] Therborn's overall interpretation of Marx is a particular kind of understanding. This does not mean that it is in any way a mispunctuation. Especially, as exhibited by this quote, many of Therborn's explanations provide for a greater understanding of certain Marxian ideas.

wanted "to state the predicament of *spiritually* and *socially* alienated men in the modern world" (Aiken 1957: 185).

Historical materialism was intended as a punctuation for understanding social change (ibid.: 186). In this sense Marx and Engels were influenced by the work of Ludwig Feuerbach (1804-1872).[25] Feuerbach rejected speculative philosophy, and held the belief that god and the after life could not be rationally justified, but that this belief in an omnipotent being could be explained "in terms of the unfulfilled needs of men whose lives are frustrated by an oppressive social order" (Acton 1967: 389).

In *The Essence of Christianity* (1841), Feuerbach had criticized Hegel as being an 'apologist for Christianity.'

> [The Absolute Idea] which was supposed to have incorporated itself in *matter* for the purpose of realizing reason had been a gratuitous presupposition which Hegel was unable to prove. Let us forget about the Absolute Idea; let us start an investigation with man and the world as we find them. When we do so, it becomes perfectly obvious that legends and the rituals of religion are merely the expressions of human minds (cited in Wilson 1972: 148-49; emphasis mine).

One notion put forward by Feuerbach, and one specifically endorsed by Engels, was the argument concerning the 'contradiction' between idealism and materialism. For as Feuerbach explained it, idealism held that matter is created by mind. Materialism,[26] however, holds that matter is dominant, and

---

[25] Ludwig Feuerbach was a supporter of the Hegelian left, who wanted to put "Hegel's theory into practice." He denied the "sacred origin or royal authority." By identifying him with the "Hegelian left," it should be understood that when Hegel died, contradictions concerning his philosophy "divided his followers into 'Hegelians of the Right' and 'Left'. The Left defended their teacher's most progressive ideas, the Right stuck Hegel's spiritual side . . . That's when (1830) the terms Left and Right came into use" (Rius 1976: 22).)

[26] Materialism evolved in ancient Greece, with the philosophy of Democritus of Abdera (460-360 B.C.E). He is recognized as having developed "the first important materialist philosophy of nature . . ." (Runes 1970: 75). It was, however the teachings of Rene Descartes (1596-1650) and Benedict Spinoza (1632-1677) that introduced the ideas known as Mechanistic Materialism.

"In the seventeenth and eighteenth centuries, the greatest scientific discoveries were made in the areas of mathematics and *mechanics* of celestial bodies. And so, materialism became 'mechanistic'. . . . In other words,

mind subordinate.[27] Marx and Engels were in profound disagreement with the "theory of reductive materialism" which stated that mind was a form of matter (Acton 1967: 390-91).

Although Marx agreed with Feuerbach's basic assumptions concerning materialism and the rejection of Hegelian idealism, he identified in Feuerbach's philosophy similar problems as those found in Hegel's formulations. In fact, Marx and Engels criticized Feuerbach's notions—specifically those concerned with history—as being too rigid and fixed.

In his *Theses on Feuerbach,* written in 1845, we find that Marx is talking about mispunctuation on the part of both materialists and idealists, and is attempting to demonstrate how *different levels of experience and realities can aid in the repunctuation of our knowledge of the world.* Moreover, the fundamental importance of translating certain ideas—from Hegelian idealism and materialism (both traditional and Feuerbachian)—were central to both Marx and Engels' development of an epistemology which could attempt to deal with the *complex nature of real social relations.* Indeed, Marx and Engels' insistence on understanding the world in a truly dialectical way resembles closely the underlying assumptions found in a critical semiotic meta-theoretical approach (or to be more accurate, the "calculus" for a critical semiotic meta-theoretical approach closely resembles the dialectical materialism[28] proposed by Marx and Engels).

---

the materialist philosophers examined both nature and social life from a mechanical point of view" (Ruis 1976: 68).

27 This is not to say that idealism and materialism are in opposition to one another. For s Coe and Wilden point out, materialism and idealism are not "logically independent of each other." Although both 'materialism' and 'idealism' ultimately pertain to the explanation of the same general world context, they are treated by the dominant epistemology as if they were two separate systems of explanation. i.e., as if they were *closed information systems.* In reality they are not closed off from, but dialectically interrelated with both each other and the socioecological context in which they arose" (1978: 51).

28 Although Marx or Engles never used the term dialectical materialism to describe their works, it is often associated with their teachings nevertheless. Indeed, the labels dialectical materialism and historical materialism are sometimes confused.

The manner in which these terms are being employed stems from the descriptions developed by Althusser (as provided by Therborn). Historical materialism is "the specificity of Marxist theory of society . . . as a *science*".

The manner in which Marx and Engels chose to incorporate and translate certain aspects of Hegelian philosophy provides us with more evidence for the necessity and importance of a pedagogy for media literacy. For what Marx and Engels were concerned with, in their formulation of a dialectical epistemology for explaining real concrete relations, was *understanding levels of patterns of relationship in context*. Marx and Engels' major concentration in their development of historical materialism was on the levels (and metalevels) of material relations of humans and society. It is here that the Hegelian notion of history becomes essential for Marx and Engels. Unlike many of their materialist contemporaries, Marx and Engels refused to accept the thesis that 'history repeats itself.'[29] For example, Feuerbach reasoned that "nature augments only in quantity while always raining the same . . ." (Rius 1976: 69).

Like Hegel, Marx and Engels conceived of the dialectical form as a rule for analysis and the understanding of change (Aiken 1957: 186-87). For Marx, "history is a non-repetitive process within which, at certain critical junctures, there occur radical, unprecedented transformations of material bases of social organization" (ibid.: 187).

In fact, the question of history has been defined as the "central dilemma" in the development of Marx and Engels' political and theoretical works. As Marx notes in his oft-quoted statement:

Dialectical materialism is "the specificity of Marxism as a *philosophy* . . . as distinct from science, politics, and ideology" (Therborn 1976: 55). Or, as Rius explains it, dialectical materialism is the "philosophical doctrine formulated by Marx and Engels, so called because of its *dialectical* manner of confronting, studying and understanding natural phenomena; and *materialist* by its manner of interpreting phenomena and drawing up its theory" (1976: 149). Historical materialism sees in the development of material goods necessary to human existence the primary force (*sic*) which determines (*sic*) all social life (and which conditions the transition from one kind of social order to another)" (ibid.).

[29] Rius explains that this type of position is, in fact, metaphysical. "Those who thought like this about nature, could think the same way about society too. Society changes very little for the metaphysician, except by repeating itself mechanically, e.g., wars, hunger, governments, etc. . . . and mankind really can't do anything to change things" (1976:69).

> People make their own history, but they do not make it just as they please, they do not make it under circumstances chosen by themselves . . . (Marx, cited in Appelbaum and Chotiner 1979: 71).

Indeed, Marx is referring to political-social and economic contexts and is insisting that *the recognition of context is essential to the understanding of historical change.*

The Hegelian dialectic proved fundamental to this contextual and relational notion of historical materialism, yet Marx's treatment of the dialectic indicates that it is not as abstract and mystical as Hegel would lead us to believe. In fact, Marx and Engels claimed that they took the Hegelian dialectic "off its idealistic head and placed it on its materialistic feet" (Wilson 1972: 212; Aiken 1967: 191; Holland 1977: 143). They were referring here, of course, to Hegel's belief that all historical changes are steps towards the realization of the "Absolute Spirit" in history. As Marx explained in *Das Kapital* (1867):

> For Hegel the process of thought, which, under the name of the idea, he even transforms into an independent subject, is the demiurge of the real world, while the real world is only its external appearance. With me, on the contrary, the ideal is nothing other than the material after it has been transposed and translated inside the human head (cited in Wilson 1972: 212).

What Marx and Engels were trying to demonstrate was that ideas are "only" human, and that therefore all ideas are related to specific social environments, which had initially been produced by human relations in and for *specific material conditions* (ibid.). Marx, in his rejection of Hegel's idealist interpretation of history (which ascribed a predetermined power to the ideas affording social change), could now see the development of thought—be it philosophical, political, or religious—as being necessarily affected by (and, at other levels, affecting) change in the modes of material production and organization (Aiken 1957: 188, 191). This had the effect of facilitating all examinations of contradictions between the ideal and the practical; that is to say, the ideational superstructure (e.g. the state, institutions, courts, schools, government) could be viewed *relationally* as expressions of real changes in the social system.

For Marx, then, all social change had to reflect a change in the material modes of economic production. His exploration into the more all-encompassing terrain of the "social" incorporated aspects of the writings and teachings of both idealists, especially Hegel, and materialists such as Feuerbach.

Marx and Engels' methods of investigating the development of human society, known as historical materialism, involved the examination and translation of a variety of ideas, experiences, and conceptualizations (e.g., aspects of materialism, the rejection of an Absolute Spirit, concern with the creation of material production; dialectics; the notions of patterns of levels of relations and change; the realities of contradictions; context; historical, social, and economic conditions; the modes of production, and so on). This radical explanation (punctuation) of historical development could never have evolved if Marx and Engels had allowed themselves to be constrained by what has been defined as either-or methodologies. Indeed, historical materialism reflects the necessity of perceiving relations in a dialectical manner.

DIALECTICAL MATERIALISM

It is at this point in the analysis that both the complexities and importance of the notion dialectics should be becoming more apparent. Within this context an examination of the dialectic within the framework of what is called dialectical materialism necessitates some form of clarification.[30]

Even though Marx wrote in *Das Kapital* that "my dialectic method is not only different from Hegelian, but is its direct opposite" (cited in Sherman 1976: 62), what Marx was communicating (in the real sense of the word) was a dialectical *shift* which:

> . . . saw the categories of method as *reflections* of the process of development of human knowledge, which in turn reflects the processes of natural and social development (ibid.; emphasis mine).

---

[30] Because dialectical materialism refers to the more general philosophy of Marx and Engels, certain relations of historical materialism may be reiterated and/or incorporated in this explanation.

Here, Marx and Engels were not only concerned with translating certain Hegelian notions, but also with applying them to real concrete relations. One important notion, which finds its antecedents in Hegel but which is radically transformed by Marx and Engels, includes the social behavior of individuals. Marx's social theory (or metatheory) required that social behavior could not be explained as a function of autonomous, rational decisions, but must be perceived as a reflection of "socially conditioned roles as members of an economic class" (Aiken 1957: 188). The necessity of understanding relations in their context is thus reinforced. Marx and Engels continued to borrow from, and translate, certain Hegelian concepts for what is today called dialectical materialism.

The Hegelian dialectic was thus transposed from an abstract process, mediated by a "Cosmic Spirit," to a practical application of social relations. As has been illustrated, Hegel's use of the dialectic had no concrete material basis for ascribing a causal connection between "thesis," "antithesis," and "synthesis." Marx, however, reinterpreted Hegel's dialectic in an attempt to explain and predict certain relations. Consequently, Hegel's dialectic was transformed from an apparently arbitrary *law* of thought into a *rule-governed means of discussing and explaining human behavior in relation to social, political, and economic contexts*.

In taking over the principle of the dialectic, Marx and Engels were able to recognize and better understand contradictions in capitalist society. Instead of the abstractions of Hegel's "Being and Nothing," Marx and Engels chose to discuss the "thesis" as bourgeois society "which had originally been a unification out of disintegrating feudal regime" (Wilson 1972: 211); the "antithesis" as the proletariat[31] (those who sell their labor

---

[31] As Marx and Engels explained this relationship in *The Communist Manifesto* of 1848: "The slave is sold once and for all. The proletarian must sell himself by the hour or by the day. Each individual slave, being the direct property of a master, has his existence assured, be that existence ever so wretched, if only because of the interest of the slave owner. Each individual proletarian, the property as it were of the whole bourgeois *class*, whose labor is sold only when it is needed by the owning class has no security of life. Existence is merely guaranteed to the working *class* as a whole. The slave is excluded from competition; the proletarian is beset by competition

creativity to those who own the means of production); and the "synthesis" which would be the communist society. The communist society:

> . . . would result from the conflict of the working class with the owning and employing classes and the taking-over of the industrial plant by the working class, which would represent a higher unity because it would harmonize the interests of all mankind (ibid.).

In other words, the struggle between the capitalist class (thesis) and the working class (antithesis) is supposed to result in a synthesis (White 1957: 14).[32] This leads to an expansion of how the dialectic was translated by Marx and Engels.

Marx was not bothered by the fact that Hegel confused logical contradictions with material conflict (in other words, confused logical types):

> The dialectical law of thesis, antithesis and synthesis provided Marx with first-rate clues for unraveling the threads of historical development. By interpreting it 'materialistically,' rather than as a mere law of thought, he was showing for the first time, *how the dialectic really operates* (Aiken 1957: 189; emphasis ours).

And so, in assuming a dialectical approach, Marx and Engels could look at the relationships between *people* rather than the Hegelian notion of looking at *individuals*. Whereas the usage of the term "individual" presumes that all people are equal, Marx and Engels understood that the key for a human science lay in recognizing both the existence of and the contradiction (not

---

and is prey to all its civil society; the proletarian is recognized as a person, as a member of civil society. The slave may therefore be able to secure better conditions of life than can the proletarian, but the proletarian belongs to a higher state of development of society than the slave. The slave frees himself by rupturing, of all relations of private ownership, only one, the relation of slavery and by this act becomes himself a proletarian; the proletarian can only achieve emancipation by abolishing private property in its entirety" (cited in Rius 1976: 111).

32 The real essence of the ensuing contradiction between labor and capital is highly complex. Suffice it to say that: the contradiction between the bourgeois and the proletarian is "not a contradiction between individuals and groups, but between the structure of the productive forces—their even greater socialization—and the structure of the relations of production—the private ownership of the productive forces" (Godelier 1966: 351).

opposition, which assumes equal but different) between *classes*.[33]

It would seem, then, that in using the dialectic, Marx and Engels were able to both identify and resolve (repunctuate) a contradiction inherent in Hegelian doctrine: the seemingly contradictory notion of the impossibility of individual purposes determining the course of social development; yet the existence of an "Absolute Being or Spirit" controlling and determining all action.

It was materialism which aided Marx and Engels in their reinterpretation and ability to ground the dialectic in reality (Aiken 1957: 189). Matter, for Marx, does not "refer to an underlying substratum or substance, but rather to the *observable 'materials'* with which [people] work and upon which they expend their energy . . ." (Aiken 1957: 189). The following statement is representative of the marriage of the dialectic, minus the idealism, and materialism, minus the mechanism:

> In the social production which men carry on they enter into definite relations that are indispensable and independent of their will; these relations of production correspond to a definite stage of development of their material powers of production. The totality of these relations of production constitutes the economic structure of society—the real foundation, on which legal and political superstructures arise and to which definite forms of social, political, and spiritual processes of life. It is not the consciousness of men that determines their being, but, on the contrary, their social being determines their consciousness (Marx 1859, cited in Bottomore and Rubel 1956: 67).

It has been previously indicated that *a very special type of materialism* was acceptable to Marx and Engels. Since conflict in human life can only be understood by an institutional (level-oriented) approach to the study of society, then all fundamental conflicts are social, and the basic form of social conflict is *class struggle* (Aiken 1957: 188). Therefore, materialism for Marx and Engels had to be far more complex than the simple assumption

33 Hegel did not, however, commit the error of so many of his contemporaries in interpreting the individual's role in society as purely a result of inherent choices, but analyzed social development in institutional terms (Aiken 1957: 188). Indeed, the interpretations of Marx and Engels, concerning class struggle, exploitation, and alienation can be viewed, in part, as translations of this radical Hegelian concept.

that humans are a product of individual circumstances and that society is more than an aggregation of human atoms, bound together by conscious decisions (ibid.).[34]

Although it may seem at first like a point of departure, the following discussion provides us with a deeper insight into dialectical materialism and a greater appreciation of Marx and Engels's criticism and rejection of certain materialist misconceptions.

VULGAR MATERIALSTS

Marx and Engels consistently emphasized that the traditional materialistic view of society seemed to preclude any hopes for radical change of the material circumstances of human life. For the early materialists held an atomistic theory of matter, which was usually accompanied by an analogous social theory. This social theory basically asserted that society was made up of individuals whose relations to one another were made up of individual decisions or interests. These materialists were labeled "vulgar"[35] by Engels (Acton 1967a: 391).

"Vulgar materialists" referred primarily to a group of German writers who argued that "materialism was the inevitable consequence of natural science and of physiology in particular" (ibid.). Engels criticized these writers, in *Socialism: Utopian and Scientific* (1892), for wasting too much time in arguing that god doesn't exist and for their lack of recognition of the *social* implications of materialism (ibid.). His primary objection to their works, however, was that theirs was largely a *mechanical* materialism (a mispunctuated materialism). The notion of mechanical materialism, for Engels, referred to the type of materialism

---

[34] In other words, any analyses of the semiotics of human communication must involve a metacommunicational, or meta-theoretical (both/and) punctuation which recognizes—and applies—the notions of contextual levels of patterns of relationship.

[35] The adjective "vulgar" is also employed to describe a specific type of theorist, known as a "vulgar Marxist." Vulgar Marxist Theory reduces (symmetrizes) all explanations of social relation to strictly economic relations.

that developed out of the natural science which was mechanics.[36]

Although we are conscious of the fact that what are perceived as radical and new ideas often find their roots in past discourse, it is both surprising and exciting to discover (or rediscover) what is considered to be a contemporary argument in earlier works. This is the case in Engels' critique of mechanical materialism. One of the major themes prefigured in this chapter is that a critical semiotic meta-theoretical approach rejects linear and atomistic theories applied to social relations. It now becomes apparent that in his explanation of the dangers of applying mechanistic methods, as grounded in studies within the natural sciences, Engels replicates and practically applies arguments previously discussed in reference to the revelations and necessity of a semiotic meta-theoretical approach.[37] What immediately comes to surface in Engels' holistic explanation is the existence of contradiction, and thus the dialectic.

Engels argued that the mechanistic (also referred to as "metaphysical," which asserted that there could be no contradictions in nature) rested upon the assumption that "things were static."[38] However, if a critical semiotic meta-theoretical approach is adopted—i.e., "things" in movement and relation to

---

[36] Once more, the detrimental implications of either-or logic is indicated.

[37] This refusal to repunctuate relations in a dialectical manner (recognizing, at least, the realities of contextual levels of patterns of relationship) is still in evidence in many contemporary modes of thought. For as Wilden points out:

> "... on both the right and left in Western society one still finds it assumed that (critical) sciences, social and physical, signifies a non-ideological or equivalently 'value-free' state of affairs. Given the awesome power of the dominant ideology and the dominant forms of communication in our society, the sources of this somewhat romantic belief are readily understandable. In a society dominated by commoditized relations and alienated values, the attempt to close science off from its relations with the values of its contexts makes a tortuous kind of sense. All the same, however, this undialectical activity seems ultimately to betray and implicit allegiance to a now venerable religious, psychological, and philosophical tradition: THE QUEST FOR THE ABSOLUTE (as the early nineteenth century phased it)" (1980:xxvii).

[38] Thus, the metaphysical views—as it is explained by Engels—provides us with yet another example of either-or mechanistic logic.

one another—then the dialectical view must be adopted. *For movement itself is a contradiction.*

THE "LAWS" OF DIALECTICS

In discussing the dialectic, Engels laid out some "laws" for its application in *Anti-Duhring* (1878) and *Dialectics of Nature* (1872: 82). In fact, Engels himself applied the laws of dialectics "as a method to provide an approach with profound insights into natural and social processes" (Sherman 1976: 58). What Engels attempted was to "codify 'material dialectics' as a way of understanding the dialectics of natural history and social life" (Wilden 1977a: 93).

For the purpose of the central argument of this chapter two of these so-called laws will be discussed in detail: those known as "Unity of Opposites" and "Negation of the Negation."

The "interpenetration of opposites," or "unity of opposites," was never discussed in great detail by Engels. Basically, this stalled law seemed to be intended as an explanation of *why change occurs*. The general idea behind it was that without tension, everything would remain the same, since there would be nothing to promote change. The purpose of this law was to explain, in a deeper and more contextual manner, and to, in fact, repunctuate and thus metacommunicate about the complexity of dialectical relations (levels of communication) involved *in and with* society. It is an attempt at reminding us that the world does not consist of isolated entities, but of relations (or "forces") in opposition, unification, and contradiction with one another (the "thesis," "antithesis," "synthesis").[39] In other words, "opposition" and/or "contradiction" is the necessary relation for change.

> Further, we find upon closer investigation that the two poles of an antithesis, positive and negative, e.g., are as inseparable as they are opposed, and that despite all their opposition they mutually interpene-

[39] Many of the characteristics of a pedagogy for media literacy (e.g., context, relationship, punctuation of patterns of relation, levels of communication and, of course, contradiction) and the more all-encompassing essence of a critical semiotic meta-theoretical approach, are easily associated with this explanation.

trate. And we find, in like manner, that cause and effect are conceptions which hold good only in their application to individual cases; but as soon as we consider the individual cases in their general connection with the universe as a whole they run into each other, and they become confounded when we contemplate that universal action and reaction in which causes and effects are eternally changing places, so that what is effect here and now will be cause there and then, and vice versa (Engels 1892: 84-85).

Much debate has ensued due to the ambiguity of Engels' explanation of "opposition." "Opposition" would seem to imply "symmetrical"—i.e., distinct but equal-relations. The most fundamental problem, which is painfully explicit in the above passage, is Engels' use of "opposition," "cause-effect," "positive-negative," to describe relations which may not be in opposition at all. Thus, one could convincingly argue (if one took Engels at face value) that hierarchically different relations, such as slave "vs." slave-owner or woman "vs." man, are in the same type of opposition to each other as the two poles of a magnet. At any event, to even use the term "versus" implies a symmetrized opposition, rather than a hierarchical *contradiction* which, in reality, exists. The use of the term "opposition" as a catch-all phrase for describing relations which are, in actuality, not opposed, *has had serious repercussions for examining social relations*.[40]

For example, the usage of such phrases as "the battle of the sexes," places the relationship of the sexes in an *imaginary* opposition to each other. In doing this, the hierarchical contradiction existing between the relations of men and women is *neutralized;* the two sexes are being placed in a false identity of opposites (Coe and Wilden 1977: 32; cf. Wilden 1988). This process is one which Wilden (1980) has termed *symmetrization*.[41]

---

40 In other words, the use of opposition to explain relations which are, in actuality, relations of contradiction once again reinforces the dangers of mispunctuation (which evolve from symmetrization).

41 The idea of "a false identity of opposites" provides us with greater insight into the notion of symmetrization (a predominant type of mispunctuation). As a result of this symmetrization of levels, distinct socioeconomic levels which contradict each other in the Real will commonly be perceived and acted on as if the various levels were simply in a single-level opposi-

In reality, no such identity and no such opposition actually exists (ibid.: 33). What exists is a *conflict* or struggle. The same can be said for the "opposition" between "capital" and "labor." Although one can still imagine the dialectic in terms of "thesis," "antithesis," and "synthesis," one *cannot* assume that the "thesis" and "antithesis" are *always* in opposition. As it happens, in most cases concerning organic relations (as in the relation between capital and labor) a contradiction or conflict exists between the "antithesis" and "thesis."

The term "unity of contradiction" implies, then, that the relationships being described involve *at least* two levels, one of which is dominant over the other (ibid.).

> The reason for substituting 'unity' for 'identity' is, first, to correct the notion that the relationship is symmetrical ('equal and opposite') by indicating its fundamental asymmetry; and second, to include within the description the reality that 'male' and 'female'—like 'capital' and 'labor' in our present economic system are interdependent . . . (ibid.).

The phrase "identity of opposites" is, however, appropriate for expressing such relationships as:

---

tion to each other (man opposes woman, capital opposes labor, white opposes nonwhite , and so on)" (Wilden 1980a: 77).

Symmetrization involves the ideological and epistemological process of making hierarchically distinct levels of relationship appear to be "equal" or on the same level, when in reality one class is of a different logical type than another. An example of symmetrization in male and female relationships is found in the phrase, "my wife and I are equal." Here the wife is being portrayed as an "independent" individual. The statement, in fact, represents the reality of power relationships as defined by the sociopolitical and economic context. Since in a patriarchal system the relationship between men and women is one of master and slave (in a psycho-social sense) one of the significations of the expression—whether deliberate or not—is that masters and slaves are equal. In pretending this equality, in actuality, this statement is reaffirming the inequality of the real relationship, i.e., men are dominant and women are subordinate.

Wilden provides further clarification of this notion of symmetrization by explaining: "No symmetrical equation can legitimately be made between epithets 'Honkie' and 'Nigger'—even though they are commonly treated as the 'two sides' of an Imaginary and symmetrical question, like 'Anti-Semite' and 'Jew,' like 'Man' and 'Woman,' like 'Business' and 'Labor.' Because each term and each image in each pair refers to distinct levels—then the two terms (and the states they refer to) are not exchangeable equivalents in our society. 'Honkie' cannot 'negate' white in the way that 'Nigger' 'negates' black" (1980a: 105-106).

1. A relation involving a polarity of two items of the same logical level of reality, "such as that between positive and negative electrical potential" (ibid.: 31), and;
2. A relationship in which the structural identity is constituted such that the distinction between the two poles is based entirely on an oppositional sign of the same type as the other; such as +2 and –2 (ibid.).

V. I. Lenin (1870-1924) is generally regarded as "the chief exponent of dialectical materialism" after Marx and Engels (Runes 1960: 167). However, it would seem that Lenin followed in Engels' footsteps in clouding the "issue of relationships between dialectics and living and social systems" (Coe and Wilden 1978: 35). For in describing "identity of opposites" he listed:

In mathematics:	+ and – Differential and integral.
In mechanics:	action and reaction.
In physics:	positive and negative electricity.
In chemistry:	the combination and disassociation of atoms.
In social science:	*The Class Struggle* (ibid.; emphasis mine).

The "class struggle," however, cannot be equated with positive and negative electricity, as it is incorrect to make an analogy between the mechanics of the physical world to the non-mechanical relationship of living and social systems (ibid.).

This is just one more example of a mechanistic perspective, whereby a misinterpretation of hierarchical relations places them in imaginary opposition to one another, which results in a mispunctuation of "real" communicational phenomena.

As Coe and Wilden point out, Marx had in the *Grundrisse* criticized the position of confusing hierarchically different relations with relations existing in bilateral opposition ("Foundations of the Critique of Political Economy," 1857-58) (1978: 37). This was in respect to the erroneous assumption that production and consumption are "equal."[42]

---

[42] As Marx explained it in his "Introduction" to the "Foundations Critique of Political Economy" (1857-58), "consumption produces production by creating the necessity for new production, i.e., by providing the ideal, inward, impelling cause which constitutes the prerequisite of production.

The notion of "identity of opposites" is a necessary concept in understanding a dialectical, and concurrently, critical semiotic meta-theoretical approach. An important lesson about context and punctuation is implicit in the lengthy discussion concerning this so-called law. When confronted with relations which seem to be in opposition, one should "adjust one's vision" to recognize, not just the context of the particular relation, *but the overall context which has defined the question in the first place.* In other words, a relationship which is, in reality, hierarchical, may, as a result of socialized assumptions, be treated—or mispunctuated—as a single-level opposition. The distinction between an "identity of opposites" and a "unity of contradiction" is often a fine one to make; however, a necessary one in the on-going process of understanding change.

Coe and Wilden discuss four different types of relations which are often seen as falling under the heading of "Identity of Opposites":

A. Unity of Differences	The rippled surface of a lake; direction is multi-dimensional space.
B. Unity of Distinctions	The alphabet in writing; the whole number system; . . . compass headings.
C. Unity of Oppositions	Positive and negative electric potential (in which the two poles are structurally identical).
D. Unity of Contradictions	('A' dominant): An economic system with 'A' standing for 'business; 'B' standing for 'peasantry,' and 'C' standing for industrial workers' (1978: 43).

Consumption furnishes the impulse for production as well as its object, which plays in production the part of its guiding aim. It is clear that while production furnishes the material object of consumption, consumption provides the ideal object of production, as its image, its want, its impulse, and its purpose. It furnishes the object of production in its subjective form. No wants, no production. But consumption reproduces the want" (Sweezy: 1942: 173).

Sweezy translates this somewhat esoteric definition by discussing "the fundamental contradiction" of capitalism:

> ". . . production entirely lacks an objective unless it is directed towards a definite goal in consumption, but capitalism attempts to expand production without any reference to the consumption which alone can give it meaning" (ibid.: 174-175).

Therefore, an essential understanding, evoked by a dialectical perspective, is that when confronted with a relation which initially seems to be, or is defined as, an "Identity of Opposites," one must study that relation in a dialectical fashion (examine the original punctuation in light of the patterns of relationship, the metacontextual levels of constraint, and take into consideration the possibility of mispunctuation) in order to ascertain if it is, in reality, the case.

More specifically emphasized by Engels was the so-called law of the "negation of the negation." If we turn once again to the structure of "thesis," "antithesis," and "synthesis" remembering Hegel's original explanation ("A" and "not-A") the "negation of the negation" takes on new meaning when given *real* characteristics. Marx, in *Das Kapital*, explained that:

> ... when, as a result of competition between capitalists, the few remaining giant capitalist enterprises find themselves confronted by a poverty-stricken proletariat, the latter will rise and expropriate the former, the expropriators will be expropriated (in Acton 1967a: 393).

The "antithesis," then *negates* the "thesis," resulting in the "negation of the negation" producing the "synthesis."

It has been argued that the label "negation of the negation" is an appropriate way to discuss contradiction, conflict, and change in material social relations. But in outlining this so-called law, it would seem that Engels failed to make a consistent distinction between inorganic, organic, and socioeconomic systems (Wilden 1977a: 94). In *Anti-Duhring* (1978), Engels asserts:

> ... our purpose here ... to show that negation of the negation *really does take place* in both (the plant and animal) kingdoms of the organic world. Furthermore, the whole of geology is a series of successive shatterings of old and deposits of new rock formations (cited in Wilden 1977a: 94).

The confusion between organic, socioeconomic and inorganic systems is another illustration of the process of symmetrization. For hierarchical and complex levels of relations, according to this explanation, can mistakenly be oversimplified (i.e., reduced) and thus neutralized.[43] The inherent dangers of classi-

---

[43] Indeed, what is taking place in this type of mispunctuation is a confusion of logical types, as inorganic, organic and socioeconomic systems represent different levels of contextual constraint.

fying all such relations, as those previously put forward as "Unity of Differences," "Unity of Distinctions," "Unity of Oppositions," and "Unity of Contradictions" under the rubric of "Interpenetration of Opposites" or "Identity of Opposites," would also hold true for the manner in which "negation of the negation" is commonly interpreted. (Mispunctuations can, of course, also arise if the relations which "thesis" and "antithesis" represent are not seen in their proper context.)

In clarification it would seem that for the purposes of discussing the relations between Hegelian ideal concepts, the triadic processes of change called "thesis," "antithesis" and "synthesis"—are both appropriate and necessary. However, in view of the repunctuations of the Hegelian dialectic into a way of understanding systems in conflict *with* systems, or conflicts *between* subsystems (e.g., socioeconomic classes) within the whole system making up society in history the "thesis," "antithesis,' "synthesis" analogy proves to be *just too linear a model* (Wilden 1977a: 95; 1987). The notion of negation of the thesis by the antithesis "applies a one-dimensional construct to a multidimensional reality" (ibid.).

In another light, this model makes it all too easy to fall into some of the ideological myths regarding relations in false opposition (the symmetrization of levels of complexity). In order for the so-called law of "negation of the negation" to make sense, "A" and "not-A" would have to be of different *logical types* or in a relation of a "unity of contradiction."

> 'A' stands for some particular item, some particular relation, or some particular pattern. "Not-A,' in contrast stands for every other item, relation, or pattern in the universe except 'A'. As a *generality*, 'not-A' cannot properly be regarded as being of the same type of a particular, such as 'A'. To put the point another way, the difference in levels between 'A' and 'not-A' results from the circumstances that 'not-A' is not simply the 'negative' of 'A'. 'Not-A' is the *environment* of 'A' (Coe and Wilden 1978: 45).[44]

---

[44] This explanation is an apt criticism of the notion of the "law of the excluded middle," whereby a relation cannot be "A" and "not-A" at the same time. For what is being emphasized is that "A" and "not-A" are of different logical types (and exist in a relation of contradiction) so that "not-A" can be perceived as providing the context for, and therefore encompassing, "A".

The "negation of the negation" should be perceived as simply a guide or punctuation available for reminding one to recognize hierarchically different levels of relations, which are often confused with "what we are taught" are opposing systems of relations or subsystems of relations.[45]

Wilden (1987: 276) notes that the "dialectic is not simply a way of knowing; it is the way of life itself." He describes the term "dialectic" as "rereading in a new context", a "reframing of logical types", a "shift in levels of communication", or an "emergence of novelty 'after-the-event'." Wilden claims that the law of non-contradiction is not violated in the dialectic. That is, dialectical logic includes and uses analytic (or static) logic as its necessary complement. Without the "either-or" of analytic logic, Wilden claims that decision is impossible. Analytic logic is also "both/and" logic in the sense that it is a secondary relationship derived by addition from its basic operation of division, either-or. The perspective of analytic logic is thus "*either* either-*or* both/and."

However, the "both/and" of dialectical logic is different. This type of logic is a relationship derived by connection from relations between levels, such as the both/and relation between open systems and environment. As Wilden notes, dialectical logic is not based on choosing between one 'side' or the other of pairs of mutually exclusive alternatives in a single dimension

---

As Wilson Bryan Key (1989) describes it:

> "The *law of the excluded middle* was one of Aristotle's more imaginative ideas. It can be briefly explained as 'Every-thing must either be or not be.' . . . Those who know and obey this law can fantasize that they know precisely at any given moment where everything either is or is not. The fantasy that there are only two sides to every question makes truth easily attainable. The world will never be such a simplistic place. When objects or people are perceived as either this or that, neither this nor that, they project into simplistic two-valued reality illusions (134).

45 Wilden explains that:

> . . . these imaginary symmetrizations will usually contain enough of a half-spoken truth about the real relationship to make the pseudo-symmetry believable. Indeed all ideological mispunctuations and misrepresentations of real relations in our society do tell some kind of truth about some aspect of our relationships. These misrepresentations of reality are rarely outright lies—and this is what makes them so difficult to deal with (1980a: 77).

but refers to the framing of new contexts and the repatterning and restructuring of the old order.

Wilden (1987: 249) reports that dialectical logic can be seen in Bateson's concept of levels of learning:

> In Bateson the concepts of levels of learning, at the first level the mere reception of information (zero learning), then the comprehension of the information by putting it into the context of other information (learning), then the comprehension of the diversity of contexts to put the information in (learning how to learn) has the same dialectic form, including the apparent discontinuity between levels. In Marx, Engels, Eisenstein, Mao, and others the key is learning through conflict. In Latin learning is *docendo didici:* 'I learnt by teaching'.

A DIALECTICAL UNDERSTANDING OF SOCIAL PROBLEMS

What was—and often still is—called "race wars between blacks and whites" in the U.S.A. is a good illustration of the symmetrized mispunctuation which was referred to in the previous section. A case in point is the so-called desegregation laws passed in 1954 by the Supreme Court. Five court cases, concerning the unconstitutional practice of segregating public school children solely on the basis of race—under the official name of *Brown vs. Board of Education*—initiated this Supreme Court decision (Quarles 1964: 268).

The so-called desegregation laws are often mispunctuated as being the *result* of the *opposition* between blacks and whites concerning the unconstitutional and racist practice of separate (and unequal) education (i.e., of placing in false opposition relations which are, in actuality, relations of contradiction). The resolution of this "problem," through a State decision, was supposed to have the affect of solving the "inequities" inherent in the system and, more importantly, to put an end to black protest. However, this "paper" change had curious repercussions in regards to ideological change. For instead of "pacifying" public displays of black "discontent," this legal decision was partially responsible for a "raising of consciousness" (or a repunctuation) for both blacks and whites.

> . . . The Brown decision meant that America would have to look anew at its colored citizens. '*The abiding subconscious of the Negro turned overnight*

> *into an acute and immediate awareness of the Negro,'* wrote James Jackson Kilpatrick, editor of the *Richmond News Leader* (Quarles 1964: 238).

Awareness and subsequent shock prevailed, as whites began to realize that the black "problem" was far from being solved, but was in fact escalating. Many blacks, on another level, recognized that this token appeasement was just symptomatic of the insurmountable injustices and violence directed at black people in America through sociopolitical and economic hegemonic constraints.

> You need some proof? Well, then, why was it that when Negroes did start revolting across America, virtually all of white America was caught up in surprise and even shock? I would hate to be general of an army as badly informed as the American white man has been about the Negro in this country (Malcolm X 1964: 273-74).

As far as the "effectiveness" of the so-called desegregation laws is concerned, we need only look at unemployment statistics; northern ghettos in such places as Detroit, Baltimore, or Washington, D.C. (see McLaren and Dantley 1989); the quality of education the majority of black children are receiving; or pay a visit to the southern states to witness the effectiveness of these laws.

> No *sane* man really wants integration! No sane white man really wants integration! No sane black man really believes that the white man ever will give the black man anything more than token integration . . . Human rights! Respect as *human beings!* That's what America's black masses want. That's the true problem. The black masses want not to be shrunk from as though they are plague-ridden (ibid.: 245-46).[46]

The common *error* of the dominant ideology is once more apparent; the never-ending mythical practice of putting *contradictory* relations in symmetrical opposition. In a real and dialectical perspective, it is immediately obvious that to place the races in opposition, i.e., black vs. white, is to posit a *false rela-*

---

[46] Indeed, what Malcolm X is emphasizing is that the idea of integration—within a white dominated society—is a symmetrization of hierarchical levels of constraint (an attempt to resolve a mispunctuated understanding of relations between blacks and whites; mispunctuated because it confuses logical types, and decontextualizes and thus neutralizes reality). Malcolm X's statement is, in fact, a metacommunication.

tion.[47] The implementation of the desegregation laws reflects not a society based on a symmetrical (binary, single- level, two-sided) opposition between whites and blacks, but rather a unity of contradictions, a social hierarchy dealing with levels of relation, with "blacks versus white" representing two sides of an imaginary equation, such as "upper class versus lower class" (in which a real conflict between social levels and levels of power is neutralized). As Wilden (1987:22) notes, the dominant ideology creates the impression that symmetrical confiict or opposition is the fundamental (natural) conflict lying behind most kinds of relations. This deflects questions away from issues dealing with illegitimate power, privilege, domination and oppression.

> Unless we call one white man, by name, a 'devil,' we are not speaking of any *individual* white man. We are speaking of the *collective* white man's *historical* record. We are speaking of the collective white man's cruelties, and evils, and greeds, that have seen him *act* like a devil towards the non-white man. Any intelligent, honest, objective person cannot fail to realize that this white man's slave trade, and his subsequent devilish actions are directly *responsible* for not only the *presence* of this black man in America, but also for the *condition* of which we find this black man here. You cannot find *one* black man, I do not care who he is, who has not been personally damaged in some way by the devilish acts of the collective white man (Malcolm x, 1964).

One notion which immediately comes to mind in this moving quotation, is Malcolm X's concern with distinguishing between the "individual" and the "collective." This distinction is another fundamental relation which is often reduced to an "either-or," "oppositional" model within the dominant social code. How often have we heard arguments like: "But I'm not a racist, some of my best friends are black," or "I'm not a sexist; my wife and I are equal." In such cases, we are taught to confuse the "individual" with the "collective." The "collective" refers to the Dominant Other[48] and/or the dominant code (ideology). This

---

[47] Within the context of this explanation, it can now be noted that the idea of "reverse discrimination," in reality, cannot exist. For it is just an extension of the mispunctuation of placing blacks and whites in a relation of false opposition, and is thus a confusion of logical types.

[48] The notion "Dominant Other" is a useful term for metacommunicating about relations of oppression. Dominant Others refer to the collective

dominant "Other" is represented by the individual, who is a part of the oppressing (exploiting) class, race, and/or sex. Since this code is of a higher level or logical type than the individual it constrains, to reduce the "collective" to the "individual" is again to posit a false opposition. And, since an individual is defined by relations to others—both real and imaginary—and to the social, political, and economic context (e.g. class, race, sex) it is impossible for the dominant discourse not to be ingrained in the individual. It is the dominant ideology—the capitalist system, in this case—which should be recognized as a *collective expression* of racism.

Within this context, the appropriateness of a critical semiotic meta-theoretical approach for a pedagogy of media literacy becomes evident. As the emancipatory nature of a dialectical analysis allow for a translation from this notion—of imaginary opposition (and thus colonial relationships)—to the depiction of this pathological reality in contemporary media. Hence the practical applications of this emergent epistemology are realized.

The problem with representing racism from the perspective of "equal but opposite" relations is evident in Spike Lee's treatment of this concept in his recent film, *Do the Right Thing*. This film would serve as a good example for teachers, to employ a pedagogy of media literacy in their classrooms, to illustrate the construction of racist ideology. Lee is commenting on how the structure of racism in American society is expressed subjectively (and contradictorily) in the social and cultural patterns of everyday life among various ethnic groups. It is the dominant, predominately white culture, that serves to constrain blacks, forcing them on a collective basis to exist as a subaltern caste. Although tied to a limited perspective of identity formation as primarily linked to race at the expense of gender and class, and while portraying a rather stereotypical image of black males encysted in a universe of a white supremacist capitalist patriarchy (hooks 1989), *Do the Right Thing* does illustrate the

---

oppression of one group, class, and/or sex by the dominant (more powerful) class, race and/or sex. Under capitalism, the Dominant Other is represented by the white, gentile, (straight), capitalist male.

logic of oppression working as a structural constraint which along with economic, social, and cultural constraints, reproduces an asymmetry of power and privilege in relation to the life chances of the subaltern in the political and corporate arena. We may deplore the uncritical acceptance of sexist-constructions of masculinity and the brand of black nationalism which excludes black women in the struggle for social justice (ibid.) found in *Do the Right Thing,* yet we can nevertheless appreciate its dialectical articulation of human agency as being hierarchically inscribed by relations of domination. It is not, as hooks argues, an "us against them film," it is an us (whites) "over" them (blacks) film. Breaking down the larger economies of power, privilege and the social apparatuses of sexism and racism that positions black men and women as naturally inferior and responsible for their own plight means understanding this process not as a symmetrical war of the races but as a form of race, class, and gender domination within a hierarchical level of hegemonic constraints. However, it must be noted that Lee resorts to symmetrized reductionism in his montage of representatives of different hierarchical groups stereotyping (in oppositional fashion) one another.

Indeed, Wilden provides us with an example which demonstrates the impossibility of "equal but opposite" relations between hierarchically different levels of relation:

> In the real world supported and maintained by real labor, and where words may also be forms of violence, potential and actual, we know that one white person's 'Nigger!' does incalculable damage to the 'self concept' of the black, whereas one thousand or one million blacks responding to an original white assault by means of 'Honkie!' has no necessary or significant effect on the white at all. Such 'negation' and 'counter-negation' cannot under state and private capitalism be reciprocal or symmetrical because the white *collectivity* represents a dominant Other for the black . . . (1979: 9).

To cite another example, what is still considered by many teachers as the opposition between critical theory and practice is another illustration of symmetrized mispunctuation. This amounts to placing in false opposition relations which are in actuality relations of *contradiction.* In teacher education programs it is often practice (hands on experience)—which dominates educational programs. A cult of technology and efficiency militates against providing students with a critical language which will enable them to understand the presuppositions which inform their practice. Instead of looking at theory and practice in "either-or" terms, an understanding of the dialectical relationship between theory and practice can help educators understand how these concepts constitute classroom *praxis*.

The same is true of teaching about social life within patriarchy. It is inaccurate for educators to symmetrize "male" vs. "female" as if they are equal but opposite positions in the arena of social struggle. Rather, the regime of maleness (patriarchy) serves to constrain that of the female in Western capitalist societies, and in most other societies as well. The employment of imaginary oppositions helps to perpetuate the liberal myth which often gets translated into an identitarian logic of abstract equality. Such assumptions are embedded in a denial of the importance of both women's roles both in and outside the family as well as the valorization of women's experience (Mills 1987). This dimension of the dialectic that can distinguish hierarchical relations and which recognizes the danger of symmetrization can help teachers and students contest society's prescribed set of gender-linked role expectations.

In his now classic text, *Ideology, Culture and the Process of Schooling,* Henry Giroux asserts that "any emancipatory notion of the dialectic has to be grounded in the process of critique and praxis" (p. 116). By employing a dialectical language to analyze contemporary trends in educational theorizing and practice, Giroux is able to subvert the conventional hierarchy which privileges practice and "raw" unreflexive experience over theory and which ensures oneself against recognizing the contingency and plurality of subjectivity and the importance of otherness. Giroux employs the dialectic to show teachers that their experiences within the classroom are never innocent but must be mediated by a critical language which enables the contradictions within the classroom and the larger society to be exposed. In this way teachers can attempt to bridge the gap between the equality schooling professes to bring and the inequality that gets reproduced in its name. In this way,

Giroux's concept of the dialectic deconstructs and transforms the tendency of school programs and practices to inexorably privilege instrumentalism, procedure, and practice and to judge these by the single criteria of efficiency and production.

What is emphasized in Giroux's *dialectical theory of dialectics,* is transformative *praxis,* that is, a recognition of the contradictions which exist in all institutional sites and pedagogical practices and an attempt to transform them in the interests of social change and the creation of a more democratic life. In this way, a pedagogical approach that defines itself as truly critical must also be dialectical.

An understanding of the dialectical nature of social life can help teachers recognize the danger in positing a false opposition between what is essentially a hierarchical relation—e.g., black/white, man/woman, theory/practice. Yet there is another slant on the dialectic that is especially helpful for teachers. In his pathbreaking work, *Negative Dialectics,* Theodor Adorno follows Hegel's recognition that consciousness and social practices are mutually constitutive yet, like Marx, he does not follow Hegel's assertion that there can be a form of thought free from social processes. Negative dialectics, according to Adorno, is a mode of critical thought which attempts to remain aware of its own social shaping while at the same time seeks to reveal the true relations between language and reality. Negative dialectics not only reveals that any dimension of reality has been historically shaped, but that it contains within "images" or "possibilities" of what it might become (Gibson 1986).

Thus, term "dialectics" refers to the constant interplay between subject and object or language and reality while the term "negative" refers to the contradictions, negations, or potentialities implied in the reality under analysis (Gibson 1986).

Rex Gibson (1986) offers a succinct example of negative dialectics in his example of the contradiction between the concept of "freedom" and the actualities of everyday classroom life. When teachers speak of students' "free time," negative dialectics shows that the relationship between the concept of "free activity" and the reality of the classroom is nonidentical because the social inequalities of power between children and teachers negate what freedom implies. Yet it does *imply* the conditions (or reveal the potentialities) which *would apply* if 'activity' were *really* 'free.' Negative dialectics therefore can identify those social factors which prevent freedom from being realized. Gibson is worth quoting at length:

> In practice, a child's 'free activity' is heavily circumscribed by the materials the teacher provides and the behavior she allows. Both materials and behavior are closely controlled by her ideology, that is, her beliefs about children, learning, schooling, and so on. We see here the *dialectic:* the movement between the particular (*this* classroom, *this* teacher) and the general (the concept of 'free activity'). We also see negation: the revealing of disjunction between concept and object, appearance and reality, and the identification of what would genuinely characterize 'free activity.' This process of the *negative dialectic* is critical theory for it identifies the discrepancies between is and *ought;* between what is claimed and what might be; between actuality and potential (p. 27).

Media literacy educators can employ the dialectic in a number of ways: in recognizing the mutually constitutive nature of theory/practice; in helping students to analyze the hierarchical positioning of individuals within the social order on the basis of race, class, gender and sexuality; and in acknowledging the asymmetrical ways in which power operates in the larger society to reproduce the interests of the dominant culture organized as a town hierarchy and marred by competitiveness and corporate greed. Of course, we are speaking here of a critical use of the dialectic (a critical semiotic meta-theoretical approach); one which is attentive to the dangers inherent in vulgar Hegelianism which universalizes the concept of liberation through a conception of an androcentric, autonomous, Cartesian subject. We argue that a critical pedagogy of media literacy needs to appropriate a reading of the dialectic which avoids a masculist conception of the self and Eurocentric and patriarchal narratives of emancipation based upon a vulgar Hegelian confrontation with and negation of the Other.

Rethinking the dialectic from a standpoint such as the one developed in this chapter will, hopefully, help to provide new explanatory categories from which to gain a more contextual understanding of past and present political and cultural struggles. The development of such categories may place us in a more advantageous position from which to appreciate the recent challenge of Ernesto Laclau (1988): transforming current forms of identification and constructions of subjectivity by searching not only for cultural forms which reveal the universal in the contingent, but also the contingent in the universal (p. 22). By so focusing on the "dignity of the specific" we may be able to "reduce the world to its 'human scale,'" avoiding the "essentialist tidiness" of conceiving contemporary social life which has brought upon us so much pain and strife.[49]

Understanding reality dialectically can also help us to make more critical choices as citizens, recognizing the distinction between necessity and desire, and making a commitment to freedom. It can also provide the foundation for a political-cultural mode of inquiry aimed at transforming the larger collective political and cultural world as it contests the given range of thought and action that defines who we are and what we might become.[50]

---

[49] It is imperative that Peter McLaren be credited for his seminal contributions which include the Analysis of Spike Lee's "Do the Right Thing," Giroux's and Laclau's notions on dialectics and the significant explication of negative dialectics.

[50] The need for a critical semiotic dialectical meta- theoretical approach for a pedagogy of media literacy is even more urgent in light of contemporary technological innovations which have serious implications for both the nature and role of television as we currently know it. By 1994 most, if not all, U.S. cable companies will switch from analog to "compressed-digital transmission," and the largely American-owned Canadian cable industry will follow suit with a system they have labeled "universal addressability." Digital video compression (DVC) will increase channel capacity to 500 (possibly 1000, if a U.S. digital-broadcast satellite service is successfully launched in 1994) (Dibbel, 1993: 55). Yet this is only one, of a plethora of "Jetsonesque" telecommunications developments which promises to radically transform television within the next 5 years. These include: "Direct broadcast satellites" (DBS)—'affectionately' dubbed Deathstars, by the Canadian cable industry—which will offer consumers 80—100 channels of "near-video-on-demand" (special sports and concerts, direct-to-video movies, etc.) for the price of a "special decoder, an 18-inch satellite receiver (about $1000.00) and a monthly subscription fee (about $25.00)" (Quill, 1993: G1). And, eventually, "supercompression and fiberoptics" brought to us courtesy of our friendly neighbourhood oligopoly.

> "Earlier this year, months if not years before it was expected, the FCC approved the entry of the nation's telephone companies into the TV industry.

> The change could be seismological: If the telcos get around to threading our country with fibre optic lines [a technology which conveys information in the form of laser light along thin threads of glass], Americans may soon live in homes where their TVs, computers, and telephones become interchangeable" (Dibbel, 1992: 55).

The gloves are off, and every multi-national in town will be competing for the consumers dime. But alas, this is only the tip of the iceberg in regards to the "shape of things to come." Chris Whittle's Channel One Network (a so-called educational video news service, complete with commercials!) has already infiltrated thousands of U.S. public schools, nationwide. In 1991, Whittle launched the 2.5 billion dollar Edison project; a plan to construct a national system of profit schools, which "Russel Jacoby refers to as 'McSchool Franchises' or 'educational boutiques'. . . fast food versions of the comprehensive high school where rows of Whittle TV monitors can replace important human resources such as teachers" (McLaren 1993).

Thus, we will be bombarded in a multitude of dimensions, with such exponential speed and frequency, through a variety of media forms and forums, that our already weakened comprehensive and critical skills will, I fear, be even further decimated. Indeed, the underlying premise of Neil Postman's 1985 seminal text, on the nature of ideology in television entertainment, *Amusing Ourselves To Death*, will take on a new, and more terrifying meaning.

> "The truth is, though, you don't have to be the reincarnation of George Orwell to sense dystopia lurking in the digital future. In fact, it probably helps if your aren't—anyone haunted by the specter of totalitarian repression isn't going to hear the creepier nuances of such healthy-sounding notions as 'pluralism' and 'personal empowerment.' And when the former becomes just code for a corporate-controlled media sphere that isolates consumers into ever-narrower pigeonholes of taste and cash flow, and the latter means little more than the consumer's right to participate in narrowing the focus, than an ability to sift through such bullshit will be crucial" (Dibbell 1992: 56, 60).

There is little doubt that the television we love to hate will be replaced with a television we will hate to love; one so slickly packaged and seductively hyped that it promises to entice even the most elitist anti-t.v. "pomo-ironist." The myth of individualism could be embraced with a fervor reminiscent of those golden days of televangelistic yore; except this time the audience could transcend educational and political boundaries. And with the death of television, as we understand it, will be the obsolescence of most mass media theories which have presumed to explain it (many of which, we must add—especially those vulgar deterministic models taught in too many communications schools—have long out-lived their usefulness). Within this context, our hope lies in an educational commitment to a critical pedagogy of media literacy which embraces a practical application of the theoretical domain, and encourages guerrilla cam-corder activism, ham-video production and counter-hegemonic transmission and distribution. For without it, Huxley's vision of *A Brave New*

REFERENCES

Acton, H. B. (1967). Hegel, Georg Wilhelm Freidrich. In P. Edwards (ed.), *The Encyclopedia of Philosophy* (pp. 435-51). New York: Crowell Collier and MacMillan, Inc.

________ (1967a). "Dialectical Materialism". In P. Edwards (ed.), *The Encyclopedia of Philosophy* (pp. 389-97). New York: Crowell Collier and MacMillan, Inc.

Adorno, T. W. (1973). *Negative Dialectics.* New York: Seabury Press.

Aiken, Henry D. (1957). "Dialectics and Materialism: Karl Marx (1818-1883) and Friedrich Engels (1820-1895)". In *The Age of Ideology: The Nineteenth Century Philosophers.* (pp. 183-201). New York; George Braziller, Inc.

Appelbaum, Richard P. and Chotiner, Harry (1979 July/August). "Science, Critique, and Praxis in Marxist Method". *Socialist Review,* 9 (4): 71-108.

Aronowitz, Stanley (1981). *The Crisis of Historical Materialism.* New York: Praeger Press.

Bateson, Gregory (1972). *Steps to an Ecology of Mind.* New York: Ballantine Books.

________ (1979). *Mind and Nature: A Necessary Unity.* New York: Ballantine Books.

Bateson, Gregory, Jackson, Don D., Haley, Jay, and Weakland, John H. (1976). In C. Sluzki and D. Ransom (eds.) *Double Bind—The Foundation of the Communicational Approach to the Family.* New York: Grune and Stratton.

________ (1976). "Foreword: A Formal Approach To Explicit, Implicit, And Embodied Ideas And To Their Forms Of Interaction". In C. Sluzki and D. Ransom (eds.), *Double Bind-The Foundation of the Communicational Approach to the Family* (pp. xi-xvi). New York: Grune and Stratton.

Bottomore, T. B., and Rubel, Maximilien (eds.) (1956). *Karl Marx: Selected Writings In Sociology And Social Philosophy* (1856). Harmondsworth, England: Penguin Books.

Carey, James C. (1989). *Communication as Culture.* Boston: Unwin Hyman.

Carroll, Lewis (1960). *Alice's Adventures in Wonderland* (1865) In *The Annotated Alice.* New York: New American Library.

Caute, David (1967). Introduction and notes to *Essential Writings of Karl Marx.* London: Panther Books Ltd.

Cocks, Joan (1988). *The Oppositional Imagination.* New York: Routledge.

Coe, Richard M. (1975 December). Logic, Paradox and Pinter's *Homecoming, Educational Theatre Journal:* 488-97.

________ (1981). *Form And Substance: An Advanced Rhetoric.* New York: John Wiley & Sons.

Coe, Richard M. and Wilden, Anthony (1978). "Error". In R. Romana (ed.), *Encyclopedia,* 5: 682-711. Turin: Einaudi.

Crites, Stephen D. (1967). Hegelianism. In P. Edwards (ed.), *The Encyclopedia of Philosophy* (pp. 451-59). New York: Crowell Collier and MacMillan, Inc.

World will surely reign, in a fashion, unimaginable by today's standards. "As he saw it, people will come to love their oppression, to adore the technologies that undo their capacities to think" (Postman, 1986: vii).

Daly, Mary (1978). *Gyn/Ecology: The Metaethics of Radical Feminism.* Boston: Beacon Press.
Dibble, Julian. (1992). "It's End Of TV As We Know It: And I Feel Wired". In *The Village Voice,* December 22, 1992 (pp. 55, 60).
Engel, Mark (1972). Preface to•*Steps To An Ecology Of Mind* by Gregory Bateson. New York: Ballantine Books.
Engels, Friedrich (1959). "Socialism: Utopian And Scientific" (1892). In L.S. Feuer (ed.), *Marx and Engels: Basic Writings On Politics And Philosophy* (pp. 68-111). New York: Anchor Books.
Freud, Sigmund (1967). *Dora: An Analysis Of A Case Of Hysteria (1905).* Edited by Philip Rieff. New York: Collier Books.
Gerbner, George. "Media Literacy: TV vs. Reality." In: *Adbusters,* Winter 1989-90, Vol. 1, No. 12, p. 12.
Gibson, Rex (1986). *Critical Theory and Education.* London: Hodder and Stoughton.
Giroux, Henry (1983). *Theory and Resistance in Education.* South Hadley, MA: Bergin and Garvey.
_________ (1981). *Ideology, Culture, And The Process Of Schooling.* Philadelphia: Temple University Press.
Godelier, Maurice (1972). "Structure And Contradiction In Capital". In R. Blackburn (ed.), *Ideology In Social Science: Readings In Critical Social Theory* (pp. 334-68). Great Britain: William Collins Sons and Co., Ltd.
Goulet, Denis (1974). *Introduction to Education:* "The Practice Of Freedom By Paulo Freire". London: Writers and Readers Publishing Cooperative.
Haley, Jay (1976). "Development Of A Theory: A History Of A Research Project". In C. Sluzki and D. Ransom (eds.), *Double Bind-The Foundation of the Communicational Approach to the Family* (pp. 59-104). New York: Grune and Stratton.
Hall, Roland (1967). "Dialectic". In P. Edwards (ed.), *The Encyclopedia of Philosophy* (pp. 385-98). New York: Crowell Collier and MacMillan, Inc.
Hammer, Rhonda and Wilden, Anthony (1987). "Women In Production: The Chorus Line". In A. Wilden (ed.), *The Rules Are Not Game: The Strategy of Communication.* London and New York: Routledge and Kegan Paul.
Hartsock, N. (1984) "Gender And Sexuality: Masculinity, Violence, And Domination". *Humanities in Society,* 7 (1 & 2), 19- 46.
Holland, Ray (1977). *Self and Social Context.* London: The MacMillan Press Ltd.
hooks, bell (1989 October). "Counterhegemonic Art: The right thing". *Z Magazine,* 31-36.
Key, Wilson Bryan. (1989). *The Age Of Manipulation.* New York: Henry Holt And Company.
Laclau, Ernesto (1988). "Building A New Left: An Interview With Ernesto Laclau". *Strategies* (No. 1, Fall): pp. 10-28.
Leach, Mary (in press). "An Interview with Peter L. McLaren." In *Journal of Educational Reform.*
Macedo, Donald (1992). "Foreward." In: Gee, James Paul, *The Social Mind: Language, Ideology, and Social Practice.* New York: Bergin & Garvey, pp. vii-xiv.
Malcolm X (1964). *The Autobiography of Malcolm X: With the assistance of Alex Haley.* New York: Ballantine Books.

Mandel, Ernest (1970). *An Introduction to Marxist Economic Theory.* New York: Pathfinder Press.
Mao Tse-Tung (1967). "On Contradiction". In *Selected Works of Mao Tse-Tung,* 1, pp. 311-45. Peking: Foreign Languages Press.
Marx, Karl (1967). *Essential Writings of Karl Marx.* London: Panther Books. Selected with introduction and notes by D. Caute.
McLaren, Peter (1989). *Life in Schools.* New York: Longman, Inc.
Mills, P. (1987). *Woman, Nature and Psyche.* New Haven: Yale University Press.
Mortenson, D. (1973). "Introduction". In D. Mortenson (ed.), *Basic Readings in Communication Theory* (pp. 1-3). New York: Harper and Row.
Nichols, Bill (1981). *Ideology and the Image: Social Represenation in the Cinema and Other Media.* Bloomington: Indiana University Press.
O'Brien, Mary (1983). *The Politics of Reproduction.* Boston: Routledge & Kegan Paul.
Ollman, B. (1986). "The Meaning Of Dialectics". *Monthly Review,* (pp. 43-55).
Postman, Neil. (1985). *Amusing Ourselves To Death: Public Discourse in the Age of Show Business.* New York: Penguin Books.
Quarles, Benjamin (1964). *The Negro in the Making of America.* New York: Collier Books.
Quill, Greg. "Zapping The Deathstar". *The Toronto Star,* February 27, 1993. (pp. G1, G6).
Rius, Eduardo Del Rio (1976). *Marx for Beginners* (trans. Richard Appignanesi). London: Writers and Readers Publishing Cooperative.
Runes, Dagobert D. and 72 Authorities (1960). *Dictionary of Philosophy.* Littlefield, Adams and Co.
Schwoch, James; White, Mimi; Reilly, Susan (1992). *Media Knowledge: Readings in Popular Culture, Pedagogy, and Critical Citizenship.* USA: State University of New York Press.
Sherman, Howard (1976 Summer). Dialectics as a Method. *The Insurgent Sociologist,* VI (4): 57-64.
Sweezy, Paul M. (1942). *The Theory of Capitalist Development: Principles of Marxian Political Economy.* New York: Modern Reader Paperbacks.
Therborn, Goran (1976). *Science, Class And Society: On The Formation Of Sociology And Historical Materialism.* London: NLB.
Watzlawick, P., Beavin, J., and Jackson, D.D. (1967). *Pragmatics of Human Communication.* New York: W.W. Norton.
White, Morton (1957). "The Decline And Fall Of The Absolute". In *The Age of Analysis: Twentieth Century Philosophers* (pp. 13-21). New York: George Braziller, Inc.
Wilden, Anthony (1972). *System and Structure: Essays in Communication and Exchange.* London: Tavistok Publications.
_________ (1976). *Communications in Context.* Burnaby: Simon Fraser University. Mimeographed.
_________ (1977). *Communication in Context: A Systems Perspective,* Part I. Burnaby: Simon Fraser University. Mimeographed.
_________ (1977a). *Communication in Context: A Systems Perspective,* Part II. Burnaby: Simon Fraser University. Mimeographed.
_________ (1979 Spring). "Culture and identity. The Canadian question, Why?" *Cine-Tracts,* 2, no.2 (pp. 1-27).

_________ (1980). Introduction (1980) to *System and Structure: Essays in Communication and Exchange,* 2nd. edition by A. Wilden. London: Tavistock Publications.

_________ (1980a). *The Imaginary Canadian.* Vancouver Pulp Press.

_________ (1980b). Additional notes (1980). In A. Wilden (ed.), *System and Structure: Essays in Communication and Exchange* (2nd edition). London: Tavistock Publications.

_________ (1981). "Semiotics as Praxis: Strategy and Tactics." In: *Researches Semiotiques / Semiotic Inquiry,* Vol. 1, No. 1, pp. 1- 34.

_________ (1987). *The Rules Are No Game: A Strategy of Communication.* London and New York: Routledge and Kegan Paul.

_________ (1987a). *Man And Woman, War And Peace: The Strategist's Companion.* London and New York: Routledge and Kegan Paul.

Wilden, A. and Wilson, T. (1976). "The Double-bind: Logic, Magic And Economics". In C. Sluzki and D. Ransom (eds.), *Double Bind-The Foundation of the Communicational Approach to the Family* (pp. 263-86). New York: Grune and Stratton.

Wilder, Carol (1978). "The Palo Alto Group: Difficulties and Directions of the 'Interactional View' for Interpersonal Communication Research." Paper presented at the Annual Meeting of the International Communication Association, Chicago, Illinois, April.

Williams, Raymond (1976). "Dialectics." In: *Keywords: A Vocabulary of Culture and Society*. Great Britain: Fontana Paperbacks, pp. 106-8.

Wilson, Edmund (1972). *To the Finland Station: A Study in the Writing and Acting of History.* New York: Farrar, Straus and Giroux.

Chapter III

White Terror and Oppositional Agency: Towards a Critical Multiculturalism

Peter McLaren

Nothing can be denounced if the denouncing is done within the system that belongs to the thing denounced.

Julio Cortázar
Hopscotch, Chapter 99

As we approach the year 2000, we are increasingly living simulated identities that help us adjust our dreams and desires according to the terms of our imprisonment as schizo-subjects in an artificially-generated world. These facsimile or imitative identities are negotiated for us by financial planners, corporate sponsors, and marketing strategists through the initiatives of transnational corporations, enabling a privileged elite of white Euro-Americans to control the information banks and terrorize the majority of the population into a state of intellectual and material impoverishment. With few, if any, ethically convincing prospects for transformation—or even survival—we have become cyber-nomads whose temporary homes become whatever electronic circuitry (if any) is available to us. In our hyper-fragmented and postmodern culture, democracy is secured through the power to control consciousness and semioticize and discipline bodies by mapping and manipulating sounds, images and information and forcing identity to take refuge in forms of subjectivity increasingly experienced as isolated and separate from larger social contexts. The idea of democratic citizenship has now become synonymous with the private, consuming citizen and the increasing subalternization of the "other." The representation of reality through corporate sponsorship and promotional culture has impeded the struggle to establish democratic public spheres and furthered the dissolution of historical solidarities and forms of community, accelerating the experience of circular narrative time and the postindustrial disintegration of public space. The proliferation and phantasmagoria of the image has hastened the death of modernist identity structures and has interpellated individuals and groups into a world of cyborg citizenry in which "other" individuals are reconstituted through market imperatives as a collective assemblage of "them" read against our "us."

THE DEBATE OVER MULTICULTURALISM

It is no secret, especially after the Los Angeles uprising—or what Mike Davis calls the "L.A. Intifada" (Katz and Smith, 1992)—that the white-controlled media (often backed by victim-blaming white social scientists) have ignored the economic and social conditions responsible for bringing about in African-American communities what Cornel West has called a "*walking nihilism* of pervasive drug addiction, pervasive alcoholism, pervasive homicide, and an exponential rise in suicide" (cited in Stephanson, 1988: 276). They have additionally ignored or sensationalized social conditions in Latin and Asian communities, polemicizing against their value systems and representing them as teleologically poised to explode into a swelter of rioting and destruction. Such communities have been described as full of individuals who lash out at the dominant culture in an anarcho-voluntaristic frenzy in a country where there are more legalized gun dealers than gas stations. In this view, agency seams to operate outside of forces and structures of oppression and policing discourses of domination and social practices. Subalternized individuals appear politically constituted outside of discursive formations and are essentialized as the products of their pathological 'nature' as drug or alcohol users and as participants in crime.

Furthermore, the white media has generated the racially pornographic term, "wilding," to account for recent acts of violence in urban centers by groups of young African-Americans (Cooper, 1989). Apparently the term "wilding," first reported by New York City newspapers in relation to the Central Park rapists, was relevant only to violence committed by black male youths since the term was conspicuously absent in press reports of the attack by white male youths on Yusef Hawkins in Bensonhurst (Wallace, 1991). Thus the postmodern image which many white people now entertain in relation to the African American underclass is one constructed upon violence and grotesquerie-a population spawning mutant youths who, in the throes of bloodlust, roam the perimeter of the urban landscape high on angel dust, randomly hunting whites with steel pipes. In addition to helping to justify police "attitude adjustments" inflicted upon black people in places such as L.A., Detroit, and Hemphill in Sabine County, Texas, this image of minorities has engendered hostility to their efforts to articulate their own understanding of race relations and to advance a conception of democracy in a way that is compatible with a critical multiculturalism.

FORMS OF MULTICULTURALISM

This paper attempts to advance a conception of "critical multiculturalism" by exploring various positions held within the debate over multiculturalism which I have termed conservative or corporate multiculturalism, liberal multiculturalism and left-liberal multiculturalism. These are, to be sure, ideal-typical labels meant to serve only as a "heuristic" device. In reality the characteristics of each position tend to blend into each other within the general horizon of our social lifeworld. As with all typologies and criteriologies, one must risk monolithically projecting them onto all spheres of cultural production and instantiating an overly abstract totality that dangerously reduces the complexity of the issues at stake. My effort should be understood only as an initial attempt at transcoding and mapping the cultural field of race and ethnicity so as to formulate a tentative theoretical grid that can help discern the multiple ways in which difference is both constructed and engaged.

Conservative Multiculturalism

Conservative multiculturalism can be traced to colonial views of African-Americans as slaves, servants, and entertainers, views which were embedded in the self-serving congratulatory and profoundly imperialist attitude of Europe and North America. Such an attitude depicted Africa as a savage and barbaric continent populated by the most lowly of creatures who were deprived of the saving graces of Western civilization.[1] It

---

[1] Africa is still demonized as a land uncivilized, corrupt, and savage and divided into countries that are viewed as not evolved enough to govern themselves without Western guidance and stewardship. We shamefully ignore Africa's victims of war and famine in comparison, for instance, to the 'white' victims of Bosnia. When the U.S. media does decide to report on Africa, much of the images it reinforces depicts a land of jungle, wildlife, famine, poachers, and fierce fighting among rival tribal/factions (Naureckas, 1993). The white supremacist and colonialist discourses surrounding the recent intervention in Somalia by heroic U.S. troops and relief workers (referred to by Colin Powell as sending the "cavalry") is captured in comments made by Alan Pizzy of CBS when he described the intervention in 'humanitarian' terms as "just a few good men trying to help another nation in need, another treacherous country where all the members of all the murderous factions look alike" (cited in Jim Naureckas, *Extra*, March, 1993, p. 12). Described as a land populated by helpless and history-less victims and drug-crazed thugs high on khat (a mild stimulant) who ride around in vehicles out of a Mad Max movie, an implicit parallel is made between Somalia youth and the cocaine-dealing gangs of toughs who participated in the L.A. rioting. (Naureckas, ibid.) This 'othering' of Africa encouraged a preferred reading of Somalia's problems as indigenous and camouflaged the broader context surrounding the famine in Somalia and its subsequent 'rescue' by U.S. marines. Occluded was the fact that the U.S. had previously obstructed U.N. peacekeeping efforts in Somalia, Angola, Namibia, and Mozambique because it was too costly (the U.S. still owes 415 million to the U.N. , including 120 million for peacekeeping efforts)—a factor absent in nearly all the media coverage (Naureckas, *ibid.*). From a U.S. foreign policy perspective, Somalia still plays an important role geopolitically, not simply because of its potential interest to Israel and Arab nations, but because of its rich mineral deposits and potential oil reserves. As Naureckas notes, Amoco, Chevron and Sunoco are engaged in oil exploration there (*ibid.*)

The media have rarely reported on other factors surrounding the famine in Somalia. For instance, they have virtually ignored the U.S. support (to the sum of 200 million in military aid and half a billion in economic aid) to the Siad Barre regime (1969-1991). The U.S. ignored its corruption and human rights abuses because the dictatorship kept Soviet-allied Ethiopia embroiled in a war. Naureckas also points out that until the 1970's, Somalia was self-sufficient in grain and its agricultural land productive enough to withstand

can also be located in evolutionary theories which supported U.S. Manifest Destiny, imperial largesse, and Christian imperialism. And it can further be seen as a direct result of the legacy of doctrines of white supremacy which biologized Africans as 'creatures' by equating them with the earliest stages of human development. Africans were likened by whites to savage beasts or merry-hearted singing and dancing children. The former stereotype led a ten year-old black boy—Josef Moller—to be exhibited at the Antwerp Zoo at the turn of the century. Closer to home and less remote in time is the case of Ota Benga, a 'pygmy' boy exhibited in 1906 at the Monkey House in the Bronx Zoo as an "African homunculus" and as the "missing link" and encouraged by zoo keepers to charge the bars of his cage with his mouth open and teeth bared (Bradford and Blume, 1992). In less sensational guise, this attitude continues right up to the present time. For instance, in 1992, the Secretary of Health and Human Services in the Bush Administration appointed Frederick A. Goodwin, a research psychiatrist and career federal scientist, as Director of the National Institute for Mental Health. Goodwin used animal research findings to compare youth gangs to groups of "hyperaggressive" and "hypersexual" monkeys and commented that "maybe it isn't just the careless use of the word when people call certain areas of certain cities, 'jungles'" (*Observer*, p. 20).

Whether conceived as the return of the repressed of Victorian puritanism, a leftover from Aristotelian hierarchical discourse or colonial and imperialist ideology, it remains the terrible truth of history that Africans have been forcibly placed at the foot of the human ladder of civilization. (Pieterse, 1992). As Jan Nederveen Pieterse notes, America historically has been the "white man's country," in which institutional and ideological patterns of the supremacy of white over black, and of men over women, supplemented and reinforced one another" (1992, p. 220).

While I do not wish to lapse into either an essentialized nativism which sees non-Western indigenous cultures as homogeneous or a view of the West that sees it as all of one

---

famine. However, U.S. and international agencies like the IMF pressured Somalia to shift agriculture from local subsistence to export crops (*ibid.*)

piece—a monolithic block—and unaffected by its colonized subjects, or solely as an engine of imperialism, I need to affirm the fact that many conservative multiculturalists have scarcely removed themselves from the colonialist legacy of white supremacy. Although they would like to officially distance themselves from racist ideologies, conservative multiculturalists pay only lip-service to the cognitive equality of all races and charge unsuccessful minorities with having 'culturally deprived backgrounds' and a 'lack of strong family-oriented values.' This "environmentalist" position still accepts Black cognitive inferiority to whites as a general premise and provides conservative multiculturalists with a means of rationalizing why some minority groups are successful while other groups are not. This also gives the white cultural elite the excuse they need for unreflectively and disproportionality occupying positions of power. They are not unlike the *inscripti* of the right-wing Roman Catholic organization, *Opus Dei*, who attempt to intellectually and culturally sequester or barricade their members from the tools for a critical analyses of social life in order to shore up their own power to manipulate and propagandize.

One particularly invidious project of conservative or corporate multiculturalism is to construct a common culture—a seamless web of textuality—bent on annulling the concept of the border-through the delegitimization of foreign languages and regional and ethnic dialects, a persistent attack on nonstandard English, and the undermining of bi-lingual education (Macedo, 1995). Gramsci's understanding of this process is instructive, and is cogently articulated by Michael Gardiner:

> For Gramsci, the political character of language was most apparent in the attempt by the dominant class to create a common cultural 'climate' and to 'transform the popular mentality' through the imposition of a national language. Therefore, he felt that linguistic hegemony involved the articulation of signs and symbols which tended to codify and reinforce the dominant viewpoint. Thus, Gramsci argued that there existed a close relationship between linguistic stratification and social hierarchization, in that the various dialects and accents found within a given society are always rank-ordered as to their perceived legitimacy, appropriateness, and so on. Accordingly, concrete language usage reflects underlying, asymmetrical power relations, and it registers profound changes which occur in the cultural, moral, and political worlds.

> Such changes were primarily expressed through what Gramsci termed 'normative grammar'; roughly, the system of norms whereby particular utterances could be evaluated and mutually understood . . . which was an important aspect of the state's attempt to establish linguistic conformity. Gramsci also felt that the maintenance of regional dialects helped peasants and workers partially to resist the forces of political and cultural hegemony . . . (Gardiner, 1992, p. 186).

In addition to its position on common culture and bi-lingual education, there are further reasons why corporate multiculturalism needs to be rejected. First, conservative or corporate multiculturalism refuses to treat whiteness as a form of ethnicity and in doing so posits whiteness as an invisible norm by which other ethnicities are judged. Second, conservative multiculturalism—as in the positions taken by Diane Ravitch, Arthur Schlesinger, Jr., Lynne V.B. Cheney, Chester Finn, and others—uses the term 'diversity' to cover up the ideology of assimilation that undergirds its position. In this view, ethnic groups are reduced to "add-ons" to the dominant culture. Before you can be "added on" to the dominant U.S. culture you must first adopt a consensual view of culture and learn to accept the essentially Euro-American patriarchal norms of the 'host' country. Third, as I mentioned earlier, conservative multiculturalism is essentially monolingual and adopts the position that English should be the only official language. It is often virulently opposed to bi-lingual education programs. Fourth, conservative multiculturalists posit standards of achievement for all youth that are premised on the cultural capital of the Anglo, middle-class. Fifth, conservative multiculturalism fails to interrogate the high status knowledge—knowledge that is deemed of most value in white, middle-class U.S.—to which the educational system is geared. That is, it fails to question the interests that such knowledge serves. It fails, in other words, to interrogate dominant regimes of discourse and social and cultural practices that are implicated in global dominance and are inscribed in racist, classist, sexist and homophobic assumptions. Conservative multiculturalism wants to assimilate students to an unjust social order by arguing that every member of every ethnic group can reap the economic benefits of neo-colonialist ideologies and corresponding social and economic practices. But a pre-requisite to "joining the club" is to become denuded, deracinated and culturally stripped.

Recent popular conservative texts set firmly against liberal, left-liberal, and critical strands of multiculturalism include Richard Brookhiser's *The Way of the Wasp: How It Made America, and How It Can Save It, So to Speak*, Arthur Schlesinger, Jr.'s *The Disuniting of America: Reflections on A Multicultural Society*, and Laurence Auster's *The Path to National Suicide: An Essay On Immigration and Multiculturalism.* According to Stanley Fish (1992), these texts, which appeal to national unity and a harmonious citizenry, can readily be traced to earlier currents of Christianity (which proclaimed that it was God's wish that the future of civilization be secured in the United States) and social Darwinism (U.S. Anglo-Saxon stock is used to confirm the theory of natural selection). Reflecting and enforcing the assumptions made by the authors (whom Fish describes as racist not in the sense that they actively seek the subjugation of groups but who perpetuate racial stereotypes and the institutions that promote them) is the SAT test used in high school for college admission. Fish notes that one of the authors of this test, Carl Campbell Brigham, championed in his *A Study of American Intelligence* a classification of races which identified the Nordic as the superior race and, in descending order, located the less superior races as Alpine, Mediterranean, Eastern, New Eastern, and Negro. This hierarchy was first expounded by Madison Grant in *The Passing of the Great Race* (Fish, 1992) and reflected in earlier European works such as *Essai sur l'inégalité des races humaines*, a four-volume testament to the racial superiority of the Germanic race by Joseph Arthur (Comte de Govineau) and Edward Gibbon's *Decline and Fall of the Roman Empire*, a work which blamed miscegination for the decline of civilization (Pieterse, 1992). Not surprisingly, this hierarchy is confirmed in Brigham's later comparative analysis of intelligence. The library at the Educational Testing Service compound still bears Brigham's name (Fish, 1992). Also problematic, as Mike Dyson points out, are theories linking white racism to biological determinism, such as recent discussions of "melanin theory" in which black researchers view whiteness as a genetic deficiency state that leads whites to act violently against Blacks because of white feelings of color inferiority (Dyson, 1993).

When we contrast Brookhiser's key WASP virtues with non-WASP virtues (those of the Asians, or African Americans or Latinos) we see the Western virtues of the former—Conscience, Anti-sensuality, Industry, Use, Success, and Civic Mindedness—being distinguished as more American than the lesser virtues of the latter—Self, Creativity, Ambition, Diffidence, Gratification and Group Mindedness. This also reflects a privileging of Western languages (English, French, German, and ancient Greek) over non-Western languages (see Fish, 1992). Supposedly, Western European languages are the only ones sophisticated enough to grasp truth as an 'essence.' The search for the 'truth' of the Western canon of 'Great Works' is actually based on an epistemological error that presumes there exists a language of primordial Being and Truth. This error is linked to the phenomenalist reduction of linguistic meaning which endows language (through analogy) with sense perceptions and thereby reduces the act of interpretation to uncovering the 'true understanding' that reciprocally binds the truth of the text to the pre-understanding, tacit knowledge, or foreknowledge of the reader (Norris, 1990). From this view of the mimetic transparency of language, aesthetic judgments are seen as linked directly to ethics or politics through a type of direct correspondence (Norris, 1990). Language therefore becomes elevated to a "truth-telling status" which remains exempt from its ethico-political situatedness or embeddedness. It is this epistemological error that permits conservatives to denounce totalitarianism in the name of its own truth and serves as a ruse for expanding present forms of domination. It is not hard to see how racism can become a pre-condition for this form of conservative multiculturalism in so far as Western virtues (which can be traced back as far as Aristotle's Great Chain of Being) become the national-aestheticist ground for the conservative multiculturalist's view of civilization and citizenship. The power of conservative multiculturalism lays claim to its constituents by conferring a space for the reception of its discourses that is safe and sovereignly secure. It does this by sanctioning empiricism as the fulcrum for weighing the "truth" of culture. What discursively thrives in this perspective is an epistemology which privileges the logic of cause-and-effect narrative construction (see Norris, 1990). In this case, intelligence quotients and test scores become the primary repository of authoritative exegesis in what constitutes successful school citizenship. Fortunately, as Foucault points out, subjectivity is not simply constituted through discourses and social practices of subjugation. Liberal, left-liberal, and critical forms of multiculturalism envisage a different "practice of the self" and new forms of self-fashioning and subjectivity based on more progressive conceptions of freedom and justice.

Liberal Multiculturalism

Liberal multiculturalism argues that a natural equality exists among whites, African-Americans, Latinos, Asians and other racial populations. This perspective is based on the intellectual "sameness" among the races, on their cognitive equivalence or the rationality imminent in all races that permits them to compete equally in a capitalist society. However, from the point of view of liberal multiculturalism, equality is absent in U.S. society not because of black or Latino cultural deprivation but because social and educational opportunities do not exist that permit everyone to compete equally in the capitalist marketplace. Unlike their critical counterparts, they believe that existing cultural, social, and economic constraints can be modified or "reformed" in order for relative equality to be realized. This view often collapses into an ethnocentric and oppressively universalistic humanism in which the legitimating norms which govern the substance of citizenship is identified most strongly with Anglo-American cultural-political communities.

Left-Liberal Multiculturalism

Left-liberal multiculturalism emphasizes cultural differences and suggests that the stress on the equality of races smothers those important cultural differences between races that are responsible for different behaviors, values, attitudes, cognitive styles, and social practices. Left-liberal multiculturalists feel that mainstream approaches to multiculturalism occlude characteristics and differences related to race, class, gender, and sexuality. Those who work within this perspective have a tendency to essentialize cultural differences, however, and ignore the historical and cultural 'situatedness' of difference. Difference is understood as a form of signification removed from social and historical constraints. That is, there is a tendency to ignore difference as a social and historical construction that is constitutive of the power to represent meanings. It is often assumed that there exists an authentic 'Female' or 'African-American' or 'Latino' experience or way of being-in-the world. Left-liberal multiculturalism treats difference as an 'essence' that exists independently of history, culture, and power. Often one is asked to show one's identity-papers before dialogue can begin.

This perspective often locates meaning through the conduit of 'authentic' experience in what I feel to be the mistaken belief that one's own politics of location somehow guarantees one's 'political correctness' in advance. Either a person's physical proximity to the oppressed or their own location as an oppressed person is supposed to offer a special authority from which to speak. What often happens is that a populist elitism gets constructed as inner city teachers or trade unionists or those engaged in activist politics establish a pedigree of voice based on personal history, class, race, gender and experience. Here the political is often reduced only to the personal where theory is dismissed in favor of one's own personal and cultural identity. Of course, one's lived experience, race, class, gender and history is important in the formation of one's political identity but one must be willing to examine personal experience and one's speaking voice in terms of the ideological and discursive complexity of its formation.

Of course, when a person speaks it is always from somewhere (Hall, 1991) but this process of meaning production needs to be interrogated in order to understand how one's identity is constantly being produced through a play of difference linked to and reflected by shifting and conflicting discursive and ideological relations, formations and articulations (see Giroux, 1992; Scott, 1992). Experience needs to be recognized as a site of ideological production and the mobilization of affect and can be examined largely through its imbrication in our universal and local knowledges and modes of intelligibility and its relationship to language, desire, and the body (an issue that I have explored elsewhere in McLaren, 1990). As Joan Scott notes, "experience is a subject's history. Language is the site of history's enactment." (1992:34). Of course, I am not arguing against the importance of experience in the formation of political identity, but rather pointing out that it has become the new imprimatur for legitimating the political currency and uncontestable validity of one's arguments. This has often resulted in a reverse form of academic elitism. Not only is the authority of the academic under assault (and rightly so, in many cases) but it has been replaced by a populist elitism based on one's own identity papers.

Critical and Resistance Multiculturalism

Multiculturalism without a transformative political agenda can just be another form of accommodation to the larger social order. I believe that because they are immersed in the discourse of "reform," liberal and left-liberal positions on multiculturalism do not go nearly far enough in advancing a project of social transformation. With this concern in mind, I am developing the idea of critical multiculturalism from the perspective of a resistance poststructuralist approach to meaning, and emphasizing the role that language and representation play in the construction of meaning and identity. The poststructuralist insight that I am relying on is located within the larger context of postmodern theory—that disciplinary archipelago that is scattered through the sea of social theory—and asserts that signs and significations are essentially unstable and shifting and can only be temporarily fixed, depending on how they are articulated within particular discursive and historical struggles. From the perspective of what I am calling "critical multiculturalism," representations of race, class, and gender are understood as the result of larger social struggles over signs and meanings and in this way emphasizes not simply textual play or metaphorical displacement as a form of resistance (as in the case of left-liberal multiculturalism) but stresses the central task of a transforming the social, cultural, and institutional relations in which meanings are generated.

From the perspective of critical multiculturalism, the conservative and liberal stress on sameness and the left-liberal emphasis on difference is really a false opposition. Both identity based on "sameness" and identity based on "difference" are forms of essentialist logic: in both, individual identities are presumed to be autonomous, self-contained and self-directed. Resistance multiculturalism also refuses to see culture as non-conflictual, harmonious and consensual. Democracy is understood from this perspective as busy—it's not seamless, smooth or always a harmonious political and cultural state of affairs (Giroux and McLaren, 1991; 1991a; 1991b). Resistance multiculturalism doesn't see diversity itself as a goal but rather argues that diversity must be affirmed within a politics of cultural criticism and a commitment to social justice. It must be attentive to the notion of 'difference.' Difference is always a product of history, culture, power, and ideology. Differences occur *between* and *among* groups and must be understood in terms of the specificity of their production. Critical multiculturalism interrogates the construction of difference and identity in relation to a radical politics. It is positioned against the neo-imperial romance with monoglot ethnicity grounded in a shared or 'common' experience of 'America' that is associated with conservative and liberal strands of multiculturalism.

Viewed from the perspective of a critical multiculturalism, conservative attacks on multiculturalism as separatist and ethnocentric carry with them the erroneous assumption by white Anglo constituencies that North American society fundamentally constitutes social relations of uninterrupted accord. The liberal view is seen to underscore the idea that North American society is largely a forum of consensus with different minority viewpoints simply accretively added on. We are faced here with a politics of pluralism which largely ignores the workings of power and privilege. More specifically, the liberal perspective "involves a very insidious exclusion as far as any structural politics of change is concerned: it excludes and occludes global or structural relations of power as 'ideological' and 'totalizing' " (Ebert, in press). In addition, it presupposes harmony and agreement-an undisturbed space in which differences can coexist. Within such a space, individuals are invited to shed their positive characteristics in order to become disembodied and transparent American citizens (Copjec, 1991; Rosaldo, 1989) a cultural practice that creates what David Lloyd (1991;70) calls a "subject without properties." In this instance, citizens are able to occupy a place of "pure exchangeability." This accords the universalized white subject a privileged status. Yet such a proposition is dangerously problematic. Chandra Mohanty (1989/90) notes that difference cannot be formulated as negotiation among culturally diverse groups against a backdrop of benign variation or presumed cultural homogeneity. Difference is the recognition that knowledges are forged in histories that are riven with differentially constituted relations of power; that is, knowledges, subjectivities, and social practices are forged within "asymmetrical and incommensurate cultural spheres" (1989/90: 181).

Homi K. Bhabha makes the lucid observation that in attributing the racism and sexism of the common culture solely to "the underlying logic of late capitalism and its patriarchal overlay," leftists are actually providing an alibi for the common culture argument. The common culture is transformed in this instance into a form of ethical critique of the political system that supposedly fosters unity within a system of differences. The concept of cultural otherness is taken up superficially to celebrate a "range of 'nation-centered' cultural discourses (on a wide axis from right to left)" (1992, p. 235). It is worth quoting at length Bhabha's notion of common culture as the regulation and normalization of difference:

> Like all myths of the nation's "unity," the common culture is a profoundly conflicted ideological strategy. It is a declaration of democratic faith in a plural, diverse society and, at the same time, a defense against the real, subversive demands that the articulation of cultural difference-the empowering of minorities-makes upon democratic pluralism. Simply saying that the "nation's cement" is inherently sexist or racist-because of the underlying logic of late capitalism and its patriarchal overlay-ironically provides the "common culture" argument with the alibi it needs. The vision of a common culture is perceived to be an ethical mission whose value lies in revealing, prophylactically, the imperfections and exclusions of the political system as it exists. The healing grace of a culture of commonality is supposedly the coevality it establishes between social differences-ethnicities, ideologies, sexualities-"an intimation of simultaneity across homogeneous empty time" that welds

these different voices into a "unisonance" that is expressive of the "contemporaneous community of the national culture." (1992, pp. 234-235).

Too often liberal and conservative positions on diversity constitute an attempt to view culture as a soothing balm-the aftermath of historical disagreement-some mythical present where the irrationalities of historical conflict have been smoothed out (McLaren, in press). This is not only a disingenuous view of culture, it is profoundly dishonest. It overlooks the importance of engaging in some instances in dissensus in order to contest hegemonic forms of domination, and to affirm differences. The liberal and conservative position on culture also assumes that justice already exists and needs only to be evenly apportioned. However, both teachers and students need to realize that justice does not already exist simply because laws exist. Justice needs to be continually created and constantly struggled for (Darder, 1992; McLaren and Hammer, 1992). The question that I want to pose to teachers is this: Do teachers and cultural workers have access to a language that allows them to sufficiently critique and transform existing social and cultural practices that are defended by liberals and conservatives as unifyingly democratic?

CRITICAL MULTICULTURALISM AND THE POLITICS OF SIGNIFICATION

Since all experience is the experience of meaning, we need to recognize the role that language plays in the production of experience (McLaren, in press a; Giroux and McLaren, in press). You don't have an experience and then search for a word to describe that experience. Rather, language helps to constitute experience by providing a structure of intelligibility or mediating device through which experiences can be understood. Rather than talking about experience, it is more accurate to talk about "experience effects," (Zavarzadeh and Morton, 1990).

Western language and thought are constructed as a system of differences organized *de facto* and *de jure* as binary oppositions —white/black, good/bad, normal/deviant, etc.—with the primary term being privileged and designated as the defining term or the norm of cultural meaning, creating a dependent hierarchy. Yet the secondary term does not really exist outside the first, but, in effect, exists inside of it, even though the phallogocentric logic of white supremacist ideology makes you think it exists outside and in opposition to the first term. The critical multiculturalist critique argues that the relationship between signifier and signified is *insecure* and *unstable*. Signs are part of an ideological struggle that attempts to create a particular regime of representation that serves to legitimate a certain cultural reality. For instance, we've witnessed a struggle in our society over the meaning of terms such as "negro," "black" and "African-American."

According to Teresa Ebert (1991a), our current ways of seeing and acting are being disciplined for us through forms of signification, that is, through modes of intelligibility and ideological frames of sense-making. Rejecting the Saussurian semiotics of signifying practices (and its continuing use in contemporary post-structuralism) as "historical operations of language and tropes," Ebert characterizes signifying practices as "an ensemble of material operations involved in economic and political relations" (p. 117). She maintains, rightly in my view, that socioeconomic relations of power require distinctions to be made among groups through forms of signification in order to organize subjects according to the unequal distribution of privilege and power.

To illustrate the politics of signification at work in the construction and formation of racist subjects, Ebert offers the example of the way in which the terms "negro" and "black" have been employed within the racial politics of the United States. Just as the term "negro" became an immutable mark of difference and naturalized the political arrangements of racism in the 1960s, so too is the term "black" being refigured in the white dominant culture to mean criminality, violence, and social degeneracy. This was made clear in the Willie Horton campaign ads of George Bush and in the Bush and David Duke position on hiring quotas. In my view this was also evident in the initial verdict of the Rodney King case in Los Angeles.

Carlos Muñoz, Jr. (1989) has revealed how the term "Hispanic" in the mid-1970s became a "politics of white ethnic identity" that de-emphasized and in some cases rejected the Mexican cultural base of Mexican Americans. Muñoz writes that the term "Hispanic" is derived from "Hispania" which was the name the Romans gave to the Iberian peninsula, most of which became Spain, and "implicitly emphasizes the white European culture of Spain at the expense of the nonwhite cultures that have profoundly shaped the experiences of all Latin Americans" (p. 11). Not only is this term blind to the multiracial reality of Mexican Americans through its refusal to acknowledge "the nonwhite indigenous cultures of the Americas, Africa, and Asia, which historically have produced multicultural and multiracial peoples in Latin America and the United States" (p. 11), it is a term that ignores the complexities within these various cultural groups. Here is another example of the melting pot theory of assimilation fostered through a politics of signification. So that we might ask ourselves what signifieds (meanings) will be attached to certain terms such as "welfare mothers?" Most of us know what government officials mean when they refer derisively to "welfare mothers." They mean black and Latino mothers.

Kobena Mercer has recently described what he calls "black struggles over the sign" (1992, p. 428). Mercer, following Volosinov, argues that every sign has a "social multi-accentuality" and it is this polyvocal character that can rearticulate the sign through the inscription of different connotations surrounding it. The dominant ideology always tries to stabilize certain meanings of the term "black". Mercer writes that for over four centuries of Western civilization, the sign "black" was "structured by the closure of an absolute symbolic division of what was white and what was non-white" (1992, p. 428) through the "morphological equation" of racial superiority. This equation accorded whiteness with civility and rationality and blackness with savagery and irrationality. Subaltern subjects themselves brought about a reappropriation and rearticulation of the "proper name"—Negro, Colored, Black, Afro-American —in which a collective subjectivity was renamed. Mercer notes that in the sixties and seventies, the term "ethnic minorities" connoted the black subject "as a minor, an abject childlike figure necessary for the legitimation of paternalistic ideologies of assimilation and integration that underpined the strategy of multiculturalism" (p. 429). The term "black community" arose out of a reappropriation of the term "community relations". The state had tried to colonize a definition of social democratic consensus designed to "manage" race relations through the use of "community relations."

The examples discussed above underscore the central theorectical position of critical multiculturalism: that differences are produced according to the ideological production and reception of cultural signs. As Mas'ud Zavarzadeh and Donald Morton point out, "Signs are neither eternally predetermined nor panhistorically undecidable: they are rather 'decided' or rendered as 'undecidable' in the moment of social conflicts" (1990, p. 156). Difference is not "cultural obviousness" such as black versus white or Latino versus European or Anglo-American; rather, differences are historical and cultural constructions (Ebert, 1991).

Just as we can see the politics of signification at work in instances of police brutality, or in the way Blacks and Latinos are portrayed as drug pushers, gang members, or the minority sidekick to the white cop in movies and television, we can see it at work in special education placement where a greater proportion of Black and Latino students are considered for 'behavioral' placements whereas white, middle-class students are provided for the most part with the more comforting and comfortable label of 'learning disabled' (McLaren, 1989). Here, a critical multiculturalist curriculum can help teachers explore the ways in which students are differentially subjected to ideological inscriptions and multiply-organized discourses of desire through a politics of signification.

A critical multiculturalism suggests that teachers and cultural workers need to take up the issue of 'difference' in ways that don't replay the monocultural essentialism of the 'centrisms'—Anglocentrism, Eurocentrism, phallocentrism, androcentrism, and the like. They need to build a politics of alliance-building, of dreaming together, of solidarity that moves beyond the condescension of, say, 'race awareness week' that actually serves to keep forms of institutionalized racism in tact. A solidarity has to be struggled for that is not centered around market imperatives but develops out of the imperatives of freedom, liberation, democracy, and critical citizenship.

The notion of the citizen has been pluralized and hybridized, as Kobena Mercer notes, by the presence of a diversity of social subjects. Mercer is instructive in pointing out that "solidarity does not mean that everyone thinks the same way, it begins when people have the confidence to disagree over issues because they 'care' about constructing a common ground" (1990, p. 68). Solidarity is not impermeably solid but depends to a certain degree on antagonism and uncertainty. Timothy Maliqualim Simone calls this type of multiracial solidarity "geared to maximizing points of interaction rather than harmonizing, balancing, or equilibrating the distribution of bodies, resources, and territories" (1989, p. 191).

Whereas left-liberal multiculturalism equates resistance with destabilizing dominant systems of representation, critical multiculturalism goes one step further by asserting that all representations are the result of social struggles over signifiers and their signifieds. This suggests that resistance must take into account an intervention into social struggle in order "to provide equal access to social resources and to transform the dominant power relations which limit this access according to class privilege, race,and gender" (Ebert, 1991, p. 294). Differences *within* culture must be defined as political difference and not just formal, textual or linguistic difference. Global or structural relations of power must not be ignored. The concept of totality must not be abandoned but rather seen as an *overdetermined structure of difference.* Differences are always *differences in relation,* they are never simply free-floating. Differences are not seen as absolute, irreducible or intractable, but rather as undecidable and socially and culturally relational (see Ebert, 1991).

Resistance or critical multiculturalism does not agree with those left-liberal multiculturalists who argue that difference needs only to be interrogated as a form of rhetoric, thereby reducing politics to signifying structures and history to textuality (Ebert, 1991). We need to go beyond destabilizing meaning, by transforming the social and historical conditions in which meaning-making occurs. Rather than remaining satisfied with erasing the privilege of oppressive ideologies that have been naturalized within the dominant culture, or with restating dangerous memories that have been repressed within the political unconscious of the state, critical multiculturalist praxis attempts to revise existing hegemonic arrangements. A critical multiculturalist praxis does not simply reject the bourgeois decorum that has consigned the imperialized other to the realm of the grotesque but effectively attempts to remap desire by fighting for a linguistically multivalenced culture and new structures of experience in which individuals refuse the role of the omniscient narrator and conceive of identity as a polyvalent assemblage of (contradictory and over determined) subject positions. Existing systems of difference which organize social life into patterns of domination and subordination must be reconstructed. We need to do more than unflaggingly problematize difference as a condition of rhetoric, or unceasingly interrogate the status of all knowledge as discursive inscription, because, as Ebert notes, this annuls the grounds of both reactionary and revolutionary politics. Rather, we need a rewriting of difference as *difference-in-relation* followed by attempts to dramatically change the material conditions that allow relations of domination to prevail over relations of equality and social justice. This is a different cultural politics than one of simply reestablishing an inverse hierarchical order of blacks *over* whites or Latinos *over* whites. Rather it is an attempt to transform the very value of hierarchy itself, followed by a challenge to the material structures that are responsible for the overdetermination of structures of difference in the direction of oppression, injustice, and human suffering. However, this is not to claim that individuals are oppressed in the same ways since groups are oppressed non-synchronously in conjunction with systems such as class, race, gender, age, ethnicity, sexuality, etc., (McCarthy, 1988). People can be situated very differently in the *same totalizing structures of oppression.* We need to analyze and challenge both the specific enunciations of micro-differences within difference and the macro-structure of difference-in-relation (Ebert, 1991a). We need to refocus on "structural" oppression in the forms of patriarchy, capitalism, and white supremacy—structures that tend to get ignored by liberal multiculturalists and their veneration of difference as identity. As educators and cultural workers, we must critically intervene in power relations that organize difference.

WHITENESS: THE INVISIBLE CULTURE OF TERROR
The Myth of Embranquecimento ("Whitening")

Educators need to critically examine the development of pedagogical discourses and practices that demonize Others who are different (through transforming them into absence or deviance). Critical multiculturalism calls serious attention to the dominant meaning systems readily available to students and teachers, most of which are ideologically stitched into the fabric of Western imperialism and patriarchy. It challenges meaning systems that impose attributes on the Other under the direction of sovereign signifiers and tropes. And this means not directing all our efforts at understanding ethnicity as 'other than white," but by interrogating the culture of whiteness itself. This is crucial because unless we do this—unless we give white students a sense of their own identity as an emergent ethnicity—we naturalize whiteness as a cultural marker against which Otherness is defined. Coco Fusco warns that "To ignore white ethnicity is to redouble its hegemony by naturalizing it. Without specifically addressing white ethnicity there can be no critical evaluation of the construction of the other" (cited in Wallace, 1991, p. 7). White groups need to examine their own ethnic histories so that they are less likely to judge their own cultural norms as neutral and universal. The supposed neutrality of white culture enables it to commodify blackness to its own advantage and ends. It allows it to manipulate the "other" but not see this "otherness" as a white tool of exploitation. 'Whiteness' does not exist outside of culture but constitutes the prevailing social texts in which social norms are made and remade. As part of a politics of signification that passes unobserved into the rhythms of daily life, and a "politically constructed category parasitic on 'Blackness'" (West, 1990, p. 29), "whiteness" has become the invisible norm for how the dominant culture measures its own worth and civility.

Using an ethnosemiotic approach as a means of interrogating the culture of whiteness and to understand ethnicity as a rhetorical form, Dean MacCannell, in his new book, *Empty Meeting Grounds*, raises the question: "In their interactions with others, how can groups in power manage to convey the impression that they are less ethnic than those over whom they exercise their power; in other words, how can they foster the impression that their own traits and qualities are correct, while the corresponding qualities of others are 'ethnic' "(1992: 121-122)? Furthermore, asks MacCannell, how does the consensus that is achieved in this matter structure our institutions? His answer leads us to explore the secret of power in discourse—that simply because language is essentially rhetorical (i.e., free of all bias because it is pure bias) we cannot escape the fact that rhetoric and grammar always intersect in particular ideological formations which makes language unavoidably a *social relation*. And every social relation is a structurally located one that can never be situated outside of relations of power. MacCannell locates this power in the ability of the speaking subject to move into the position of "he" without seeming to leave the position of "I" or "you" (which are empty or "floating" signifiers that have no referent outside the immediate situation). The personal pronoun "he," refers to an objective situation outside of the immediate subjectively apprehended situation. MacCannell asserts that whites have mastered interactional forms that permit them to operate as *interactants* while seeming to be detached from the situation, to be both an "I" or a "you" and a "he" at the same time-both to operate within the situation *and* to judge it. Dominant groups will always want to occupy the grammatical power position; that is, assume the external objective and judgmental role of the '*he*' by suggesting that their use of language is free of bias. White culture, according to MacCannell, is an enormous totalization that arrogates to itself the right to represent all other ethnic groups. For instance, binary oppositions such as 'white as opposed to nonwhite' always occupy the grammatical position of "him", never "I" or "you", and we know that in white culture, "whiteness" will prevail and continue to be parasitic on the meaning of "blackness."

Cornel West (1990: p. 29) remarks that "'Whiteness' is a politically constructed category parasitic on 'blackness'." He further asserts that "One cannot deconstruct the binary oppositional logic of images of Blackness without extending it to the contrary condition of Blackness/Whiteness itself." According to Jonathan Rutherford

> Binarism operates in the same way as splitting and projection: the centre expels it anxieties, contradictions and irrationalities onto the subordinate term, filling it with the antithesis of its own identity; the Other, in its very alieness, simply mirrors and represents what is deeply familiar to the centre, but projected outside of itself. It is in these very processes and representations of marginality that the violence, antagonisms and aversions which are at the core of the dominant discourses and identities become manifest-racism, homophobia, misogyny and class contempt are the products of this frontier. (1990: p. 22).

Of course, when binarisms become racially and culturally marked, *white* occupies the grammatical position of *him*, never *I* or *you* and, notes MacCannell, "always operates *as if* not dependent on rhetoric to maintain its position." (p. 131). Rhetoric is aligned with *non-truth* and whiteness is perceived as neutral and devoid of interest. Of course, "whiteness" projects onto the term "blackness" an array of specific qualities and characteristics such as wild, exotic, uncontrolled, deviant and savage. Whiteness is founded on the principle of depersonalization of all human relationships and the idealization of objective judgement and duty. MacCannell is worth quoting at length on this issue:

> To say that White Culture is impersonal is not the same thing as saying that it does not function like a subject or subjectivity. But it is the kind that is cold, the kind that laughs at feelings while demanding that all surplus libido, energy and capital be handed over to it...White culture begins with the pretense that it, above all, does not express itself rhetorically. Rather, the form of its expression is always represented as only incidental to the "truth." And its totalizing power radiates from this pretense which is maintained by interpreting all ethnic expression as 'representative,' and therefore *merely* rhetorical. (1992: p. 130)

When people of color attack white ground rules for handling disputes, or bureaucratic procedures, or specific policies of institutionalized racism, these are necessary oppositional acts, but insufficient for bringing about structural change because, as MacCannell notes, this work is "framed by the assumption of the dominance of white culture" (p. 131). This is because white culture is predicated upon the universalization of the concept of 'exchange values'-systems of equivalences, the transcribability of all languages, the translatability of any language into any other language, and the division of the earth into real-estate holdings in which it is possible to precisely calculate and calibrate the worth of every person. MacCannell is quite clear on this. Within such a totalization brought about by white culture, indigenous groups can only belong as an 'ethnicity.' As long as white culture, as the defining cultural frame for white-ethnic transactions, sets the limits on all thought about human relations, there can be no prospect for human equality.

Richard Dyer (1988) has made some useful observations about the culture of whiteness, claiming that its property of being both 'everything' and 'nothing' is the source of its representational power in the sense that white culture possesses the power to colonize the definition of the normal with respect to class, gender, heterosexuality, and nationality. Perhaps white culture's most formidable attribute is its ability to mask itself as a category. Whites will often think of their Scottishness, Irishness, or Jewishness, and so on, before they think of their whiteness. Michael Goldfield (1992) argues that white supremacy has been responsible for holding back working class struggle in the United States, as labor groups tragically failed to grasp the strategic importance for labor in fighting the system of white supremacy, missing an opportunity-especially during the Reconstruction-for changing the face of U.S. politics.

In her recent book, *Black Looks*, bell hooks notes that white people are often shocked when black people "critically assess white people from a standpoint where 'whiteness' is the privileged signifier" (p.167). She remarks that

> Their [white people's] amazement that black people match white people with a critical "ethnographic" gaze, is itself an expression of racism. Often their rage erupts because they believe that all ways of looking that highlight difference subvert the liberal belief in a universal subjectivity (we are all just people) that they think will make racism

> disappear. They have a deep emotional investment in the myth of "sameness," even as their actions reflect the primacy of whiteness as a sign informing who they are and how they think. Many of them are shocked that black people think critically about whiteness because racist thinking perpetuates the fantasy that the Other who is subjugated, who is subhuman, lacks the ability to comprehend, to understand, to see the working of the powerful. Even though the majority of those students politically consider themselves liberals and anti-racist, they too unwittingly invest in the sense of whiteness as mystery. (pp. 167-168).

hooks discusses the representation of whiteness as a form of terror within black communities and is careful not simply to invert the stereotypical racist association of whiteness as goodness and blackness as evil. The depiction of whiteness as 'terrorizing' emerges in hooks' discussion not as a reaction to stereotypes but, as she puts it, "as a response to the traumatic pain and anguish that remains a consequence of white racist domination, a psychic state that informs and shapes the way black folks 'see' whiteness." (p. 169).

THE POLITICS OF MULTICULTURAL RESISTANCE

Critical pedagogy needs to hold a non-reductionist view of the social order, that is, society needs to be seen as an irreducible indeterminacy; the social field is always open and we must explore its fissures, fault-lines, gaps and silences. Power relations may not always have a conscious design, but they have unintended consequences which define deep structural aspects of oppression even though every ideological totalization of the social is designed to fail. This is not to affirm Schopenhauer's unwilled patterns of history but rather to assert that while domination has a logic without design in its sign systems and social practices, it does operate through overdetermined structures of race, class, and gender difference. Resistance to such domination means deconstructing the social by means of a reflexive intersubjective consciousness-what Freire terms 'conscientizaçao.' With this comes a recognition that ideology is more than an epistemological concern about the status of certain facts, but the way in which discourse and discursive systems generate particular social relations as well as reflect them. A reflexive intersubjective consiousness is the beginning-but only the beginning-of revolutionary praxis.

We also need to create new narratives-new 'border narratives' in order to re-author the discourses of oppression in politically subversive ways as well as create sites of possibility and enablement. For instance, we need to ask: How are our identities bound up with historical forms of discursive practices? It is one thing to argue against attacks on polyvocal and unassimilable difference and on narrative closure or to stress the heterogeneity of contemporary culture. But in doing so we must remember that dominant discourses are sites of struggle and their meanings are linked to social struggles and labor/economic relations and then naturalized in particular textual/linguistic referents. Consequently, self-reflection alone-even if it is inimicably opposed to all forms of domination and oppression—is only a necessary but not nearly sufficient condition for emancipation. This must go hand-in-hand with changes in material and social conditions through counter-hegemonic action (Hammer and McLaren, 1991; 1992). The socio-historical dynamics of race, clan, and gender domination must never be left out of the equation for social struggle or take a back seat to the sociology seminar room. We need a language of criticism as an antidote to the atheoretical use of 'personal experience' in advancing claims for emancipatory action. Common sense consciousness is not enough. However, this needs to be followed by the development of truly counter-hegemonic public spheres. We need more than rhetorical displacements of oppression but strategic and co-ordinated resistance to racist patriarchal capitalism and gender-divided labor relations. According to Teresa Ebert (in press), what is needed is an intervention into the system of patriarchal oppression at both the macropolitical level of the structural organization of domination (a transformative politics of labor relations) and the micropolitical level of different and contradictory manifestations of oppression (cultural politics).

Those of us working in the area of curriculum reform need to move beyond the tabloid reportage surrounding the political correctness debate and take the issue of difference seriously and challenge the dimissive undercutting of difference by the conservative multiculturalists. First we need to move beyond admitting one or two Latin American or African American books into the canon of great works. Rather, *we need to legitimize multiple traditions of knowledge.* By focusing merely on diversity we are actually reinforcing the power of the discourses from the Western traditions that occupy the contexts of social privilege. Second, curriculum reform requires teachers to interrogate the discursive presuppositions that inform their curriculum practices with respect to race, class, gender, and sexual orientation. In addition, they need to unsettle their complacency with respect to Eurocentrism. Third, what is perceived as the inherent superiority of whiteness and Western rationality needs to be displaced. The very notion of the 'West' is something that critical educators find highly problematic. Why is Toni Morrison, for instance, denounced as non-Western simply because she is African-American? (This is complicated by the fact that conservative multiculturalists often retort with the insinuation that any attack on Western culture is an attack against being American.) Fourth, curriculum reform means recognizing that groups are differentially situated in the production of Western high-status knowledge. How are certain groups represented in the official knowledge that makes up the curriculum? Are they stigmatized because they are associated with the Third World? Are we, as teachers, complicitous with the oppression of these people when we refuse to interrogate popular films and TV shows that reinforce their subaltern status? Educators would do well to follow bell hooks in dehegemonizing racist discourses such that "progressive white people who are anti-racist might be able to understand the way in which their cultural practice reinscribes white supremacy without promoting paralyzing guilt or denial" (p. 177). In addition, curriculum reform means affirming the voices of the oppressed; teachers need to give the marginalized and the powerless a preferential option. Similarly, students must be encouraged to produce their own oppositional readings of curriculum content. And lastly, curriculum reform must recognize the importance of encouraging spaces for the multiplicity of voices in our classrooms, and creating a dialogical pedagogy in which subjects see others as subjects and not as objects. When this happens, students are more likely to participate in history rather than become its victims.

In taking seriously the irreducible social materiality of discourse and the fact that the very semantics of discourse is always organized and interested, critical pedagogy has revealed how student identities are differentially constructed through social relations of schooling that promote and sustain asymmetrical relations of power and privilege between the oppressors and the oppressed. And it has shown that this construction follows a normative profile of citizenship and an epistemology that attempts to reconcile the discourse of ideals with the discourse of needs. Discourses have been revealed to possess the power to nominate others as deviant or normal. Dominant discourses of schooling are not laws. Rather, they are strategies —disciplined mobilizations for normative performances of citizenship. Ian Hunter (1992) has shown that the concept of citizenry taught in schools has less to do with ethical ideals than disciplinary practices and techniques of reading and writing and the way students are distributed into political and aesthetic spaces. We are being aesthetically and morally reconciled with the governing norms of a civic unconscious. The 'unconscious' is not a semiotic puzzle to be opened through the discovery of some universal grammar but is rather an ethical technology designed to 'complete' students as citizens. Pedagogically, this process is deceptive because it uses liberal humanism and progressive education to complete the circuit of hegemony. The liberal position on pedagogy is to use it to open social texts to a plurality of readings. Because we live in an age of cynical reason, this pedagogy provides a "knowing wink" to students which effectively says: "We know there are multiple ways to make sense of the world and we know that you know, too. So let's knowingly enter this world of multiple interpretations together and take pleasure in rejecting the dominant codes." Consequently, teachers and students engage in a tropological displacement and unsettling of normative discourses and revel in the semantic excess that prevents any meaning from becoming transcendentally fixed. The result of this practice of turning knowledge into floating signifiers circulating in an avant-garde text (whose discursive trajectory is everywhere and nowhere and whose meaning is ultimately undecidable) is simply a re-containment of the political. By positing undecidability in advance, identity is reduced to a form of self-indexing or academic "vogue-ing." Liberation becomes transformed into a form of discursive 'cleverness,' of postmodern transgressive-chic grounded in playfully high vogue decodings of always already constructed texts.

I would also like to argue, in conclusion, that students need to move beyond liberal pedagogy and be provided with opportunities to construct border identities. Border identities are intersubjective spaces of cultural translation—linguistically multivalanced spaces of intercultural dialogue. It is a space where one can find an overlay of codes, a multiplicity of culturally inscribed subject positions, a displacement of normative reference codes, and a polyvalent assemblage of new cultural meanings (see Hicks, 1991; Giroux, 1992; McLaren, in press; in press a).

Border identities are produced in sites of 'occult instability' and result in "un laberinto de significados." Here, knowledge is produced by a transrepresentational access to the real—through reflexive, relational understanding amidst the connotative matrixes of numerous cultural codes. It is a world where identity and critical subjectivity depend upon the process of translating a profusion of intersecting cultural meanings (Hicks, 1991; Giroux, 1992). We need to remember than we live in a repressive regime in which identities are teleologically inscribed towards a standard end—the informed, employed citizen. There is a tension among students to "reterritorialize" this narrative in which schools have attempted to install in them through normative pedagogical practices and the nonlinear narratives that they 'play out' in the world outside of the school. But students and even their often well-intentioned teachers are frequently incapable of intervening.

Especially in inner-city schools, students can be seen as inhabiting what I call 'border cultures.' These are cultures in which, while there is a repetition of certain normative structures and codes, these often 'collide' with other codes and structures whose referential status is often unknown or only partially known. In Los Angeles, for instance, it is possible that an inner-city neighborhood will contain Latino cultures, Asian cultures, and Anglo cultures and students live interculturally as they cross the borderlines of linguistic, cultural and conceptual realities. Students, in other words, have the opportunity to live multidimensionally. Living in border cultures is an anticentering experience as school time and space is constantly displaced and often a carnivalesque liminal space emerges as bourgeois linear time is displaced. Because the dominant models of multiculturalism in mainstream pedagogy is of the conservative or liberal variety, the notion of sameness is enforced and cultural differences that challenge white Anglo cultures are considered deviant and in need of enforced homogenization into the dominant referential codes and structures of Euro-American discourse.

I am in agreement with critics who assert that border identity cannot be subsumed under either dialectical or analytic logic (Hicks, 1991). It is, rather, to experience a deterritorialization of signification (Larsen, 1991) in a postnationalist cultural space—that is, in a postcolonial, postnational space. It is an identity structure that occurs in a postimperial space of cultural possibility. The postcolonial subject that arises out of the construction of border identity is non-identical with itself. It acquires a new form of agency outside of Euro-American Cartesian discourses. It is not simply an inverted Eurocentrism but one that salvages the modernist referent of a liberation from oppression for all suffering peoples. I am here stressing the universality of human rights but at the same time criticizing essentialist universality as a site of transcendental meaning. In other words, I am emphasizing the universality or rights as historically produced. Social justice is a goal that needs to be situated historically, contextually, and contingently as the product of material struggles over modes of intelligibility as well as institutional and social practices. I need to be clear about what I mean by a referent for social justice and human freedom. I mean that the project underlying multicultural education needs to be situated from the standpoint not only of the *concrete other* but also the *generalized other*. All universal rights in this view must recognize the specific needs and desires of the concrete other without sacrificing the standpoint of a generalized other, without which it is impossible to speak of a radical ethics at all. Selya Benhabib distinguishes between this perspective—what she refers to as an "interactive universalism"—and a "substitutionalist universalism": "Substitutionalist universalism dismisses the concrete other behind the facade of a definitional identity of all as rational beings, while interactive universalism acknowledges that every generalized other is also a concrete other" (1992: 165). This position speaks neither exclusively to a liberal humanist ethics of empathy and benevolence nor a ludic postmodernist ethics of local narratives or "les petits recits," but one based on engagement, confrontation and dialogue, and collective moral argumentation between and across borders. It takes into account both macro and micro theory (Best and Kellner, 1991) and some degree of normative justification and ajudication of choices. As Best and Kellner note (1991), "one needs new critical theories to conceptualize, describe, and interpret macro social processes, just as one needs political theories able to articulate common or general interests that cut across divisions of sex, race, and class" (p. 301). In this sense I take issue with "ludic" voices of postmodernism that proclaim an end both to self-reflective agenthood and the importance of engaging historical narratives and which proclaim the impossibility of legitimizing institutions outside of an "immanent appeal to the self-legitimation of 'small narratives'" (Benhabib, 1992: 220). Rather, a critical multiculturalism must take into account the "methodological assumptions guiding one's choice of narratives, and a clarification of those principles in the name of which one speaks" (p. 226).

A border identity is not simply an identity that is anti-capitalist and counterhegemonic but is also critically utopian. It is an identity that transforms the burden of knowledge into a scandal of hope. The destructive extremes of Eurocentrism and national-cultural identities (as in the current crisis in what was formerly Yugoslavia) must be avoided. We need to occupy locations between our political unconscious and everyday praxis and struggle but at the same time guided by a universalist emancipatory world view in the form of a provisional utopia or contingent foundationalism (See Butler, 1991). A provisional utopia is not a categorical blueprint for social change (as in fascism) but a contingent utopia where we anticipate the future through practices of solidarity and community. Such a utopian vision demands that we gain control of the production of meaning, but in a post-nationalist sense. We can achieve this by negotiating with the borders of our identity—those unstable constellations of discursive structures—in our search for a radical otherness that can empower us to reach beyond them.

Border identities constitute a bold infringement on normalcy, a violation of the canons of bourgeois decorum, a space where we can cannibalize the traces of our narrative repression or engage them critically through the practice of cultural translation—a translation of one level of reality into another, creating a multidimension reality that I call the *cultural imaginary*, a space of cultural articulation that results from the collision of multiple strands of referential codes and sign systems. Such collisions can create hybrid significations through a hemorrhage of signifiers whose meanings endlessly bleed into each other or else take on the force of historical agency as a new *mestizaje* consciousness. Mestizaje consciousness (Anzaldúa, 1987) is not simply a doctrine of identity based on cultural bricolage or a form of bric-a-brac subjectivity but a critical practice of cultural negotation and translation that attempts to transcend the contradictions of Western dualistic thinking. As Chandra Talpade Mohanty remarks

> A mestiza consciousness is a consciousness of the borderlands, a consciousness born of the historical collusion of Anglo and Mexican cultures and frames of reference. It is a plural consciousness in that it requires understanding multiple, often opposing ideas and knowledges, and negotiating these knowledges, not just taking a simple counterstance. (1991, pp. 34-35).

Anzaldúa speaks of a notion of agency that moves beyond the postmodernist concept of "split subject" by situating agency in its historical and geopolitical specificity (Mohanty, 1991, p. 37). Borders cannot simply be evoked in an abstract transcendental sense but need to be identified specifically. Borders can be linguistic, spacial, ideological and geographical. They not only demarcate otherness but stipulate the manner in which otherness is maintained and reproduced. A mestizaje consciousness is linked, therefore, to the specificity of historical struggles (Mohanty, 1992, p. 38).

A critical multiculturalism needs to testify not only to the pain, suffering, and 'walking nihilism' of oppressed peoples, but also to the intermittent, epiphanic ruptures and moments of *jouissance* that occur when solidarity is established around struggles for liberation. As I have tried to argue, with others, elsewhere (McLaren and Hammer, 1989, Giroux and McLaren, 1992), we need to abandon our pedagogies of protest (which, as Houston Baker reminds us, simply reinforces the dualism of 'self' and 'other' and reinstates the basis of dominant racist evaluations, and preserves the 'always already' arrangements of white male hegemony; see Baker, 1985) in favor of a politics of transformation. Those of us who are white need also to avoid the "white male confessional" that Baker describes as the "confessional *manqué* of the colonial subject" (Baker, 1985, p. 388).

White male confessionals simply 'induce shame' rather than convince people to change their axiology, yet still employ the language and "shrewd methods of the overseers." It is the type of confessional that proclaims that oppressed people of color are "as good as" white people. It simply asserts that subaltern voices measure up to dominant voices and that African Americans are merely 'different' and not deviant. In contrast, Baker calls for a form of "*supraliteracy*" or "guerrilla action" carried out *within* linguistic territories. This constitutes an invasion of the dominant linguistic terrain of the traditional academic disciplines—an invasion that he describes as a "deformation of mastery." From this perspective, critical pedagogy needs to be more attentive to the dimension of the vernacular—"to sound racial poetry in the courts of the civilized" (p. 395). Teachers need to include non-literary cultural forms into our classrooms —such as video, film, popular fiction, and radio—and a critical means of understanding their role in the production of subjectivity and agency.

Concentrating on the reflexive modalities of the intellect or returning to some pre-theoretical empirical experience are both bad strategies for challenging the politics of the white confessional. The former is advocated mostly by academics while the latter is exercised by educational activists suspicious of the new languages of deconstruction and the fashionable apostasy of the post-structuralists whose intellectual home is in the margins. Academic theorists tend to textualize and displace experience to the abstract equivalence of the signified while activists view "commonsense" experience as essentially devoid of ideology or interest. We need to understand experience from a radical contextualist standpoint as constructed within cultural alliances and contexts articulated to and by asymmetrical relations of power and privilege.

Critical social theory as a form of multicultural resistance must be wary of locating liberatory praxis in the realm of diachrony—as something to be resolved dialectically in some higher unity outside of the historical struggle and pain and suffering to which we must serve as pedagogical witnesses and agents of radical hope. Yet at the same time, critical pedagogy needs to be wary of forms of populist elitism that privilege only the reform efforts of those who have direct experience with the oppressed. After all, no single unsurpassable and 'authentic' reality can be reached through 'experience' since no experience is pre-ontologically available outside of a politics of representation and power.

As multicultural educators informed by critical and feminist pedogogies, we need to keep students connected to the power of the unacceptable and comfortable with the unthinkable by producing critical forms of policy analysis and pedagogy. In tandem with this, we must actively help students to challenge sites of discursive hierarchy rather than delocalizing and dehistoricizing them, and to contest the ways that their desires and pleasures are being policed in relationship to them. It is important that as critical educators we do not manipulate students simply to accept our intellectual positions nor presume at the same time to speak *for* them. Nor should our critical theorizing be simply a service to the culture of domination by extending student insights into the present system without at the same time challenging the very assumptions of the system. We cannot afford to just temporarily disengage students from the *doxa*—the language of commonsense. If we want to recruit students to a transformative praxis, students must not only be encouraged to choose a language of analysis that is undergirded by a project of liberation but must affectively invest in it.

If we are to be redeemed from our finitude as passive supplicants of history we must, as students and teachers, adopt more directly oppositional and politically combatative social and cultural practices. The destructive fanaticism of present day xenophobia is only exacerbated by the current ethical motionlessness among many left constituencies. Insurgent intellectuals and theorists are called to steer a course between the monumentalization of judgment and taste and riding the postmodern currents of despair in a free-fall exhilaration of political impotence.

The present historical moment is populated by memories that are surfacing at the margins of our culture, along the faultlines of our logocentric consciousness. Decolonized spaces are forming in the borderlands—linguistic, epistemological, intersubjective—and these will affect the classrooms of the future. Here saints and Iwa walk together and the Orishas speak to us through the rhythms of the earth and the pulse of the body. The sounds produced in the borderlands are quite different from the convulsive monotones that echo from the schizophrenic boundaries of Weber's iron cage. Here it is in the hybrid polyrhythms of the drum that the new pulse of freedom can be felt. Within such borderlands our pedagogies of liberation can be invested once again with the passion of mystery and the reason of commitment. This is neither a Dionysian rejection of rationality nor a blind, pre-rational plunge into myth but rather an attempt to embrace and reclaim the memories of those pulsating, sinewed bodies that have been forgotten in our modernist assault on difference and uncertainty.

REFERENCES

Anzaldúa, Gloria (1987). *Borderlands/La Frontera,* San Francisco: Spinsters/Aunt Lute.

Auster, Laurence (1990). *The Path to National Suicide: An Essay on Immigration and Multiculturalism.* American Immigration Control Foundation.

Baker, Houston A. (1985). "Caliban's Triple Play." In Henry Louis Gates, Jr. (Ed.) *"Race," Writing and Difference.* Chicago, Illinois, The University of Chicago Press, 381-395.

Benhabib, Seyla (1992). *Situating the Self: Gender, Community and Postmodernism in Contemporary Ethics.* London and New York: Routledge.

Best, Steven and Kellner, Douglas (1991). *Postmodern Theory: Critical Interrogations.* New York: the Guilford Press.

Bhabha, Homi K. (1992). "A Good Judge of Character: Men, Metaphors, and the Common Culture." In Toni Morrison (editor) *Race-ing Justice, En-gendering Power*. New York: Pantheon Books, pp. 232-249.

Butler, Judith (1991). "Contingent Foundations: Feminism and the Question of 'Postmodernism.' *Praxis International*, vol.11, no.2, pp. 150-165.

Bradford, Phillips Verner and Blume, Harvey (1992). *Ota Benga: The Pygmy in the Zoo*. New York: St. Martin's Press.

Brookhiser, Richard (1991). *The Way of the WASP: How It Made America, and How It Can Save It, So to Speak*, New York: Free Press.

Cooper, B. M. (1989). "Cruel and the Gang: Esposing the Schomburg Posse." *The Village Voice*, 34(19), 27-36.

Copjec, Joan (1991). "The Unvermogender Other: Hysteria and Democracy in America," *New Formations* 14(Summer): 27-41.

Cortázar, Julio (1963). *Hopscotch*. Trans. Gregory Rabassa. New York: Random House.

Darder, Antonia (1992). *Culture and Power in the Classroom*. South Hadley, Mass.: Bergin and Garvey.

Dyer, Richard (1988). "White," *Screen*, vol. 29, no. 4, pp. 44-64.

Ebert, Teresa (1991). "Writing in the Political: Resistance (Post) Modernism." *Legal Studies Forum*, vol xv, no. 4: 291-303.

_________ (1991a). "Political Semiosis in/of American Cultural Studies," *The American Journal of Semiotics*, vol. 8, no. 1/2, 113-135.

_________ (in press). "Ludic Feminism, the Body, Performance and Labor: Bringing Materialism Back into Feminist Cultural Studies," *Cultural Critique*.

Estrada, Kelly and McLaren, Peter (in press). "A Dialogue on Multiculturalism and Democracy." *Educational Researcher*.

Fish, Stanley (1992). "Bad Company." *Transition*, 56, pp. 60-67.

Gardiner, Michael (1992). *The Dialogics of Critique: M.M. Bakhtin and the Theory of Ideology*. London and New York: Routledge.

Giroux, Henry (1992). *Border Crossings*. London and New York: Routledge.

Giroux, Henry and McLaren, Peter (1992). "Writing From the Margins: Geographies of Identity, Pedagogy, and Power." *Journal of Education*, vol. 174, no. 1, pp. 7-30.

_________ (1991). "Radical Pedagogy as Cultural Politics: Beyond the Discourse of Critique and Anti-Utopianism." In D. Morton and M. Zavarzadeh (eds.). *Theory/Pedagogy/Politics*. Chicago: University of Illinois Press, pp. 152-186.

_________ (in press). "Paulo Freire, Postmodernism, and the Utopian Imagination: A Blochian Reading." In Jamie Owen Daniel and Tom Moylan (eds.) *Bloch In Our Time*. London and New York: Verso.

_________ (1991a). "Media Hegemony." Introduction to *Media Knowledge* by James Schwoch, Mimi White, and Susan Reilly. Albany New York: State University of New York Press, pp. xv-xxxiv.

_________ (1991b). "Leon Golub's Radical Pessimism: Toward a Pedagogy of Representation." *Exposure*, vol. 28, no. 12, pp. 18-33.

Goldfield, Michael (1992). "The Color of Politics in the United States: White Supremacy as the Main Explanation for the Pecularities of American Politics from Colonial Times to the Present." In Dominick LaCapra (Ed.) *The Bounds of Race*. Ithaca and London: Cornell University Press, pp. 104-133.

Hall, Stuart (1991). "Ethnicity: Identity and Difference," *Radical America*, Vol. 23, no. 4, 9-20.

Hammer, Rhonda and McLaren, Peter (1992). "Spectacularizing Subjectivity: Media Knowledges and the New World Order." *Polygraph*, No. 5, pp. 46-66.

_________ (1991). "Rethinking the Dialectic." *Educational Theory*, vol. 41, no. 1, pp. 23-46.

Hicks, D. Emily (1991). *Border Writing*. Minneapolis, University of Minnesota Press.

hooks, bell (1992). *Black Looks.* Boston, MA: South End Press.

Hunter, Ian (1988). *Culture and Government: The Emergence of Literary Education*, Houndmills, Basingstoke, Hampshire and London: The MacMillan Press, Ltd.

Katz, Cindi and Smith, Neil (1992). "L.A. Intifada: Interview with Mike Davis." *Social Text*, 33, pp. 19-33.

Larsen, Neil (1991). "Foreword" to *Border Writing* by Emily Hicks, Minneapolis: University of Minnesota Press, pp. xi-xxi.

Lloyd, David (1991). "Race Under Representation," *Oxford Literary Review*, vol. 13, nos. 1-2, 62-94.

MacCannell, Dean (1992). *Empty Meeting Grounds: The Tourist Papers.* London and New York: Routledge.

Macedo, Donaldo (1995). *Literacies of Power*. Boulder, CO: Westview Press

McCarthy, Cameron (1988). "Rethinking liberal and radical perspectives on racial inequality in schooling: Making the case for nonsynchrony. *Harvard Educational Review*, 58 (3), 265-279.

McLaren, Peter and Hammer, Rhonda (1992). "Media Knowledges, Warrior Citizenry, and Postmodern Literacies." *Journal of Urban and Cultural Studies*, vol. 2, no. 2, pp. 41-77.

_________ (1989). "Critical Pedagogy and the Postmodern Challenge: Towards a Critical Postmodernist Pedagogy of Liberation." *Educational Foundations*, vol. 3, no. 3, pp. 29-62.

McLaren, Peter (in press). "Collisions with Otherness: Multi-Culturalism, the Politics of Difference, and the Ethnographer as Nomad." *American Journal of Semiotics.*

_________ (in press a). "Border Disputes: Multicultural Narrative, Critical Pedagogy and Identity Formation in Postmodern America." In J. McLaughlin and William g. Tierney (eds.) *Naming Silenced Lives.* New York and London: Routledge.

_________ (1990). "Schooling the Postmodern Body." In Henry A. Giroux (Editor) *Postmodernism, Feminism and Cultural Politics.* Albany, New York: SUNY Press, pp. 144-173.

_________ (1989). *Life in Schools.* White Plains, NY: Longman, Inc.(Revised Edition in press).

_________ (1988). "Culture or Canon? Critical Pedagogy and the Politics of Literacy." *The Harvard Educational Review*, vol. 58. no. 2, pp. 213-234.

_________ (1986). *Schooling as a Ritual Performance: Towards a Political Economy of Educational Symbols and Gestures.* London and New York: Routledge (Revised Edition in press).

_________ (1985). "Contemporary Ritual Studies: A Post-Turnerism Perspective." *Semiotic Inquiry*, vol. 5, no. 1, pp. 78-85.

Mercer, Kobena (1992). "1968: Periodizing Politics and Identity." In *Cultural Studies* (Lawrence Grossberg, Cary Nelson and Paula Treichler (Eds) London and New York: Routledge, pp. 424-449.

________ (1990). "Welcome to the Jungle: Identity and Diversity in Postmodern Politics," in Jonathan Rutherford (Ed.), *Identity: Community, Culture, Difference.* London, Lawrence and Wishart, 43-71.

Mohanty, Chandra Talpade (1991). "Introduction: Cartographies of Struggle: Third World Women and the Politics of Feminism." In Chandra Talpade Mohanty, Ann Russo and Lourdes Torres (eds.) *Third World Women and the Politics of Feminism.* Bloomington: Indiana University Press, pp. 1-47.

________ (1989/90). "On Race and Voice: Challenges for Liberal Education in the 1990s," *Cultural Critique.* Winter, 179-208.

Muñoz, Carlos (1989). *Youth, Identity, Power.* London and New York, Verso.

Naureckas, Jim (1993). "The Somalia Intervention: Tragedy Made Simple." *Extra,* vol. 6, No. 2, pp. 10-13.

Nieto, Sonia. (1992). *Affirming Diversity: The Sociopolitical Context of Multicultural Education.* White Plains, NY Longman Publishers.

Norris, Christopher (1990). *What's Wrong With Postmodernism?* Baltimore, Maryland: The John Hopkins University Press.

Observer, vol. 5, no. 2, (March 1992).

Pieterse, Jan Nederveen, (1992). *White on Black: Images of Africa and Blacks in Western Popular Culture.* New Haven and London: Yale University Press.

Rosaldo, Renato (1989). *Culture and Truth: The Remaking of Social Analysis.* Boston: Beacon.

Rutherford, Jim (1990). "A Place Called Home: Identity and the Cultural Politics of Difference." In J. Rutherford (Ed.) *Identity: Community, Culture, Difference.* (pp. 9-27). London: Lawrence and Wishart.

Schlesinger, Jr., Arthur M. (1991). *The Disuniting of America: Reflections on a Multicultural Society.* Knoxville: Whittle Direct Books.

Scott, Joan W. (1992). "Experience." In Judith Butler and Joan W. Scott (Eds.) *Feminists Theorize the Political.* New York and London: Routledge, pp. 22-40.

Simone, Timothy Maliqualim (1989). *About Face: Race in Postmodern America.* Brooklyn, New York: Autonomedia.

Sleeter, Christine E. (1991). *Empowerment Through Multicultural Education.* Albany: State University of New York Press.

Stephanson, Anders (1988). "Interview with Cornel West" in Andrew Ross (Ed). *Universal Abandon? The Politics of Postmodernism.* Minneapolis: The University of Minnesota Press, 269-286.

Wallace, Michele (1991). "Multiculturalism and Oppositionality." *Afterimage.* October, 6-9.

West Cornel (1990). "The New Cultural Politics of Difference." In Russell Ferguson, Martha Gever, Trinh T. Min-ha and Cornel West (Eds). *Out There: Marginalization and Contemporary Cultures.* Cambridge, Mass.: The MIT Press and The New Museum of contemporary Art, New York, pp. 19-36.

Willis, Paul (1990). *Common Culture,* Boulder, CO and San Francisco: Westview Press.

Young, Iris Marion (1990). *Justice and the Politics of Difference.* Princeton, New Jersey: Princeton University Press.

Zavarzadeh, Mas'ud and Morton, Donald (1990). 'Signs of Knowledge in the Contemporary Academy,' *American Journal of Semiotics,* 7(4), 149-60.

Chapter IV

A Critical Analysis of the Koppel Report: D.C./Divided City

Susan Reilly and Ron Scott

The following critical analysis of a television network news program serves to illustrate what was identified theoretically in the preceding chapter as a politics of representation. In this program the media personality serves as a pedagog operating within the patterns and limits of the commercial television medium. The personality/pedagog both consciously and unconsciously marshals a set of social practices which affirm and justify racism while the program's stated intent is to denounce racism.

On the night of April 27, 1989, in what appeared to be another relatively standard Thursday evening of programs, ABC aired a news documentary titled *D.C./Divided City*. The host of this one hour program, to be followed by a special town meeting on *Nightline*, was Ted Koppel. As both the title of the show implies and the promo leads suggested, the show was to focus on the nation's capitol, Washington, D.C., and an array of problems which have divided the city into two discrete populations, one white and the other black. To entice viewers around the country to watch, the show's lead suggested that the problems of the nation's capitol were problems which every part of the nation shared. In fact, the use of the capitol as a microcosm of the various problems of drugs and racism which confront the nation was well reasoned and logical.

To begin with, the rationale of the capitol as microcosm was narratively correct. Specifically, if the problems of drugs can not effectively be dealt with in the nation's seat of power, then what element of American society can lay claim to be effectively dealing with the problem? As the national center for the major organizations (FBI, DEA, and FTC) charged with fighting the drug problem in America, and the home of a newly appointed Drug Czar (William Bennett) who had recently declared the first front in the drug war would be D.C., the show promised to be of interest to national viewers. The claim advanced by this segment of the program then, was that one element which divided the city, and by implication the nation, was the widespread use, abuse, and sale of drugs.

While drugs alone may strategically be enough to divide any city, *D.C./Divided City* went one step further and explored the issue of racism as another major dividing factor in the capitol. As with the issue of drugs, the choice of D.C. as an example of the problem which confronts America, and especially black America, appeared well-reasoned. If, given the resources and talent in the city and its place as the heart of the nation's government and judicial systems, D.C. could not transcend the issues and problems of race, what hope would any portion of the nation have in ridding itself of the vestiges of a legacy steeped in the cultural, economic, and political history of this nation? As such, the second claim advanced by special was that race or racism was a factor which divided D.C. and the nation.

Had *D.C./Divided City* simply followed up the two claims it advanced, that drugs and race divide the city and the nation, the show may not have been worthy of much critical attention, beyond acclaim for its boldness and insight, and the motives for the show may have escaped question. As this analysis will demonstrate, however, the show did not simply address the issues it raised; rather it presented the viewer with another message which directly contradicted its apparent goal and argued for the continued, if not further, division of the city and nation.

In the program's teaser or lead, shots of a black tour guide, pointing out the sites to a bus load of white tourists, are intercut with shots of a black police officer, who becomes Koppel's and the viewer's tour guide, pointing out various drug havens and talking about the influx of drugs into the area he is patrolling. After a series of cut aways and short narrative bits which set the stage for this "drug infested" area, Koppel, on a street corner, appears on camera stating:

> Only blocks from the capital eleven year old boys stand watch for fifteen year old drug dealers who are guarded by seventeen year old enforcers who kill on behalf of a twenty-four year old drug king pin.
>
> The year is not yet four months old and already more than 150 people have died in drug-related violence. Almost all of them were black. This is *D.C./Divided City*.

Consequently, as the program begins, race has already been modified as a major issue that is dividing the city. Instead of shots of black and white drug dealers, users, and victims of drug-related violence, the screen is filled with images of blacks. To add to the impression that the drug issue is confined to one segment of the population, additional images of the black community and a series of sound bites which are all related to drugs, violence, or police intervention appear. Koppel later suggests that if one were to place a grid over the city, most of the violence would be confined to the black areas of the city. As the lead concludes, Koppel appears in shot two and greets the viewer with:

> Good evening. Much of what you'll see has to do with drugs, violence, money, and young people . . . threads lead back to the Kerner Commission Report twenty-one years ago that . . . white society is deeply implicated in the ghetto. White institutions created it. White institutions maintain it and white society condones it . . . What we are about to see may appear to be just a black problem, it is not.

At best, and if taken only in isolation, the narrative in the program's lead does hint that racism is a factor which has led to some division in the city and the nation. The notions of white institutions being "deeply implicated in the ghetto" does suggest that some aspect of the drug problem in America is at least indirectly tied to the white community and even hints at some conspiracy to control, contain, or establish at least theoretical justification, based on survival, for segregation. But the language of this narrative is problematic in that it implies that blacks live exclusively in the "ghetto" or the area of the city which allegedly harbors the worst elements in every American city. By tacit suggestion the viewer is also left with the impression that the black community, or ghetto, is rampant with drugs and drug-related violence. As the narrative for this segment concludes, Koppel adds that the program may appear to be about black problems, when in fact it is not.

As previously stated, if taken at face value, this segment of the program may suggest that the problems which divide the city are, in fact, related to drugs and race. While alluding to it, this particular segment, as does the rest of the program, fails to realize that drugs are at best only a symptom of the larger problem of race. The approach taken in this segment of the program however, implies that drugs are the problem and that if they could be eliminated from the "ghetto," a major factor in the city's division would be eliminated.

There is a curious sideline of the Koppel introduction which occurs in the reference to the 1968 Kerner Commission Report. In terms of a direct relationship to the basic claims of this program, i.e., race and drugs are dividing the city of Washington, D.C., the Koppel reference to the white community's implication in the black community actually begs the issue of race as a dividing factor in favor of an argument that suggests economics may be a more tangible factor in the division. In his passing reference to the Kerner report, Koppel fails to inform the audience that the Commission did in fact warn the nation of the problems of poverty and drug addition and subsequent problems which would result. The Commission also warned that unless drastic changes in racial relations were forthcoming, the nation was heading on a course which:

> ... would lead to the permanent establishment of two societies: one predominantly white and located in the suburbs, in smaller cities, and in outlying areas, and one largely Negro located in central cities. We are well on the way to just such a divided nation.

Thus, whether deliberately or by oversight, the lead of the show does not support the notion that two elements divide the city (drugs and race); rather it presents a narrative and set of black images which suggest that any division that occurs is the result of criminal activity in the ghetto or "black side" of the city. In effect the argument that is advanced is that drugs (and all the activities associated with them) are responsible for dividing the city of Washington, D.C. The assumption is that somehow the city divided into users and dealers, who are black and those who suffer from the violence which threatens the safety of the nation's capitol, or whites. This segment ignores, both narratively and visually, the amount of white drug activity in the city by implying that only blacks are involved. This curious approach only seems to support the need for division by playing on the fears of whites by presenting images of blacks that coincide with pervasive negative stereotypes.

The Documentary

After the introduction, the documentary *D.C./Divided City* is shown. It consists of two sections. The first focuses on the effects of drug-related violence and drug addiction on a black neighborhood. It includes attempts by local residents to cope with the drug problem. The neighborhood is identified as Anacostia, located a few blocks from the White House. Three vignettes about neighborhood residents are presented. The first opens with a series of shots of a young black man lying dead on the street while his mother, restrained by the police, cries hysterically. In a voice-over Koppel tells the audience that similar scenes of death and despair are being acted out all over America. As the young man's story unfolds, Koppel interviews his mother. He talks of her son's involvement in the drug business and identifies his murderer as an employee of the Edmunds family. The mother appears not to know what he is talking about. She acts extremely naive and is unwilling to acknowledge the information. The Edmunds family is described as a successful drug organization headed by another young black man. Each member of the family is pointed out to the audience from a wedding photograph. As each person's role in the organization is described, shots of the terrible results of their enterprise are shown—more young black men dead on the street or being led away by police. The audience is told that the Edmunds family paid for fancy cars, houses, trips and other luxuries with drug profits and provided these things as perks for employees. Koppel reveals that members of the Georgetown University basketball team knew Edmunds and socialized with him. Shots of young black people dancing at a night club are shown, while a voice-over describes the club as a place that black college students, basketball players, and drug dealers frequent. The coach of the Georgetown basketball team, who is black, is interviewed. He says that upon learning of his players' association with the drug dealer, the coach arranged a meeting with Edmunds to explain his concern for the safety of his players. The vignette is concluded with scenes of the capture of the Edmunds family in a recent drug bust carried out by the Washington police, the FBI, and the Drug Enforcement Administration.

The next vignette is about two young black women who are drug addicts. The first woman is interviewed before she leaves her children with her sister and enters a drug treatment program. She explains that she turned tricks to get money for drugs. Her sister describes how her children were left to wander the streets at night alone. The doctor in the treatment program she enters identifies her as a second generation drug user, a multiple substance abuser, a high school drop out, and an unwed mother. The second woman, whose whereabouts are unknown, has left her children with her mother who now cares for them. The youngest child has been identified as testing HIV positive. Mrs. George Bush is shown holding this baby at the special home where he must be kept. The baby's grandmother describes Mrs. Bush as a wonderful woman.

The last vignette is about two community volunteers, middle-aged black men nicknamed Uncle Skeezy and Peter Bug. These men are shown talking with elementary school children, trying to convince them to avoid drugs, get a good education, and become gainfully employed. The men talk to Koppel about the need to reach children and instill good values before it's too late. They express concern that children may become addicted to making money and that may justify their becoming involved in the drug business.

During the second section of the documentary the focus shifts to racism. At a black middle class church in Georgetown, the minister talks to his congregation about Apartheid American-style. Koppel describes high infant mortality among blacks and high homicide rates, over shots of afflicted infants and the bodies of murdered young men. A series of interviews with successful black business people and attorneys reveals their concern about *de facto* segregation in housing, the corporate world, and recreational facilities in Washington. They speak of an unfulfilled American Dream. The white chairman of a large bank is asked how many black vice presidents there are in his firm and he attempts to explain why there are none. This section of the documentary concludes back in Anacostia where a resident explains that the drug business is one of the few ways for young blacks to become entrepreneurs and assume controlling interest in their own enterprises.

Finally, Koppel introduces a videotape made by three black high school students. The students have tried to demonstrate how whites are fearful of young black men. In the video, the students stop whites on the street and ask for directions to the Corcoran Museum. Whites are shown trying to avoid them or ignoring them and brushing past. The students describe the fear they sensed in the white people when they approached. The program ends with the poem, "The Invisible Man," by Ralph Ellison, which the students have included in their videotape.

The effect of this documentary is profound. The premise seems to be that the seat of national government is threatened by the drug-related violence and addiction prevalent in Washington, D.C.'s black neighborhoods. The drug business is presented as an entrepreneurial substitute for the corporate success and social integration that remains unattainable to young black men because of white racism. However, the documentary contains a retinue of images that support whites' fear of blacks. Therefore it demonstrates the correctness of white fear and reinforces the racism it intends to condemn.

The first half of the documentary introduces a number of familiar black stereotypes—the dysfunctional black family, dangerously irresponsible young black men, immoral young black women, enduring black mothers, and good, but simple, black uncles. These stereotypes, which have permeated popular media for decades in this country, are provided as examples of the people who populate the black neighborhood.

The mother of a victim of drug-related murder is shown to be unaware of her son's involvement in the drug business. Members of a ruthless criminal family who make hundreds of thousands of dollars selling drugs are implicated in over 30 drug-related murders. This chaotic black neighborhood extends to include members of the Georgetown University basketball team, forcing the coach to ask a drug dealer to leave his boys alone. Young black women prostitute themselves for money to support their drug habits. They mistreat and abandon their children to enduring grandmothers and kindly old uncles. What are missing from this portrayal of the black community in Washington, D.C. are the statistics from The National Institute on Drug Abuse that indicate that a higher proportion of white Americans are drug abusers than black Americans, suggesting that a significant drug problem occurs in white suburban and rural neighborhoods. Yet there is no section in Koppel's grid of Washington, that represents those communities. Koppel's point seems to be that the drug business substitutes for legitimate business opportunity unavailable to blacks because of white racism. However, the documentary doesn't mention census data which indicates that over 200,000 black Washingtonians are gainfully employed and not dependent on the drug industry for financial support. Without the presentation of the positive side of the black community or the negative side of the white community the audience is subtly led to believe that the drug problem that affects some residents of a black neighborhood is representative of not only all black neighborhoods in Washington, D.C., but of all black neighborhoods in all urban centers across the country.

In the second half of the documentary the issue of racism moves to the foreground. The familiar images of articulate blacks decrying *de facto* segregation and insisting on a fairer distribution of economic and social advantage are presented. Although the intent of the program is to present this critique as justified, the images of financially successful blacks demanding less tangible forms of inclusion in the dominant culture maintains the stereotype that white society is somehow intrinsically enviable. The enviable qualities are presumed and never fully delineated. The notion of equality becomes lost in the presumed desire to be with whites because their way of life is less connected to unsavory elements of society. This subtle suggestion is made by stating that successful blacks must return after work to black neighborhoods which have already been presented as riddled with drug-related violence. Missing from the documentary's approach to racism are positive elements of the black experience that would provide balance along with negative elements of white experience. An argument for an end to racism cannot be based on white guilt and a plea for white magnanimity. It must make clear the value to be gained from an integrated culture. Compelling positive aspects of the black experience are totally absent from this documentary.

Therefore, there is a great irony in the program's conclusion with the student video depicting white fear of young black men. After watching the rest of the documentary, the white audience can only empathize with the fear exhibited by whites in the videotape. Young black men have been shown repeatedly as both victims, and more importantly, as perpetrators of irrational violence.

Next, what is billed as a special edition of a live town meeting is presented to viewers. As does the initial portion of the program, this segment opens with leads, four short national reports, which allude to additional special live coverage which will appear later in the broadcast. Unlike previous segments which have focused on drug activity and racism in Washington, D.C., this segment of the program presents stories from Los Angeles, Denver, Atlanta, and New York.

After a narrator introduces the second half of the program and restates the intent of the program to explore the relationship between drugs and racism, the first of the national clips is presented. Reporting from Los Angeles, correspondent Ken Kashiwahara informs the viewer that Los Angeles, among other things, is "... a city that has become the major distribution center for more than half the nation's cocaine." He is followed by James Walker, reporting from Denver, who adds that "... in Denver the biggest concern about illegal drugs involves crack brought to the "Mile High City" by drug gangs from L.A." Having established the West Coast distribution centers, the introduction shifts to correspondent Jackie Judd in Atlanta who reports that "This (Atlanta) is a city that's become a major stopping point along the cocaine corridor. [Where] vast supplies of cocaine come up from Miami." Finally a report from New York correspondent Jeff Greenfield, among other things, establishes that "... what makes New York City's drug problem unique is what makes the city itself unique. Its sheer size ..." Each of the leads establishes drugs as a problem confronting the nation. Further support for this national problem is underscored by Koppel who addresses both the audience at home and at the town meeting and reminds them that they are "... not here to talk only about drugs and violence in Washington ... The problem is a national one, Washington has merely become the symbol."

Like the initial portions of the program, the argument presented to viewers in the introduction of this portion of the show raises some questions about the purpose and focus of the program. First, if the program is designed to explore the issue of division in the city of Washington and the nation, why are there no direct references to race as a problem in any of the news summary segments? As presented, if the viewer does not remember the initial narrator's brief reference to the show's exploration of the "... relationship between drugs and racism," nothing in the four news reports will remind the viewer of the show's purpose of exploring dual issues which divide cities.

Second, the program has chosen to focus on four cities which have substantial minority, specifically black, populations. The danger here of course, is that viewers are allowed or even perhaps led, to develop the link between large black populations and drugs, and the relationship between drugs, crime, violence, and black people. Instead of addressing an issue which may be dividing a city, blacks, because of their behavior, attitudes, and actions are presented as *the* factor which has led to the division of not only D.C., but other majors cities as well. Even though the visuals in this segment are not exclusively populated by blacks or other minorities, setting the stories in urban centers, urban again being the code for black, further supports arguments about blacks which have already been presented in the program. The program suggests that the drug problem occurs only in large inner city or urban areas and not in the more genteel suburban areas of the country. The irony here is that, while showing the urban or black areas and not presenting areas more heavily populated by whites, the show presents a segregated view of the country which, once again, seems based on tranquillity and safety vs danger and violence that is removed from the issue of race and directly tied to drugs.

Finally, the lack of a black correspondent, or any minority member of the production crew presented on screen during the entire program, raises questions about the show's understanding of its own selection of images, content, or central issues.

The National Town Meeting

The Town meeting begins immediately following the documentary. The meeting is held in a black church in the Anacostia section of Washington, D.C. Koppel begins the meeting by stating that the problem of drugs and violence is a national one and that Washington, D.C. is a symbol of that national problem. Koppel sits on an elevated platform. There are several hundred people in the church. Many different factions of the black community have been invited to participate in this town meeting—educators, police personnel, corrections officials, DEA agents, officers from the National Guard, members of the Nation of Islam, members of Alcoholics Anonymous, directors of various drug treatment programs, community organizers, and local politicians. They are seated all around Koppel. Some audience members sit on the platform behind him. These appear to be mostly young people, including the young high school students who made the videotape shown earlier at the end of the documentary. The audience in the church is identified as a gathering of community leaders. The vast majority are black. Almost immediately Kopple begins to establish some rules of order for the meeting. He does this indirectly by correcting speakers. It is unclear whether instructions were given to the audience before the meeting began and Koppel is enforcing them or whether he is correcting people spontaneously. Koppel corrects speakers if he feels they are not factual, logical, or brief enough. For example, Kopple asks Washington's Mayor Marion Barry, "Who is to blame for the drug problem." The mayor responds rhetorically that all of us are to blame. Koppel says he "doesn't have time for generalities." He instructs the mayor to "point to one, two, three segments of society that are to blame."

Koppel makes it clear that he will not accept criticism of the documentary. A high school principal begins to express concern about Koppel's depiction of young black people "destroying the city." Koppel tells her she's "got it backward," he is talking about youngsters being destroyed, not about youngsters destroying the city.

Koppel also makes clear that the audience members must defer to commercial breaks. Koppel tells a speaker to "make it quick, we have about 45 seconds before the break." As the introductory piece of the town meeting ends, Koppel tells the viewing audience that Jack Kemp, Secretary of Housing and Urban Affairs, and William Bennett, the Drug Czar, will join him at 11:30 when the Koppel Report continues after the news.

When the program resumes, during Koppel's regular *Nightline* slot, Koppel tells the audience that Jack Kemp and William Bennett can only stay for half an hour. He instructs the audience in the church to use that time productively. He then says that before audience members ask questions they "owe the courtesy" of listening first to Kemp and Bennett. Kemp talks about positive action being taken to combat drugs by community leaders and the Bush Administration. A black congressman attempts to interrupt but Koppel tells him to wait until Kemp and Bennett are finished speaking. Bennett speaks about the need to "get the bad guys off the street" by bolstering law enforcement and the penal system. Interestingly, Bennett criticizes Koppel for presenting the black community in a negative light. He says that the majority of black people in Washington are law abiding citizens who work hard for a living. Koppel tells Bennett he "missed the point" of his documentary. Koppel says he "was not representing a profile of the city of Washington," he "was representing a profile of drug violence in the city of Washington."

When Kemp and Bennett are finished speaking, Koppel selects audience members who stand up if they wish to speak. If a person raises his/her voice and begins to speak in a cadence familiarly associated with black religious rhetoric, Koppel interrupts and cuts the person off insisting that they be brief and ask a question of Bennett or Kemp. For example, at various time he says, "Sir, if everyone gets up and gives a speech here, maybe five people will have the change to speak" and "you're not asking a question" and "Forgive me, but I want to take advantage of the time these gentlemen are giving us," and "I think there's a question mark at the end of that." At times he lectures the entire audience, "we are going to have chaos here if we don't establish some kind of order" and "I'm going to give you a chance to raise your questions, if possible, but we still have to take commercial breaks. That's one of the imperatives of television" and "If it's just going to be the people with the loudest lungs, then I've got the mike, OK" and "Folks, don't be naive about it, that's how commercial television works."

Ostensibly, Koppel is being a tough, but fair moderator, controlling a potentially unpredictable and unruly audience and forcing them to abide by the rules of commercial television. But the subtext presumes that the audience will be unruly and that only a certain kind of rhetorical behavior is appropriate. First, all responses must be questions to Kemp or Bennett. This effectively forces speakers to turn over the floor repeatedly to the government officials who correct the speaker's misperceptions and keep attention focused on the correctness of government policy. Second, statements of personal belief, especially those that are emotional, are construed as bad manners or not showing proper respect for authority. Koppel conducts a meeting about a problem which he locates in the black community, invites black community leaders, holds the meeting in a black church, in a black neighborhood, and then insists on white rhetorical rules and ensures that the solutions to the problem be presented by white government officials. He justifies his attempts to enforce white rhetorical rules as a need to maintain order and manage time. The effect of this double bind is clearly unsettling to the black audience. As their frustration rises, Koppel's attempts to control the audience increase, playing out the assumption that the audience will be unruly. Koppel creates the frustration exhibited by the audience because of his own insensitivity to black rhetorical style and to the desire for community leaders to present their own solutions to the problem.

Regional Life Report #1—Atlanta

After a commercial break a live regional report is presented by correspondent Jackie Judd from Atlanta. As the segment begins, Judd, in a voice-over narrative, reports on a series of crimes which have occurred within the last twenty-four hours. On screen a shot of a housing project in Chattanooga appears. In the report (WTVC) footage of a glass storm door with bullet holes is presented as the audience is told that drug violence has occurred here. The action then moves to the small town of Milledgeville, Georgia where dozens of drug dealers are being arrested. Of the "dozens" arrested the three suspects that appear on the screen are black, and as they are placed in police cars Judd informs us that ". . . the rural South is infested." The live report and coverage continues as another drug victim is placed in a San Antonio ambulance and driven off screen to the narrative of ". . . three people killed, their punishment for having earlier shot a rival dealer." The rival dealer also appears to be black. Judd's voice-over report ends with shots from Miami and a report of crack houses being bulldozed by police.

The live coverage continues with Judd in the studio continuing to report on the impact of drugs in the south. Focusing on the Florida area, she explains that "law enforcement in Florida" is at a distinct disadvantage because 4000 prisoners a month are released from overcrowded prisons. According to the commentary, these prisoners return to the streets and a life of crime and drugs. The imagery here is significant. No shots of these prisoners that the state is "forced to release" are shown, however, if all the criminals who have committed crimes thus far have been black, why should the viewer not assume that those being released, or at least the majority of them, are black.

The image of non-white criminals is further enhanced when Judd later explains that Texas is becoming a drug hub rivaling Miami. According to Judd ". . . Colombians are teaming up with Mexicans . . . also Jamaican posses . . . and to a lesser degree L.A. gangs." Accordingly, only minorities, in what appears or is presented as an expanding totality which threatens the white community, are involved in the drug trade. When Judd explores what is happening inside the communities with children, especially the black communities, things appear to be even more critical:

> . . . and inside the poor neighborhoods of this city, one police official tells me that some parents simply aren't being tough enough on their

> kids. They say it's hard to say no to these little giants who can come home earning $300 a day . . . and can help pay some of the bills . . .

Thus, unlike whites, blacks (who live in poor neighborhoods) are not tough on their kids, are overly concerned with money, and live in communities filled with criminals who belong in jail but walk the streets.

When the show returns to the church in Anacostia, Bennett is gone, and Kemp follows shortly thereafter. Koppel calls upon Georgetown basketball coach Thompson to speak. A considerable amount of time is spent with Coach Thompson. He is a soft spoken man, who "does not wish to blame anybody." He encourages people to work together to solve the drug problem. Koppel directs the audience to ask Coach Thompson questions now that Kemp and Bennett are gone. This takes the focus off the fact that Kemp and Bennett stayed for only half an hour. After a commercial break, a second live report comes to the viewer from Chicago.

Live Report #2—Chicago

According to the narrative and the visuals presented by correspondent Judd Rose, the north central area is suffering from the same ills as the rest of the nation. Footage of a Detroit housing project shows a pair of black children standing behind a storm door that has no glass in it, as a black woman explains to a local reporter how afraid she is. In a shot that recalls the images in a previous shot from Atlanta, the glassless door is a reference to what happens in the gun battles which plague the black community. In Indianapolis, eight black drug dealers are being arrested and cut away shots of their cars, drugs, money, and jewelry are shown. The segment ends with Rose telling Koppel and the live audience of a nine year old involved in a juvenile drug ring in Des Moines, Iowa.

Perhaps the most telling element of this report occurs during an exchange between Koppel and Rose:

> Koppel: Judd, I don't even know if you can answer the question, but once again the faces we see in the piece where we see drug dealers being rounded up, they're all black . . . when you talk about organized crime [being involved in the drug trade] as we've come to know it over the years . . . are these white organized criminals?

> Judd: By and large and surprisingly no. In fact there is a large Mexican drug family, with roots in Mexico, now living here that apparently controls most of the drug trading in Chicago and then by extension throughout the mid-west. They are using black street gangs but also white organized crime, as I said, to help in sales and distribution . . . but it's Latin drug dealers in Chicago.

Judd's response to Koppel's question about the constant use of black images is that the images are essentially accurate. According to Judd, whites are only tangentially involved in the drug traffic. Thus the problem of drugs and the violence associated with it, is confined to black and brown-skinned minorities and serves as justifiable motive, again, for segregation or the division of cities in the nation.

When the show returns again to the Church in Anacostia, Koppel allows audience members to speak without addressing a question to someone. At this point the nature of the discussion changes. Audience members begin to insist that racism is the real issue and that drugs are only a symptom. When the issue of genocide is raised, Koppel responds incredulously, "How does what William Bennett proposes come down to a genocide plan?" Eventually a female black psychiatrist explains genocide in terms of white fear of annihilation by being neutralized genetically. She makes the point that this fear is historic and international in scope. She attributes the elimination of the male role in the family that occurred both in South African Apartheid and U.S. slavery as a way of insuring white superiority. She infers that insistence on incarceration for black men as an answer to the drug problem in the black community is a continuation of this strategy. When she is finished speaking the audience rises to its feet and applauds. A white man from the Rainbow Coalition accuses Koppel of showing one hour of blacks killing blacks and one half an hour of Kemp and Bennett talking about their programs. Koppel replies that the man "must have been watching another program." Koppel says the first five minutes of the documentary dealt with black people killing one another, the rest dealt with black people coping and helping one another, and that a third part of the program dealt with racism. At this point, the audience is mobilized. People begin to shout encouragement to speakers they agree with, the religious rhetorical style of call and answer begins to occur spontaneously in the church setting. Koppel cuts to a correspondent report.

Live Report #3—Los Angeles

The third live report follows the same format as the previous ones. A commentary by correspondent Ken Kashiwahara is presented as images of blacks in street gangs and drug-related activity are presented. As the narrative progresses it establishes a link between the gangs, which are black, and the drugs and crime which plague the nation's capital. The lead for this segment begins with this is ". . . a typical scene in South Central Los Angeles. A drug shooting during a drug deal tied to gangs . . . gang violence is on the upswing." While images of blacks fill the screen Kashiwahara explains that:

> Gang violence is increasing every year. For 1989 Law Enforcement Officials estimate three people will be killed every two days. The primary reason—drugs. In Los Angeles County the statistics are staggering. One drug arrest every six minutes, twenty thousand dollars worth of cocaine seized every hour . . . Many of the L.A. gangs have become entrepreneurs. Importing cocaine from South America and exporting it to every major city in the country. They started in the West. Crack houses raided in Las Vegas, Portland, Phoenix, and other cities. Today an L.A. gang has become the major supplier of crack cocaine in Washington, D.C.

As this report ends the viewer is left with the impression that drugs are in the control of minorities exclusively. It is minorities who are responsible for the spread of drugs and the violence which seems to be a natural part of the drug trade.

When the show returns to the church in Anacostia, Koppel reintroduces the videotape made by the three high school students. After the videotape is reshown the audience had thinned out considerably. Koppel asks the student director to speak about his experience making the tape. This defuses the exploration of racism that had begun in the preceding segment. It appears that discussions of racism which go beyond the bounds of what a white audience is used to and begins to introduce ideas such as those espoused by the Nation of Islam are deemed too extreme for a program such as *The Kopple Report*.

After one or two more comments by audience members, a woman is called on who identifies herself as a former drug addict and ex-convict. She says her oldest son had been recently killed in a drug-related incident. She declares that the problem is on "the inside not the outside." She describes her attempt to become a productive member of society and a good mother to her remaining son. She says she doesn't need welfare, she just needs to believe in herself. She speaks emotionally for a long time, blaming herself and vowing to improve. There are several cut-away shots to women in the audience wiping tears from their cheeks. When she finishes, Koppel says, "Folks, do me a favor and sit down. There is one thing I've learned in 26 years in the business. Every once in a while somebody says it like it is. There is not much point in saying anymore. This lady has wrapped it up."

The effect of Koppel's assessment of the last speaker's remarks wipes away the accusations of the people who talked about genocide. It wipes away government responsibility for maintaining economic and social inequities. It wipes away white responsibility for institutionalized racism. The victim assumes the blame for the drug problem. The problem is seen as one of the victim's own making and she is attempting to correct the problem through atonement and rebirth as a moral individual. This may have been a convenient exit for a television interview but it was an unfortunate closing message for the viewing audience. In the case of *D.C./Divided City*, viewers are ostensibly presented with an argument to end racism, but simultaneously presented with the visual imagery which justifies racial separation.

This analysis attempted to employ a politics of multicultural resistance to unravel a discourse of oppression disguised as journalistic objectivity. It is hoped that such analyses can begin to free racial identity from the confines of historical discursive practice. Teachers and other cultural workers are encouraged to cross borders and lay bare the damaging presuppositions imbedded in media representations of everyday life and in so doing create spaces where a new intercultural dialogue can take place and new multicultural meanings can be forged.

REFERENCES

Duster, Troy. (1970). *The Legislation of Morality: Laws, Drugs, and Moral Judgment*. New York: Free Press.

Musto, David F. (1987). *The American Disease: Origins of Narcotic Control.* New York: Oxford University Press.

Hall, Stuart. (1978). .*Policing the Crisis: Mugging, the State, and Law and Order.* London:Macmillian.

In previous ABC programs, the widespread use of drugs was portrayed in news specials titled *Drugs, A Plague Upon the Land* (April 1988) and *Drugs, Why This Plague?* (July 1988).

African American stereotypes are described in *Ethnic Notions: Black People in White Minds,* a video documentary produced and directed by Marlon Riggs and distributed by California Newsreel, San Francisco, CA.

In this program, statistics are presented by a former director of the National Institute on Drug Abuse to suggested that blacks account for less than 20% of all addicts in the USA.

Statistical information in this paper is from the *1980 U.S. Government Census;* the *1987 National Drug and Alcoholism Treatment Survey;* and the *1988 National Institute on Drug Abuse National Household Survey on Drug Abuse.*

Chapter V

Buy Our News: The Melding of News, Entertainment and Advertising in the Totalized Selling Environment of the Postmodern Market

David Sholle

It can be argued that television is the most powerful tool for the reproduction and maintenance of the normative values of dominant culture ever known, ever imagined. In the historical context of postmodern late capitalism these culture industries exhibit the added ability to subsume, diffuse and incorporate into themselves those isolated expressions of difference which represent potential sites of cultural resistance. We need to examine the ways that the mass media contribute to the continued erosion of the kind of democratic public sphere necessary for the very possibility of an emancipatory democracy and we need to understand the relations of contemporary media to everyday life; its ubiquitous presence as the source for the iconography of our own and our student's lives.

Foregrounded, here, is the nature of media as themselves *pedagogical machines*, which function in the defining of what counts as legitimate knowledge. But most theories of schooling have ignored the manner in which cultural institutions contain pedagogical practices that are as significant for learning as institutionalized education. As Phillip Corrigan (1989, 79) notes, "we need to widen our understanding of how we are taught, and how we learn, and how we know" and this involves analyzing the pedagogy of popular culture forms.

Certainly, the dominant educational medium of contemporary culture is television and the functioning of the pedagogical in this medium has a bearing on how education in general functions in our society. Lawrence Grossberg (1989, 94) demarcates the effective pedagogical terrain of popular culture, seeing it as operating at three levels: 1) the production of common sense—"the multi-layered, fragmented collection of meanings, values, and ideas that we both inherit and construct and which largely define our taken-for-granted interpretations of the world. 2) the determination of our libidinal and affective lives. 3) the production of a site where our identities and experiences are constructed.

In the light of these concerns, television can and should be looked at as a pedagogical machine, constructing identities and defining agency within a general "pedagogy of consumerism." The existence of television as an instrument for blurring differentiated social discourses to the unifying sign of the commodity can be taken as the final victory of capitalism to coopt all oppositional discourses. However, a critical pedagogy maintains that by a continual process of critical media analysis, spaces for struggle with this terrain can remain open. Given this pedagogical project, this chapter attempts to conduct a thorough critique of the manner in which television has become the preeminent "pedagogy of consumerism." This dimension of the media will be examined through looking at the quintessential form of commodity program—the tabloid.

INTRODUCTION

The current explosion of "reality-based" programs in television is a phenomenon with wide cultural implications. These shows are significant not simply because of their so-called denigration of news values, but rather in and through the way their bombardment signals the ultimate commodification of the television form. The purpose of this essay is to examine the tabloid as the limit form of the aestheticization of the cultural commodity. Tabloid television will be targeted as an instance of the postmodern market that pushes toward a totalization of commodity exchange and thus, as an instance of the generalized form of advertising which sets in motion the determinant factors that pre-figure the stance of the audience toward contemporary cultural products.

The "reality-based" series includes a number of typifications: crime reenactment, rescue and emergency reenactment, "actual" police action, home videos, entertainment news and magazine "reports." I will focus on the "genre" of tabloid magazine programs, particularly *A Current Affair, Hard Copy* and *Inside Addition*. These programs are *tabloid* in the sense that they focus, generally, on stories of moral disorder and deviance—sex, power, deviant families, corruption, greed, and victimization; and they personalize these actions through a subjective treatment, rather than the supposed objective, neutral stance of "high" journalism (Knight 1989, 94). This particular type of "reality-based" program contains elements of all the others: reenactments of crimes and other events, personalized reporting, entertainment and celebrity stories, family violence and foibles, home video segments, and police actualities.

The tabloid in its television form exists as an odd amalgamation of news reports, entertainment and advertising. It draws upon a general social sense of the ubiquity and randomness of victimization and the need for official surveillance and protection from this deviance. There is a pervasive sense of "loss of control over the outcome of events," and a corresponding call for moral normalization and official protection and control. Yet, at the same time, these programs focus on the collapse of the family in a way which points to the insufficiency of normality; and they reveal authority as hypocritical and corrupt. This contradiction is part and parcel of the tabloid form: they call forth a type of popular response and interaction, at the same time that they propose institutionalized normalization as the solution.

In a sense, these features are simply those of television in general, including all forms of journalism. The notion that tabloid TV is a vulgarization of "straight" television news does not hold water. Television news has consistently evolved in a direction that dovetails with the tabloid form. Local television news, for example, developed into its present form as a marketing effort—selling the station "image" (Knight 1989, 96) The happy talk and action news elements of local journalism have developed further and further toward a personalization of the news and a sense that the news-gatherer is involved and "at the scene." In this sense, local news uses "reality-based" imagery, i.e., it does not simply record actual events. More and more, news reports and tabloid reenactments look like each other. The style of recreating actuality has a long history in television; particularly, the current use of shaky camera and messy mise-en-scene is traceable to Hill Street Blues. This same gritty style is heavily employed in national advertising for fashion projects; another strong influence on the tabloid style.

National television news has not remained pristine in the face of this stylization of news. Its focus on the personality of the news anchor, increasing use of stylized graphics and digital effects, continual search for "images" to fit with stories, and use of reenactments (usually in cartoon or computer generated form, as in the gulf war), all point to the continuum that exists between supposed Journalism (capital J) and tabloid TV.

Nevertheless, tabloid TV pushes these elements of style and content to the extreme, where reality and simulation blend with report and spectacle. Tabloid TV, then, is a very telling site for examining the limit-point of television reality—its breaking down of the attachment to reality. Further, the tabloid form, in its movement toward an integration of all television forms into one, pushes toward the total commodification of the television environment—news and entertainment are drawn into the function of advertisement.

There are a number of characteristics of the tabloid form that rightly or wrongly have been connected to the condition of postmodernity. All of these textual and contextual characteristics center on: the blurring of the difference between image and reality, the fragmentation of meaning and the proliferation of the polysemic that follows from it, and the excess of the spectacular that neutralizes its own "specularity" into mere simulation. Taken as simply aesthetic elements of a depoliticized postmodern practice these "effects" appear only as markers of an impenetrable, incoherent chaos. Only through rearticulating these characteristics of the tabloid form through the critical tool of a commodity aesthetics does it become possible to inquire into the underlying structure responsible for the way things seem.

THEORETICAL MAP

Commodity Aesthetics

In order to describe the functioning of tabloid television we need to employ a number of theoretical components that will keep us from falling into the traps of comparing tabloid TV to "real" news, of treating it as simply a self-existent genre, and of assuming a "resistance" of the audience position based in the identification of politics with populism. By populist cultural studies I refer to the contemporary trend in cultural studies, as a whole, to turn from a critique of cultural power, discursive exclusion and economic exploitation to a celebration of the struggles of audiences with popular texts. This "audience as resistant" approach is exemplified in the work of John Fiske (1989), Ian Ang (1985), Janice Radway (1984), Mary Ellen Brown (1990), etc. For a more thorough criticism of this approach see Sholle (1990) and Morris (1988).

It is also our intention to avoid the critique of tabloids as presented by traditional journalism criticism and the media journalist's own self-serving views of the tabloid. Here, the view is that tabloid journalism is inferior because it is not objective, plays to sensationalism, uses fictional elements, and treats soft news items. In other words, tabloid journalism does not uphold the sacred canon of high journalism. This view is not only problematic in its assumptions about what 'reality' is, it also misses the main point—tabloids are commodities (as is the news). Often critiques of this kind are presented simply to defend standard news practices and to backhandly stab at the tabloids, which are stealing away ratings points. The issue of whether tabloids are a lesser form of news is not the concern, here. Instead, tabloids will be looked as a textuality that establishes a particular relationship to the viewer—that of commodity.

Our first step, is to return to critical theory and particularly to Adorno's project of dialectical critique.[1] This project is extended and altered in bringing in the work of W. F. Haug (1987) on commodity aesthetics. The problematic addressed in this theoretical step is inclusive of a number of key elements: 1) the commodity form of tabloid television and its subsumption under the general form of marketable items, 2) the practice of the televisual representation of reality as subsumed under the form of advertising, generally, 3) the audience, as fragmented and isolated, as already incorporated into the market's decisions, thus, containing and conditioning the supposed semiotic democracy of popular forms, 4) a generalized commodity aesthetics that mobilizes and assimilates the responsive satisfactions of the audience.

For Adorno and Horkheimer, any account of cultural forms must include an examination of their processes of production, reproduction, distribution, exchange and consumption. Such an account must describe in detail the internal structure of cultural forms, the manner in which the socio-economic whole and the mechanisms of reception are crystallized in them. For them, the commodities of the cultural industry can be interpreted as "a code language for processes taking place in society." The immediate objection to this "immanent critique" is that audiences do not passively imbibe cultural forms and thus, one must examine audience response if one wishes to know how the particular object is taken up and influences individuals. In other words, what is encoded in the object is not necessarily what is decoded. But this objection is based in a number of questionable assumptions. First of all, by assuming a dichotomy of passive/ active, audience studies divide the subjectivity of the "meaning maker" into rigid areas, leading to the conclusion

[1] I am well aware that returning to Adorno flies in the face of the ubiquitous knee-jerk repudiations currently fashionable in populist cultural studies. The choice is a deliberate one aimed at the current reduction of cultural studies to deliberations on "resistant" qualities of this or that audience (market) segment. Adorno has been used as a scapegoat (the evil mandarin elitist) for populist cultural studies turn away from the mechanisms of commodification and ideology. The constant pronouncements of Critical Theory's death are premature and based in superficial interpretations of a few texts of the vast body of Frankfurt school work.

that activity and self-reflection are transparent categories. Adorno, on the other hand, does not regard strict belief or naivete as a condition for the culture industry to succeed: "The triumph of advertising in the culture industry is that consumers feel compelled to buy and use its products even though they see through them" (Horkheimer & Adorno 1972, 167). This points to the second assumption—that one can read the effect of cultural forms by examining the conscious spoken reactions of audiences, as if the statements of fans and readers were straightforward accounts of meaning. Of course, in practice, the populist cultural studies, audience ethnographers do not undertake such a project. Instead, the audience's self-reports must be "interpreted." The ethnographer, then, reads the text of "interpretations," pulling out contradictions and multiple-meanings. But where does this lead? It brings in a third assumption, that the mere existence of contradictions and multiple-meanings shows that the "popular" is a sphere of resistance. That is, that the cultural product itself must fulfill gratifications and needs that "actually" exist in the popular and thus must structure itself as open to these popular contestations. The notion is, then, that cultural products exist as a semiotic democracy. In such a move, ideological critique takes a back seat to describing and interpreting the positive instances of audience resistance and self-creation.

For dialectical criticism, cultural forms do not simply transmit ideology by erasing contradictions—the process "is not one which resolves objective contradictions in a spurious harmony, but one which expresses the idea of harmony negatively by embodying the contradictions, pure and uncompromised, in its inner-most structure. Confronted with this kind of work, the verdict 'mere ideology' loses its meaning" (Adorno 1982, 32). Thus, Adorno's dialectic method attempts to overcome the temptation of treating the mind and its products as self-sufficient. What populist cultural studies misses is that audiences are relating to a commodity that must be examined as a source and effect of supra-individual relations. The commodity form leads us to focus on that which is relatively determinate, not on populist responses, as if these "active" responses could be unhinged from any determination. This is why we look at the commodity itself and the exchange process in which its cultural effects are unlocked. What audiences actually do is indeterminable; it can only be inferred from data, interpretations, etc. There is only a relative degree of further stepping back from the subject, when we look at the text.

In summation, as J.M. Berstein states,

> There is a naive, Lukasian optimism involved in the belief that mass media in reflecting, expressing and articulating social reality will, in so doing, deflate their own products, and, despite themselves, become vehicles for social critique and ideological subversion (1991, 20).

Thus, Adorno's theory calls attention to the difference between pseudo-individuality and individuality, pleasure and happiness, consensus and freedom, pseudo-activity and activity, illusory otherness and non-identical otherness. Far from a view of the media as homogeneous in its particularity, Adorno shows how that particularity participates in a larger totality that is, indeed, homogeneous through the subsumption of all activities in commodity exchange.

The work of W. F. Haug in commodity aesthetics furthers the dialectical analysis of Adorno by turning explicitly to contemporary advertising forms and by developing a theory of the psychology of commodity exchange. The populist cultural studies "audience as resistant" approach is sorely lacking in developing a theory of psychological relations with cultural industry products. It, in fact, seems to have no psychology at all, rejecting Lacanian psychoanalytic theory as well as cognitive science. In practice, the basis of these audience studies seems to be in a rather naive appropriation of the social psychology of the forties and fifties: audiences have needs which they seek to gratify, popular pleasure arises from the everyday life of viewers and is positive in and of itself, viewers construct their own meanings through a kind of self-reflective rationality, viewer "meanings" can be read from their self-reports, which are immanently interpretable and direct, etc.

What is needed is a critical psychology that attends to the manner in which the larger social environment of capitalist commodity relations structures the possibilities of engagement with media objects. Thus, agency is not a matter of straightforward appropriation, as if the agent stands outside of the general social environment and simply acts. Populist cultural studies has thrown out the baby with the bath water by positing a polysemic ocean that seems to simply open up for the viewer. Why assume this, and not that a polysemic flood washes over the viewer, covering over their little streams of resistance in a fragmenting tide?

Commodity aesthetics, instead, starts from the general relations that prefigure the potential for response: the manner in which the commodity form contains and controls the contradictions that define its relations. A commodity calls forth a response, not based in its value (particularly, not its value for building up resistance) but based upon its exchangeability. In its exchange, the commodity as substance retreats, its value is measured in an abstraction. Why does it fulfill satisfactions and needs and where is its value measured? This question is erased in the commodity's abstraction. Its value is located neither in the labor that produced it, nor in its intrinsic qualities, but rather in the comparison to all other values and ultimately to the money equivalent. Ultimately, the commodity hides or is subsumed under the general value, thus to be "bought" the commodity form must stand out. In this process, the use-value (what populist cultural studies identifies as creating the site of resistance) is supplemented and eventually replaced by the "appearance of use-value" (Haug, 1987).

As in all mass production of commodities, the cultural commodity's quality (its representational form, production values, aesthetic components, etc) is degraded. In material commodities this includes the use of lower quality materials and automation in production which leads to gaps in detail work. The object then requires a semblance to re-aestheticize it, leading to the use of subtle surface treatments that cover over the defective materials. Ultimately, the aesthetic attractiveness of the product consists solely in its packaging. The sheen of the package becomes the embodiment of the "appearance of use-value," replacing the first-order use value and aesthetic form of the object. The same de-substantiation of the object occurs in the production and circulation of cultural commodities. The packaging of the product overwhelms the communicative or aesthetic purposes and serves as the primary environment in which the product is appropriated. Thus, the function of advertising in re-aestheticizing products becomes attached to all cultural commodities, as the projection of "the image of what they are" takes over their reception (Haug 1987, 109).

The advertising of the commodity fulfills the purpose of placing the product in a position for exchange and this requires that everything that has been emptied out of it be returned to it, albeit in the form of an appearance. Thus, the purpose of advertising is: 1) to make the cultural commodity stand out, to attach an image to it that is abstractly attracting. As Marx says, "commodities cast amorous glances at potential buyers," 2) to attach and detach various values to the commodity based not on its inherent qualities or even its potential for generating reflection, but solely through the calculation of contradiction, 3) to re-subjectify the commodity, making personal that which is isn't, 4) to authenticate the object, creating the appearance that the calculation of value attachments is inherent in the object and in its potential to activate response, 5) to re-embody the cultural commodity, creating it as a visceral object, and thus retrieving the substance lost. This is accomplished not in the commodity itself, but in a general bodily impact on the consumer, i.e., through the stimulation of the buyer (Haug, 1987).

Under commodity exchange relations the audience is positioned toward needs in such a way that appropriation is prefigured. It is not that the culture industry creates needs from nowhere, it is that needs cannot be seen outside of the re-substantiation taking place in the general form of political economy. As a result, the audience's desires, interests, and pleasures are played out in the general deformation of subjectivity that Adorno describes as the loss of the individual.

Postmodernism

The theoretical map of postmodernism, rather than rejecting the account of domination forwarded by the Frankfort School, can be seen as furthering its description of the general social environment. As J. M. Bernstein points out, much of Adorno's work prefigures contemporary postmodern thought. A critical postmodernism can be built upon the insights of critical theory, adding a sharpened description of how the "meanings" of cultural commodities are unhinged from any reference to the substance of the commodity. As Bernstein notes,

> Just as art works become commodities and are enjoyed as such, the commodity itself in consumer society has become image, representation, spectacle. Use value has been replaced by a packaging and advertising (1991, 20).

Once the sign, the unit of social meaning, becomes commodified in its mode of production and exchange, so it succumbs increasingly to the effects of the law of value. Over-production and saturation become the norm, with the result that the value (meaning) recedes as its material form (signifier) proliferates. Thus, in the postmodern condition, the culture industry increases its recycling of itself as the ironic articulation of the already said. Representation and "the real" are no longer separable (if they ever were) and simulation governs the appropriation of the cultural form. Postmodernism's hyperreality is nothing other than the false reconciliation of particular and universal that Adorno railed against. The proliferation of images and signs to their saturation point, the breathlessness of style "tokens the disappearance of the distinction between distracting pleasure and emphatic happiness, underlining Adorno's view that the culture industry is pornographic and prudish at once" (Bernstein 1991, 21).

CHARACTERISTICS OF THE TABLOID FORM

The Appearance of "Reality"/ The Reality of "Appearance" [2]

We now turn to an examination of the textual and contextual characteristics of the tabloid form, first to those elements that

---

[2] The following analysis draws upon Graham Knight's treatment of the tabloid as explicitly postmodern in its creation of reality effects, drawing out obvious connections with the work of Baudrillard, Barthes, Debord, etc. Knight does attempt to square his postmodern description with commodity relations, but not as a primary focus. The present essay assumes the inherent problems in measuring 'simulation' against 'reality' and focuses instead on the construction of the cultural object as commodity. Thus, the problematic of the postmodern is not seen as an essentially new condition that escaped the analysis of the Critical Theorists.

particularly tie in to the condition of postmodernity. These elements are treated not simply as postmodern aesthetic components, but are rearticulated through the viewpoint of a commodity aesthetics.

Textual Fragmentation. Television relies on taking seriously the distinction between fiction and non-fiction and its genres have evolved on this basis. Yet, in its practice it continually mixes up fiction and non-fiction (Knight 1989, 104). Television, at times, purposively carries out this mixing, but at the same time it is careful to make sure that we are told which is which (at least, we are told which form the producers want us to consume the product as). However, progressively this telling of "the form of facticity" is breaking down, as the conventions of one form spill over into the other. Thus, *Hill Street Blues* appears as gritty reality and *Cops* as detective drama.

In the tabloid form this fragmentation of genres reaches the breaking point. Fiction and non-fiction occur not as separate treatments of meaningful content, but as packaging devices within a continuum of effects, i.e., the sign-posts of each are attached indiscriminately to varying contents. The effect on the meaning of the content of any particular moment of the presentation is not to produce appropriately fictive or non-fictive stances in the audience, but rather to package the particular moment with the technique most capable of crystallizing that moment as something of value. Thus, the tabloid borrows heavily from a variety of genres that cross fictional and non-fictional lines: horror/mystery films, television detective drama, television investigative documentary, psycho-sexual fashion commercials, music television, soap opera, the standard ENG package, etc.

The horror/mystery genre is most evident in victimization stories, particularly those involving "shocking" crimes. In reenactments of these crimes, we are given access to a "reality" through our memory of affective reactions to cinema fictions. The choice of music, camera angle, intercutting, use of lingering shots, etc. all owe something to Hitchcockian psycho-detection and "Halloweenesque" psycho-termination. A favorite detail is the lingering shot of the actual point of horror, cut up into fragmented viewpoints which reveal no actual visceral horrific content, but nevertheless signal a bloody reckoning. This voyeurism is hightened by the general framing of the story as "real." It tokens an access to the reality of the "actual" impact of deviant horrific acts. The fictive elements become attached to the non-fictional, as if the events of actual violence were staged for us. It is as if the techniques of cinematic portrayal were implemented through a complex of surveillance devices actually present at the non-fiction event. For example, in the *Current Affair* story "Feud and Lodging," we are treated to a recreation of the act of murder, signaled by a shift to grainy, black and white footage. A car is shown in slow motion drifting through the empty streets of a rural town. The previous voice over set the viewer up to see this footage as a murder scene. The scene is edited together in the style of Hitchcock, with varying views of the car as it moves to an abandoned field. The shots build up (the music swelling), the voice over builds to a climax. The scene then cuts to a long shot of the car sitting in the field and the camera slowly moves in (in fact moving slower and slower) as it approaches the car. The camera wobbles slightly and moves to a view of the seat of the car where we see the victim slumped over, laying in what could be dirt or blood. The view is actually obscured somewhat by the car window and since the scene is in black and white the "dirt-blood" is barely visible. Yet, at this point, the entire treatment has led the viewer to expect something awful, something in fact unspeakable. In fact, it is just that. We see and hear nothing much at all. Yet, through the images and techniques of the horror genre, the viewer is drawn into the scene and by connecting it to the past memory of films is likely to see it as horrifying (but in a safe way).

This blurring of the fictional and the non-fictional is not significant because it "causes" viewers to confuse the dramatization with reality. The typical viewer of tabloid is, at least upon reflection, able to distinguish quite well between fiction and non-fiction. We do not need to assume any straight-forward duping of the audience in this instance to make the claim that the blurring of fiction and non-fiction still have effects. The effect is still present even though a moment of disbelief and self-reflection occurs. It is within the visceral reaction of the moment of horror that the "reality effect" takes hold, and even if a moment later the distinction between the real and representational returns, the blurring of facticity has already worked its wonders—it has attached itself to the viewer's response through affective memory, thus drawing him/her into the product. It matters not whether the viewer believes the whole (since there is no whole anyway), rather it matters only that each moment promote itself through the fullest exploitation of particular techniques.

The fragmentation of genres is further evidenced in the manner in which television detective and investigative documentary forms are melded together in the tabloid form. In the tabloid it is not the specific contents of these genres which are important, but rather the process of detection itself, a process that again relies upon representing the access to the actual through a voyeuristic stance. Detection-itself, as a pleasure, becomes the locus of attachment to the story. The tabloid investigation, itself an actuality, unfolds through a telling of the process that draws upon the affective enjoyment of the fictional detective drama. The shock of an actually occurring crime is appropriated through the pleasure of fictional criminality which releases the viewer from any reflection upon the structural determinants that give rise to acts defined as criminal.

Many of the tabloid's segments also borrow from the soap opera form, weaving together complex plots of deception and deviance rooted in the interrelationships of recognizable "soap opera" type characters. Not only are these stories told in the "withhold/reveal" form of the soap, they employ many of its stylistic camera and editing techniques. Often stories involving celebrities are told in this fashion. Although most tabloid programs typically present three separate stories in a half hour, when the story involves celebrities and is "big enough," they will use up the entire program length. In these cases, the soap opera (melded with the mystery drama and documentary genres) dominates. The half hour is segmented between commercials with soaplike cliffhangers, promising to reveal new developments in the next segment (the Amy Fisher spectacle is a good example). Further, dramatizations show conversations focused on emotional states and relationships, instead of the usual criminal reenactment. An *Inside Addition* story about a wealthy playboy who ends up murdered, in fact, calls itself a "real life soap"and is set in Santa Barbara. The story shows no action at all, and instead dwells on home videos and reinactments showing the private entaglements of the characters—cocktails are sipped, vacations embarked on, and funerals attended. The interviewees and the narrator continually make reference to the soaplike quality of the story. In other stories the reinactments are modeled after soap opera shots, showing lots of teary faces; well-dressed, jewel bedecked woman; and romantic interludes. Again, these techniques do not serve some grand ideological purpose (or a direct manipulation of the audience's perception of reality), rather they package the material in a familiar form that peaks the audience's sense of "making meaning," i.e., the openness of the text is a sort of moveable feast. The text's polysemy is part and parcel of its commodity nature, an open "appearance of use-value" that keeps the audience "buying" the product.

The use of music video forms is also a predominant aspect of the tabloid form. The aesthetic of music video—associative montage, fast-paced editing, rhythmic connection, high-contrast lighting, use of special effects in conjunction with the jump cut, etc.—are heavily employed in intro and outro segments, as well as in promotional segments for future segments. As a genre, music video is perhaps the most purely stylistically defined form in television, making it the preeminent packaged segment. In this, the music video dovetails with the commercial ad and the cross-fertilization between ads and music video has resulted in the ultimate televisual spectacle. The tabloid's use of the music video form is an obvious choice for a genre that displaces meaning in favor of the sheen of packaging.

Dovetailing with this use of music video is the tabloid's borrowing from the psycho-sexual fashion commercial. Many of the reenactment sequences in the Tabloid rely upon the compositional and lighting techniques of these lifestyle ads. It is no coincidence that Linder's (the producer of *America's Most Wanted)* favorite director for his program also does Guess Jean's ads (Robins, 1988). These grainy, fragmented verite ad segments frequently recur in slightly altered forms as ads for the ending story of the program. Within the story the same ad segment reappears in an extended form. The overall schema is one in which we see the progressive development of an ad campaign within the show. At the finale, we discover that the ads are for the ad itself, for the story contains nothing more significant or spectacular than the same sequence of psycho-sexual display that announces its arrival. A recent example is the story on *Inside Edition* which announces in promo segments that they have a picture of Madonna that she doesn't want seen. The promos are slickly edited fragments of Madonna in various erotic poses. When the "revelation" comes, the photo in question is no more or less unflattering or "deviant" than any photo in the promo sequence. In the end, the audience most likely knows this will be the case, but "they rush in anyway lest they miss something. Exactly what is not clear, but in any case the only ones with a chance are the participants" (Horkheimer & Adorno 1972, 161).

Postmodern Spectacle. The tabloid, looked at from the perspective of its image-structure, is nearly the perfect example of the postmodern spectacle. As spectacle, the tabloid-product becomes unhinged from textuality, i.e., it no longer fits the model of representational form and content, it is pure image. In this shift out of the representational, everything becomes meaningful and thus textually meaningless. Fascination and voyeurism replace interpretation or rather structure interpretation as an act that bears no relation to a world outside the spectacle.

The tabloid scavenges the video garbage can for any and all images—home video, handheld camera shots, police video, answering machines, pornography videos, etc. Thus, the spectator takes up the stance of voyeur—not so much in the Lacanian psychoanalytic sense, but rather as a surveillant of the immediate. The pleasure of this voyeurism is located in the sheer sense of "being there," of having a look at whatever is produced as image by others in their private occupations. The perceptual effect is one of fusing image and reality—an effect of unfashioned, immediate presence; of the direct and the "live." In this saturation of images and signs, the tabloid displaces the viewer from a function of interpreting the narrative. Instead, the elements of narration are fused together. Personality, place, function, status, event, practice, issue are all elements on "this side of the camera," not pieces of a narrative structure (Knight 1989, 101). It is only the camera eye-itself that has these attributes. What matters is the personality behind the camera, the voice behind the answering machine, the place where the camera sits, the event that brought the camera operator to the scene, etc. Thus, it is not only the viewer of the tabloid that is a voyeur, those who assemble its images are already voyeurs.

This is not to say that the viewer has no entry into a narrative or that no discursive content is assessed and/or contested by the viewer. However, the entry into this interpretive stance is preformed by the presentation of "image as image." In the tabloid form "only the exaggerations are credible" (Knight 1989, 107), because they are ingrained in the voyeuristic construction of image. The content (or issues) are always in question, because they are detached from the immediate spectacle. The deadly serious attention to deviance, crime, horror, etc. is a pseudo-stance. These excesses are normalized by the tabloid, made banal, reassuring and familiar. The tabloid wavers back and forth between the stances of comic dismissal and high moral judgement, unable to settle on any stance. This non-stance is the only one available to the voyeur of voyeurism—the pleasure of looking, the horror of seeing too much.

The voyeuristic spectacle is the vehicle for the "actual stories" of the tabloid, but another type of spectacle also surfaces in the form. This is the spectacle of pure advertising gimmick that ties together the show as a whole. Here, the signal of "amusement" is stamped clearly on the whole. In *Current Affair* we have the whirling logo and the audio "kachung" that literally becomes the "stamp" of the show. In *Hard Copy* we have the whirling typeball, stamping out words that we can't see. In *Inside Edition* we have the whirling dervish of the reporters, ritually dancing in preparation for the spectacle to follow. In this postmodern spectacle, the tabloid does not turn news into entertainment, it neutralizes meaning in favor of the meaningless. In this, the tabloid is again seen to be more akin to advertising and publicity.

The Reality Effect. The spectacle is at the same time the simulation, for in the advertising aesthetic the "realness" of the object must always return in some form. The news depends on the separation of representation from reality. There must always be an "out there" that remains real in that it has actual effects on everyday life. In the postmodern, this separation breaks down—representation does not stand in for the object in reality, it overwhelms that reality. Competing codes for representing the real lead to the society of the simulation in which representation relies on a heightened realism of formal and circumstantial detail—reality effects. The thing itself is replaced with the evidence of it (Knight 1989, 97).

The *reality effect* depends on a pseudo-interaction. In the tabloid, the supposed truth-content of news judgement shifts from relying on accuracy to credibility, from what is true to what can be believed to be true. Since the "objective" eye of the camera can rarely actually be there when something happens (and even so is only ever one viewpoint of what is there), television has to substitute various *"reality effects"* for the reality. In the tabloid these *reality effects* are predominantly substituted actions. Thus, the anchor sits in the "control" room amid a panoply of technical devices that signal that they have special access to the environment; the reporters appear at the site, intoning an account that simulates "the eyewitness"; official documents, "expert" witnesses, graphic times and dates "retrieve" that which has already past; etc. Most importantly, the reenactment is pure simulation of the real event. Its authority consists in its techniques, its sheer presentation of the image. The bulk of tabloid stories consist of just such *substituted* actions. For example, a *Current Affair* segment on Jerry VanDyke's daughter, constructs a morality play of her fall from "star" offspring to pseudo-prostitute by linking a series of "star" eyewitness accounts and narration with a continually returning 10 second segment of home stag video. All the different voices become subordinated to the *reality effect* of the video (in which the daughter reveals her breasts, although not to us), i.e., the grain and shakiness of the video authorizes all the other elements—it must be true. In classic realism the problem is to authenticate veracity. This is done by suppressing the voice of the author, but this whole technique breaks down in the hyperrealism of the tabloid, where the representation no longer can stand separate from the reality. Thus, subjective voice and the technique of the video apparatus are foregrounded as themselves signs that what we are seeing is real—more real than real.

Language, Popularity and Power

The Floating of meaning: Uniquely the Same. As we have seen, the tabloid ironically articulates what is already said. Like TV in general it continually recycles itself. Yet it must create "the appearance of use value," the appearance that what is said is unique, that it is "breaking" news. As Gitlin and others have pointed out, TV is a recombinant culture. It must continually refurbish itself as attractive by constructing commodities that are *uniquely the same.* Knight (1989, 96), echoing Horkheimer and Adorno, maintains that as a cultural commodity in the market, the tabloid's relative or unit value depends on scarcity (difference), yet it must be produced under conditions which are standardized and routine (similarity). If, as Horkheimer and Adorno say, the culture industry puts the same stamp on everything, it must at the same time make sure that each stamping appears to be new and thus, immanently consumable: "The standards are the striking and the familiar, the easy yet catchy, the skillful yet simple; the object is to overpower the consumer" (1972, 163).

This effect is accomplished in the floating of meaning, of making words into signs devoid of quality. Language relapses into magic and incantation. Horkheimer and Adorno attend to how language in the cultural commodity functions to unhinge meaning:

> The result is that the word, which can now be only a sign without any meaning, becomes so fixed to the thing that it is just a petrified formula. This affects work and object alike. Instead of making the object experiential, the purified word treats it as an abstract instance, and everything else . . . fades away in reality. (. . .) Terms themselves become impenetrable; they obtain a striking force, a power of adhesion and repulsion which makes them like their extreme opposite, incantations (1972, 164).

The tabloid is full of such incantations: "lets take an inside look," "behind closed doors," "the naked truth," "the real story." All of these promotions stake a claim for the authenticity of the story to follow. The emptiness of these phrases is immediately evident when the actual content of the story is shown do be based on nothing but gossip and speculation. These words are nothing but incantations for authenticating the story as news. The incantations of the tabloid condense reality to bare *essentials*: the here, the now, the local, the immediate.

Populism. There is another twist to the tabloid's use of language which is involved in its claim to *populism*. The camp sensibility of tabloid is often sighted as part and parcel of its creation of a semiotic democracy, i.e., its popularity is rooted in its connection to the everyday lives of its viewers, especially in what is denigrated by elites as the "vulgar." Populist cultural studies reads this as the site of popular pleasure—a knowing, ironic campiness, which fosters possibilities for resistance. The audience plays along with the irony, never taking "too seriously" the overt ideology of the tabloid. Instead, the tabloid's reflection on its own camp opens a realm of interpretation for the viewer that allows for audiences to make their own meanings out of the text.

As we have seen, the tabloid relies on the history of television in general (its genres, past shows, stars, etc.) and thus any entrance into its workings requires a knowledge of the media. Tabloid is marketed to the TV generation—those "knowing" viewers who easily catch references to *Gilligan* or *Star Trek*. On the surface, the tabloid seems aware of its own construction of the real, i.e., it parodies itself as it pastiches. As Maury Povich states, "Some shows go the the edge, we take it one step further: we are the abyss." Povich evidences an ironic knowingness of his show's campiness. He goes on to say that "*Current Affair* is a steam valve for the explosive pressure building around us" (Povich, 1991). What comes through is that he believes in what he is doing, even though he doesn't. This is particularly clear in Povich's emotive range in response to *Current Affair's* stories—from mugging mockery to synthetic empathy. This contradictory emotional tone is clearly evident in its use of the pun as framing device. Stories are tagged with plays on language that are serious and parodic at once. For example: "Vice, Camera, Action," "Mean Streets to Clean Streets," "Candid Scamera," "Granny Larceny."

Populist cultural studies reads all of this as a struggle over meaning that opens up oppositional activity in the viewers. However, this "reading as resistance" approach sidesteps the greater issue: that this meaning generation occurs in a general economy of consumption. The knowledge drawn upon in camp is already commodity related. It is knowledge of cultural commodities that have become exchangeable items in the ahistorical pastiche of the postmodern. Further, the *populism* that supposedly comes forth in the tabloid/audience relationship is a passive one in terms of consequent political and/or economic action: the viewers consensus is not in what they do, but in what and how they feel (Knight 1989, 107).

Power and Deviance: Normalization and surveillance. If there is a *populism* engendered by the tabloid form it is one that cements the consensus between popular and dominant conceptions of power. The tabloid presents a world of threat and menace at the same time that it promises security and the reassurance that dangers are not endemic to the American social structure. Crime and deviance are subjectified. The causes of social disarray are located in the "bad seed syndrome" and in just plain "bad luck." Gender, race, age, economic conditions are erased.

In line with Foucault's (1980) notion of power, the tabloid, as a locus of power relationships, divides and excludes in order to produce relations of dependency, and normalization. Tabloids are fascinated with moral disorder, but this focusing in on the atypical calls attention to difference, which produces a basis for a challenge of resistance to the normal. This challenge must be managed and thus, power must consensualize and normalize. Thus, the tabloid redraws the configuration of the deviant and the normal, focusing on the subjective and personal attachments of difference. Lines of identification, meaning and feeling are produced that tend to close off any form of resistance that would challenge the originary power relationships lying behind social problems. Thus, as noted before, the tabloid tends to ask the viewer to personally get involved in solutions to deviant behavior, but only in theory. The real solution lies in solidarity with the institutional forces of police that reign in the deviant.

This contradiction between pseudo-interaction and identification with power leads to the tabloid's characteristic ambivalence: it is at once politically cynical and morally conservative (Knight 1989, 106). In the tabloid world, the powerful are corrupt and the deviant are dangerous, while "the people" are the bearers of ordinary values, bound together by shared individualism. Of course, this individualism is the same form of recognition that advertising draws upon: the viewer is encouraged to recognize herself/himself in the "individualism" of the tabloid characters. The character's victimization becomes the selling point through fictive identification.

THE PSYCHOLOGY OF COMMODITY RESPONSE: RE-EMBODIMENT, VALUE LOSS, RE-SUBJECTIVIFICATION

It should be clear by now that the preceding tabloid characteristics are related through their function in advertising and promotion. Ultimately, the tabloid is both a selling environment and a self-standing commodity in its own right. As an environment, the tabloid engenders a set of positive psychological states for the workings of selling and promotion. In the tabloid world, victims are turned into celebrities and celebrities into victims, i.e., they are all *stars* and as *stars* they attach us to the market that they stand in for. Advertisers perceive the tabloid as an environment that is seen as doing something for the public good and thus, as a setting that engenders the type of emotive and cognitive potentials that are ideal for situating their products. Even when the tabloid stories themselves deride (on the surface) the products of the market, they make the product stand out. For example, *Inside Edition* ran a story on deaths due to *Domino Pizza's* 30 minute policy. The next night *Dominos* ran an ad on the show. Thus, the tabloid environment levels all messages to an equally trivial level: death, family tragedy, pizza and furniture sales are all linkable to publicity.

In the postmodern market representation and the real become inseparable, hence the news becomes less a process of intelligence and more one of promotion. The supposed objectivity of news is irrelevant, what matters is its subjectivity (nearness, affinity). The commodity as a substance retreats, but in the very same moment it reappears as "appearance of use value"—"*the stars brought down to earth.*" The goal of the cultural commodity is to stand out, to become image. It is the need to attract the consumer that subsumes all other functions into the glistening of the stars.

The tabloid, a commodity itself, becomes the space in which secondary commodities are hawked with incessant spectacle and incantation. Celebrities sell themselves through their troubles. When their images as actors and their vehicles fail, they sell themselves as *us*—lonely, troubled, guilty, wrecked by life —"feel sorry for me, then watch my show." Products appear strewn through the tabloid environment—books, fashions, cosmetics, vacation spots, cars, food. Many tabloid stories are nothing but mini-ads for other cultural products—a star has a new film, a network a new show, Hollywood a new blockbuster. The hosts and reporters sell themselves as "up and coming," "involved," "cutting-edge." They hope to be somewhere else (perhaps on the real news, perhaps their own series, it really doesn't matter) and their "reports" become ads for themselves. The tabloid (as a whole) sells itself throughout its program length, incessantly hawking the next show—which will promise to be even better. The tabloid becomes a seamless half-hour of ads for commodification itself.

As the use-value of any and all of the products that make up the tabloid as a whole recedes, pure exchangeability comes to the for. But selling "buying" still requires that the product appear to have a use-value. Thus, the tabloid attaches and detaches various values to its product, stamping it with "the personal" and the "authentic." It is here that critical psychology locates the emotive states of audience attachment to the cultural object, in its re-embodiment as a use-value through created identifications. The tabloid fills its empty form with pure viscerality, retrieving the substance, not in the commodity itself, but in a general bodily impact on the viewer. The viewer is "empowered" by the simulation of realities that can never be lived. The tabloid comes full circle, making stories that cannot be personal to us into "our stories." Thus, mere publicity, the purest form of the emptied commodity becomes re-subjectified in a pseudo-personalization.

The audience identifies with the semblance as if it were a mirror of their own objective needs and longings. That is,

> endless successions of images, which want to be like mirrors, rush forth empathically, looking down into the depths, bringing secrets to the surface and spreading them out there. In these images the unsatisfied pages of people's natures are continuously turned open to them. The semblance offers itself as if it were announcing the satisfaction; it guesses people's nature, reads the wishes in their eyes, and brings the wishes to light on the surface of the commodity. As the semblance in which the commodities come forth deciphers people, it provides them with a language for deciphering the world. Soon there is no other language than that supplied by the commodities (Haug 1987, 117).

The tabloid's characteristics: textual fragmentation, spectacle and reality effects, floating of meaning, passive populism, and normalizing exclusion; all function to position the audience within the general stance of consumerism. Thus, the standing out of the product situates the audience in a state of attraction. Attraction while appearing to be an active quest for satisfaction is primarily constructed out of the existent desire of subjects (already constructed from the memory of image production) and reworked in order to seduce them into new modes of gratification. Thus, the tabloid relies on all of those cinematic and televisual images that borrow from and re-image psycho-sexual desire.

Thus, the tabloid and television in general, recognize the fragmentary nature of the audience and decipher their desires and deprivations. This knowledge is incorporated into its practice; it markets to the semiotic democracy, thus containing it and conditioning it. The meanings made of any particular content of the tabloid, the "seeings-through" of any particular moment of its narration, become inconsequential in light of the general mechanisms of commodification.

NOTE

Portions of this article were presented at the 1992 Speech Communication Association Conference. The author would like to thank Lisa McLaughlin for comments on drafts of this manuscript.

REFERENCES

Adorno, Theodor. 1982. *Prisms.* Cambridge: The MIT Press.

Ang, Ian. 1985. *Watching Dallas: Soap opera and the melodramatic imagination.* London: Methuen.

Brown, Mary Ellen, ed. 1990. *Television and women's culture: The politics of the popular.* London: Sage.

Corrigan, Philip (1989) "Playing ... contradictions, empowerment, and embodiment: punk, pedagogy, and popular cultural forms (on ethnography and education)", in, Henry Giroux and Roger Simon (ed.) *Popular Culture, Schooling and Everyday Life* pp. 67-90. Granby, MA: Bergin & Garvey.

Fiske, John. 1989. *Reading the Popular.* Boston: Unwin Hyman.

Foucault, Michel. 1980. *Power/Knowledge: Selected Interviews & Other Writings,* ed. Colin Gordon. New York: Pantheon.

Grossberg, Lawrence (1989) "Pedagogy in the present: politics, postmodernity and the popular" in Henry Giroux and Roger Simon (ed.) *Popular Culture, Schooling and Everyday Life* pp. 91-116. Granby, MA: Bergin & Garvey.

Horkheimer, Max, and Theodor W. Adorno. 1972. *Dialectic of Enlightenment.* New York: Continuum. (Originally published in 1944).

Bernstein, J. M. 1991. Introduction. In *The Culture Industry: Selected Essays on Mass Culture,* Theodor W. Adorno, 1-25. New York: Routledge.

Haug, Wolfgang Fritz. 1987. *Commodity Aesthetics, Ideology & Culture.* New York: International General.

Knight, Graham. 1989. Reality effects: tabloid television news. *Queens Quarterly 96(1),* 94-107.

Morris, Meaghan. 1988. Banality in cultural studies. *Discourse* 10(2), 3-29.

Povich, Maury. 1991. *Current Affairs.* New York: G. P. Putnam's Sons.

Radway, Janice. 1984. *Reading the Romance: Women, patriarchy, and popular culture.* Chapel Hill: University of North Carolina Press.

Robins, J. Max. 1988. Here come the news punks. *Channels,* September, 39-43.

Sholle, David. 1990. Resistance: Pinning down a wandering concept in cultural studies discourse. *Journal of Urban and Cultural Studies 1(1),* 87-105.

Chapter VI

Media Knowledges, Warrior Citizenry, and Postmodern Literacies

Peter McLaren
and Rhonda Hammer

The actants, those structures of narrative action, had to sustain the drama of masculine words and deeds for the most ethereal and most lusted-after of goals-to be seen by all not to have backed down, to have drawn the line in the sand and made the inscription matter. The sands turn to concrete when the manly write in them. These are old, indeed old-fashioned, tendentious, unscrupulously generalizing feminist remarks. They need to be made again, as long as *virtu*, the quality of manliness, means the readiness to kill, that is, to be a replicant, of whatever biological or technological description, in the reproductive dramas of the Father, who forever structures the action in order to produce, again and again, the sacred image of the same. *In saecula saeculorum.* And, ageless, Bush and Saddam Hussein, those two secular figure heads of secular states, each declaring holy war, figured in blinding mirror image as autocrat and democrat, are surely knowingly enmeshed in the brotherly salvation histories that have driven their two Peoples of the Book for centuries.

—Donna Haraway, 1991, pp. 42-43

The subject is constructed through acts of differentiation that distinguish the subject from its constitutive outside, a domain of abjected alterity conveniently associated with the feminine, but clearly and not exclusively so. Precisely in this recent war we see the Arab as figured as the abjected Other, a site of homophobic fantasy well made clear in the abundance of bad jokes grounded in the linguistic sliding from Saddam to Sodom.

—Judith Butler, 1991, p. 76

Postmodern wars are not fought for clearly defined goals. Combatants may well invoke pretexts, but these pretexts are subject to change. As goals change, these wars come to assume an anarchic aspect. Postmodern wars have opened up multiple discursive spaces in which individu-

> als can find agency; women who have always been part of war can find in postmodern war a space to articulate this participation. This articulation threatens to undermine the Homeric war myth, yet it is itself always threatened by the entrenchedness of that archetype. The disenfranchised who before submitted to the distortions of dominant discourse are making their voices heard and their faces seen and thus exposing the mechanisms of power consolidation.
>
> —Miriam Cooke, 1991, p. 27

MEDIA KNOWLEDGES; A BRICOLAGE

We have for some time been chilled by the recognition that we are living in an age gone mad. Such madness is of an escalating variety, not unlike that characterized by Lewis Carroll's "Mad Tea Party" where Alice's recognition of the privileging discourses of Wonderland—as pathological—was essential for her survival and ultimate escape.

News events of recent years have greatly confirmed our suspicion that the madness surrounding us functions within wider discursive practices. We have referred to the outcome of such practices as "media knowledges." As we followed the media coverage related to the Iran/Contra hearings, the expulsion of the televangelist Jim Bakker, and the ignominious fall from political grace of the Democratic Party's "great white hope," Gary Hart (coverage that was referred to as the three "gates"—specifically "Contra," "Holy," and "Forni"—that followed in the wake of Watergate), we became convinced that our liberation from Wonderland (were it at all possible) would in no way be comparable to the conditions surrounding Alice's escape. For unlike Alice, who never doubted the lunacy of Wonderland, the majority of North Americans give some semblance of credibility to the mythical landscape of representations and literacies constructed by contemporary media.

We are interested in providing conditions for educators to approach the issue of literacy critically, by recognizing that we live in a world of multiple literacies—you could call them 'postmodern literacies'—in which knowledge can be understood as a form of meaning-making. Such knowledge production consists of both our cognitive engagement with and affective investment in various cultural forms (print, film television, and radio). In this essay we want to draw on Walter Benjamin's figure of the Flaneur to discuss the role of media commentators as popular intellectuals. More specifically, we want to draw attention to the way media knowledges constitute possibilities for human agency as well as textual restraints placed on teachers as cultural workers—as workers who deal in codes, social texts, and the semiotic circuitry of classrooms and everyday life, and who act as cultural cartographers, mapping cultural life in terms of understanding whose stories are visible and whose lie buried in the established archives of history.

THE NEWS REPORTER AS POSTMODERN FLANEUR

When Walter Benjamin wrote about the nineteenth century figure of the flaneur or "street reader," the bohemian prototype of the modern intellectual whose method of literary production consisted in strolling the city streets and reflecting upon the everyday production of cultural life, he was essentially describing a particular generation of cultural workers whose "object of inquiry was modernity itself" (Buck-Morris, 1989: 304). For Benjamin, the poet Baudelaire best embodied the figure of the intellectual flaneur as teacher—a socially rebellious cultural worker who was sympathetic to the needs of the proletariat and was able to teach Benjamin's generation of intellectual producers about the social, culture, and economic conditions that informed their lived experience.

The status of the flaneur was always precarious: "Unlike the academic who reflects in his room, he walks the street and 'studies' the crowd. At the same time, his economic base shifts drastically, no longer protected by the academic's mandarin status" (p. 304). As capitalism expanded into hitherto uncommodified social and cultural realms, and further implicated itself in the signifying practices of mass communications media, fascism became its afterimage and Benjamin began to notice that the modern role of the flaneur was changing to its peril. As cultural producer, the flaneur increasingly came under the spell of the dreaming collective created by consumer capitalism" (p. 312) which removed him more and more from the historical conditions that produced his own social universe.

The transformation that the flaneur gradually underwent could be seen in the degraded incarnation of the sandwichman. As the structured unconscious of the collective (*Kollectiv*) or the masses (*die Masse*) became porous receptacles for the political phantasmagoria and staged extravaganzas of mass spectacles of Germany in the 1930s and 1940s, the most degraded caricature of the flaneur was eventually to appear in the streets of Munich in the form of Jews marching through the city bearing placards —barbaric self-advertisements which the Nazis forced upon the Jews as emblems of their ethnic disgrace (p. 312) and which become social hieroglyphs of the most profound evil of the century.

THE FLANEUR IN POSTMODERN CULTURE

Our analysis of the media production of the war against Iraq by CNN and its valorization of the viewer as "phallomilitary warrior-citizen" (Cooke, 1991; Butler, 1991) follows the observation by Susan Buck-Morss (1989) that the role of the news reporter as "flaneur-become detective [who] covers the beat" or "photojournalist [who] hangs about like a hunter ready to shoot" has changed as capitalism has expanded into hitherto uncommodified social and cultural realms and has further implicated itself in the signifying practices of mass communication media. We have followed Buck-Morss in tracing the views of Walter Benjamin towards his figure of the flaneur, the "street reader" who strolls ambiguously and ambivalently through the city streets, projecting a "distaste for the industrial labour through which he glides" (Eagleton, 1981: 26) and abandoning himself to the crowd like a commodity.

According to Buck-Morss, Benjamin saw the flaneur in shifting roles, from a "person of leisure (*Musse*)" to someone engaged in "loitering (*Mussigang*)" to the "prototype of the new form of salaried employee who produces news/literature/advertisements for the purpose of information/entertainment/persuasion" (p. 306). Buck-Morss paints a final portrait of the flaneur as someone whom Benjamin felt advertised not simply commodities but ideological propaganda. Like a "sandwichman" who is "paid to advertise the attractions of mass culture" (pp. 306-307), the flaneur as "journalist-in-uniform" advertises the state and "profits by peddling the ideological fashion" (p. 307).

Benjamin's early depiction of the flaneur, who "moves majestically against that historical grain that would decompose his body into an alien meaning, reduce his numinous presence to an allegory of loss" (Eagleton, p. 154) was a socially rebellious cultural worker, the bohemian prototype—or "ur-form"—of the modern intellectual (Buck-Morss, p. 304). His method of literary production rejected the mandarin status of the metropolitan intellectual and consisted in strolling the city streets and reflecting on the everyday production of cultural life.

Our understanding of contemporary forms of electronically produced media knowledges has been informed by what we perceive as the changing role of the flaneur in the age of late capitalism—one that is as ominous and drastic as the changes which Benjamin perceived. We suggest that the flaneur no longer provides the service of teaching his or her generation about "their own objective circumstances"; rather, we suggest that the flaneur, as global newscaster, has transmogrified into the afterimage of fascism.

Today we are living in a precarious historical moment in which the flaneur—as signifying agent—is undergoing even further metamorphosis. The postmodern flaneurs of today are corporate individuals cunningly managing and shaping the world of mass-produced images, superannuated servants of the state whose forms of knowledge production are mediated by and fastened securely to the logic of consumption. They still stroll the city streets, as they did in Benjamin's era, but this time they are accompanied by a video production crew and, in times of war, a military censor. Often salaried employees of transnational corporations and other standard bearers of imperialism, the insights served up by the global, postmodern flaneur (to audiences exceeding millions at one viewing) more often than not serve to mystify and further camouflage race, class, and gender antagonisms, and thereby hinder rather than help viewers understand the conditions of everyday existence.

As reality increasingly becomes confused with the image, and the mediascape becomes the driving force of our time, the image of the postmodern flaneur becomes embodied not in human presence but in human immanence transmuted through an electronic signal, a satellite beam roaming the earth in search of new spectacles through which to present and contain reality. We are entering an age of painful loss of everyday history and shared popular memory that has followed the development of media technology since the beginning of the century (Schwoch, White and Reilly, in press).

Media knowledges produced by the postmodern flaneur serve as a discourse about action that teleologically fulfills itself in the sense that it recounts an event, that is, in the sense that it *emplots* an event. Yet, paradoxically, it is an emplotment of a history—an event—that is manufactured not simply as narrative but also as mood, as a "structure of feeling." Often it has no real beginning (*arche*) or end (*telos*) other than the illusion created by the context of its production. The Gordian knot of history is cleaved as history is declared dead in the frozen moment of the image. For instance, the bloody aftermath of the war with Iraq continues today, although the media has officially declared the war to be over.

Media knowledges offered up by the postmodern flaneur—what we refer to as "perpetual pedagogy"—constitute a moving, circulating signwork that possesses a valorizing and legitimating function in the way that it marks off the territory of the real. In the case of the Gulf War, it was able to situate the mobile self of postmodernity in a synecdochial relation to a hyperreal, apocalyptic event, one that came ideologically unannounced yet was able to "cue" both our sign membership and our "affective investment" (Grossberg, 1988) into the political economy of patriotism and global citizenry.

COLONIZATION OF THE INTERIOR

Today's cultural and historical events bombard our sensibilities with such exponential speed and frequency, and through such a variety of media forms, that our critical comprehension skills have fallen into rapid deterioration. This collective loss of reasoning, and of history, appears to be reaching epidemic proportions, with little hope of abatement. The etiology of this "plague," many scholars argue, stems from the expanding sophistication and complexity of networks of social relations that we call "television" (Gitlin, 1986).

It is indeed a paradox that a piece of videotape has no visible image inscribed upon it since, like audiotape, it holds nothing but electrical impulses. Television works by electronic scanning in which tiny dots of light on the screen are lit up, one at a time, by the firing of cathode ray guns across alternate lines on the front of the picture tube (Nelson, 1987: 71). Joyce Nelson describes the process as follows:

> The succession of glowing dots moves rapidly across and down, along alternate lines, in a sweep that lights up the first series of phosphors. In all there are 525 such lines of miniscule dots on North American TV sets. During each one-thirtieth of a second, the scanning process completes two full sweeps of the screen, one on each alternative set of lines, to create, by electrical impulse, the whole mosaic of an instant's image. In terms of micro-seconds, however, there is actually never more than a single dot of light glowing on the screen. Our eyes receive each dot of light, sending its impulse to the brain. The brain records this bit of information, recalls previous impulses, and expects future ones. We "see" an entire image because the brain fills in or complete 99.999 percent of the scanned pattern each fraction of a second, below our conscious awareness. The only picture that ever exists is the one we complete in our brain. (1991, p. 71)

Whereas in film viewing, the viewer fills in the motion between the frames, which change twenty-four times a second, in the case of watching television, the viewer fills in the motion *and* the picture (pp. 71-72). Researchers such as Krugman (cited in Nelson, p. 71) have reported that watching television shuts down the left hemisphere of the neo-cortex of the brain (that deals with part-by-part analytical thinking and logical analysis) and disengages information processing. this occurs either because of habituation to the scanning dot or "overloading" during the scanning process. Whatever the case may be, direct access to the right hemisphere is unquestionably enabled (since it goes into an alpha rhythm state) and this promotes "evoked-recall" rather than "learned recall" as well as free associations and unconscious connections.

In effect, this opens up the private space of the individual viewer to feelings and associations that are ripe for colonization by the advertising industry. Messages are designed by advertisers that seek to match the coded expectations of viewers through the use of associative memory response, free association, rhythm, melody, rhyme, harmony, pictorial triggers, etc. (p. 77). This provides optimal conditions for advertisers to label our feelings for us: With the help of advertisements and their products, we can purchase "feeling 7-UP" and "Oh what a feeling—Toyota" or Bell Telephone's "long distance feeling" (p. 78).

As a form of knowing, of what we refer to as "perpetual pedagogy," mainstream television programming is decidedly anti-dialogical and rarely evokes acts of political refusal. Unreflective television viewing has a homogenizing, unifying force by unfixing the space of cultural enunciation through the right hemisphere and simultaneously recolonizing it through the left hemisphere—a form of double-encoding that rehistoricizes and translates heterogeneity and the instability of deep memories and associations into a mimetic correspondence with the real—like Coke, it becomes "the real thing." In effect, the television viewer becomes constructed within the pulsations of electronically mediated desire. Read against this televisually constructed and radically decentered subjectivity, we are able to conceive of the Kantian and Cartesian tradition of viewing the self as rational, unified, and autonomous as little more than a monstrosity. Within the dominant logocentric tradition, viewers are taught to mis-recognize in the private space of their phantom self the deep memories and associations that are evoked below the threshold of conscious awareness as self-conscious, autonomous, and willed desire, that is, from the perspective of the rational subject as a detached, disembodied, and sovereign (patriarchal) observer of a transparent reality. Furthermore, the illusion that televisual desire can be controlled by an autonomous, self-effulgent ego occludes from viewers the way television works as a corporate mobilization of desire for objects that are constantly misrecognized as real in that liminal space between consciousness and repression.

In fact, the television images that we see are never really there. They exist as furtive shadows that we capture as viewers through forms of televisual address that are variously shaped by our "viewing formations," that is, through our deep cultural memories, our fears, our repressions, and our anxieties. Watching television is not so much to have the self decentered or turned nomad against a totalizing regime of logocentric representation: rather it is to have one's sense of self-contained identity de-situated and deformed into concatenated levels of desire. We are not so much dealing here with regimes of signification as we are with what Larry Grossberg (1988) calls "mattering maps"—with investments of desire and pleasure.

Television viewing is like watching the world not through the rose-colored glasses of naive hope but through a glass coffin inside memory's prison house. It offers us a new means of constituting subjectivity, a new "assemblage" formed within capitalism that "reterritorializes" the relation of human and the machine (Poster, 1991, p. 136). As Deleuze and Guattari put it:

> with automation comes ... a new kind of enslavement ... one is enslaved by TV as a human machine insofar as the television viewers are no longer consumers or users, nor even subjects who supposedly "make" it, but intrinsic component pieces, "input" and "output" feedback or recurrences that are no longer connected to the machine in such a way as to produce or use it. In machine enslavement, there is nothing but transformations and exchanges of information (cited in Poster, 1991, p. 136).

But the subjectivity constructed through machine enslavement is more than the subject's positioning within the circuit of information flows or the "schizoid pulsations of the unconscious." According to Poster, there occurs a radicalization of anti-logocentric bearings of the self brought on by electronically mediated communication, and the undermining of the space/time co-ordinates that hold together the Cartesian view of the subject as autonomous and rational. In Poster's view, this "reterritorialization" of subjectivity offers the possibility for radically new and potentially emancipatory forms of community." Since, for Poster, electronically mediated communication both supplements and substitutes for existing forms of sociability (Poster, 1991: 154), there always exists a space for the construction of "new and unrecognizable modes of community." Yet, as we shall argue in the final section, whether or not these new modes of sociality and community will be emancipatory will depend to a large extent on what types of media literacy are permitted.

George Gerbner (1989/90) has made a good case for the development of critical media literacy. His research has revealed that U.S. television viewers accept a distorted picture of the real world "more readily than reality itself." According to Gerbner, television reality is one in which men outnumber women three to one, where women are usually portrayed as either mothers or lovers, rarely work outside the home, and are natural victims of violence. It is a reality in which less than ten percent of the population hold blue collar jobs, where few elderly people exist, where Black youth learn to accept their minority status as inevitable and are trained to anticipate their own victimization (they are usually cast as the white hero's comic sidekick or else as drug addicts, gang members, or killers). It is a world in which 18 acts of violence an hour occur in children's prime time programs. Violence in television, Gerbner insists, demonstrates the social power of adult white males who are most likely to get involved with violence but most likely to get away with it. It also serves as a mass spectacle reflecting and legitimating the allocative power of the state. That such an unreality could be rendered natural and commonsensical in a country that in 1990 reported the largest number of rapes against women in its history and a prison incarceration rate of Blacks that exceeds that of South Africa, where rich Angelenos are hiring private police, where wealthy neighborhoods display signs warning "Armed Response!" and where security systems and the militarization of urban life are refiguring social space along the lines of the postmodern film *Bladerunner,* is symptomatic of a moral and epistemological crisis of astonishing proportions.

DEATH AS ENTERTAINMENT: FOR PATRIOTS ONLY

A highly precipitous occasion for our reflection on these themes has been the coverage of three seemingly unrelated historical events known as the "gates." What struck us as most disconcerting was the conflation of these diverse and unrelated news worthy events into a single representative category of public consumption—namely, entertainment—and thus, of being (at least in the public eye) of equal import. To reduce the complex interactions of these events to the noun "gates" transforms these events into soap opera spectacles of individual transgression while ignoring their national, cultural, and geopolitical situatedness as social practices occurring in specific contexts at particular historical moments. What reduces these events to the same level of importance is their entertainment value: the sexual and political intrigue, the attempted cover-ups, the image value elicited by the personalities of the offenders, etc.[1] This type of reductionism is what Wilden (1987) refers to as "symmetrization." Symmetrization involves the ideological and epistemological process of making hierarchically distinct levels of relationship appear to be "equal" or on the same level when in reality one class of relationship is a different logical type than another.

In *Amusing Ourselves to Death,* Neil Postman assures us that what we have been describing is neither hallucination nor historical accident. The culprit, as Postman sees it, is the complex, multi-levelled system of communication known as the television industry. As he puts it:

> Our politics, religion, news, athletics, education, and commerce have been transformed into congenial adjuncts of show business, largely without protest or even much popular notice. The result is that we are people on the verge of *amusing ourselves to death* (1985: pp. 3-4; emphasis *ours*).

Within this context, we view these three news events as a representative metaphor for the state of news reporting in the age of the "postmodern flaneur," and an apt indicator of the shape of things to come in the state of 1990s broadcast news. Regardless of the relationships that both constrain and enable the construction of content, television's politics of representation and mode of information reduces everything from commercials, to comedy, to local, national, or international events to the same meta-form: entertainment.

---

[1] The Pathology of symmetrized and inverted levels associated with what has evolved into a multidimensional profitable industry: The O.J. Simpson saga, is further testimony to the escalating phenomenon.

PROFANE ILLUMINATION: ENTERTAINMENT AS THE STRUCTURING OF COLONIALIST MODES OF SUBJECTIVITY

> America: heroic, phallic America is dead. Great God America proclaimed itself the paramount power, the vital cultural center, and all the other gods died laughing.
>
> —McKenziew Wark, 1991, p. 48

Our previous investigations of the media (Hammer and Wilden, 1987; Giroux and McLaren, in press; 1991; Hammer and McLaren, in press; McLaren and Hammer, 1991) did little to prepare us for the violent semiotics of the media spectacle surrounding the coverage of the Gulf War, especially the way it was able to meld the apocalyptic genre of catastrophe with the nonsense genre of carnival. More specifically, we were struck by the ability of the media to transform the military campaigns in Kuwait and Iraq into a 24-hour advertising spectacle in which the newscaster as postmodern flaneur was (with the few notable exceptions of reporters who chose not to co-operate with military censors) reduced to a carnival huckster for patriotic zeal and a salesperson for machineries of destruction and death.

The propagandistic construction of the Gulf war is an extreme example of how the media serves up death for surplus consumption in a politics that centers primarily around the lifestyle industry and what Stuart Ewen (1988: 264) has termed "info-tainment." As Ewen (p. 265) notes, "in the ratings game, the news—out of economic necessity—must be transformed into a drama, a thriller, entertainment. Within such a context, the *truth* is defined as *that which sells*" (emphasis original). Especially with reference to the CNN coverage of the war, a kindred range of films and videos dealing with war at a distance (*Top Gun, Iron Eagle*, etc.) tacitly coordinated the reception of many viewers to the aerial shots of 'precision' hits through a superimposition of images and forms of emplotment-memories from postmodern war's electronic and celluloid Hollywood archive-transforming the war coverage into a type of palimpsest blending the discontinuity of war with the continuity of Western narratives about it. Mark Poster (1991: 221) remarks that there existed a "deja vu" effect with aerial shots that provoked memories of computer games of flight simulations—"Just when you are taken to the place of impact, the intensifying rhetoric of realism implodes into the hyperrealism of computer games."

The mass production of patriotic sentiment and the mobilization of consent that allowed such a disproportionate and excessive use of force to literally disintegrate hundreds of thousands of Iraqi soldiers fleeing north out of Kuwait (described as "one of the most terrible harassments of a retreating army in the history of warfare;" Ellis, Saeeda and Plott, 1991) was, in our minds, unquestionably designed as a *mass advertisement*; the hidden payoff was not the construction of a more critically informed public but rather an electronic display for showcasing weapons of mass destruction in a way that benefitted the arms dealers, the war industry, and a phallic warfare state deploying identities politically and strategically by preparing its citizenry to assume a leadership role in a "new world order."

Can we tell the difference between actual and simulated war? It is difficult when the investigative gaze of the viewer is replaced by a giddy acquiescence to the accredited expertise of visiting military experts and politicians. This is not to suggest that there exists no readings among viewers that aggravate the techno-ideological thrust of the programming but rather that the static and retrospective character of news shows is often enough to smudge the boundary between *doxa* and *episteme*. Spectacles do not invite situating information into a context. This was most evident in CNN's use of dazzling optical effects as exploding bombs and tracer bullets became luminously pock-marked against darkened skies while the Iraqi soldiers (and civilians) remained largely invisible except perhaps as oneiric battlefield abstractions that resembled the ovaloid forms of Oliver Wascow photographs.

As Jochen and Linda Schulte-Sasse point out, we are speaking here of an event that is potentially more dangerous than what Walter Benjamin referred to as the "aestheticization of politics" since we are witnessing the very process of politics itself being constructed symbolically through the imaginary of media images (1991: p. 70). Not only was the media war in the Gulf "at least in part propelled by [its] power to unify the body politic and to instill in the state's subjects the illusion of being masterful agents of history," the war itself also became an epiphenomenon the media's production of the war—what could be called "an appendex of image production, an inconvenient though unfortunately still necessary anchor in reality of media simulations" (pp. 70-71). The danger of media-produced wars turning spectators in narrator/agents of history is that it carries with it both the illusion of and addiction to omnipotence. As Jochen and Linda Shulte-Sasse remark:

> While experiencing ourselves, collectively and individually, as a unified body, we simultaneously fall prey to the illusion that we can decipher and master the world, we cover up our actual impotence as agents, which in turn worsens the nation's material situation (economy, infrastructure, educational system, etc.) and increases its dependence on images of superiority (p. 71).

The "totally administered stylistic environment" of the newscast is one of the best entertainment formats for promulgating "cognitive confusion" and geopolitical misunderstanding. Ewen (1988: 265) remarks:

> The highly stylized signature of the news program offers the only overarching principle of cohesion and meaning. Again, surface makes more sense than substance. The assembled facts, as joined together by the familiar, formulaic, and authoritative personality of "The News," becomes the most accessible version of the larger reality that most Americans have at their disposal. Consciousness *about the world* is continually drawn away from a geopolitical understanding of events as they take place in the world. As nations and people are daily sorted out into boxes marked "good guys," "villains," "victims," and "lucky ones," style becomes the essence, reality becomes appearance.

Investment in imperialism is important for the United States in order to retain its superpower status since it cannot compete successfully with Japan and Germany's demilitarized economies. We view the war coverage on CNN and other stations as a global media advertising campaign for sophisticated weapons technology—technology now being sold to countries inhabiting the Gulf region and elsewhere (i.e., Israel and Turkey). The Gulf war spectacle, in this sense, reflected the global push of transnational capital in the information-cultural sphere primarily through the transformation of the "theater" of battle into an international market economy. It was an advertisement for the "new world order" of Western-structured development and incorporation into the dominant world business order. Yet the kind of new world order to which the Gulf war pointed was framed by a gaudy sideshow of flags, emblems, and military hardware—a counterfeit democracy produced through media knowledges able to effectively harness the affective currency of popular culture such that the average American's investment in being "American" reached an unparalleled high which has not been approximated since the years surrounding the post-WWII McCarthy hearings.

DOUBLESPEAK: THE NEW LANGUAGE OF DEMOCRACY

The success of the advertising campaign surrounding both the "selling" and the "displaying" of the Gulf war was largely due to the strategic use of doublespeak to disguise from television viewers the extent of the real terror and carnage of the military campaign against Iraq. When a euphemism is used to mislead or deceive, it becomes doublespeak. William Lutz (1981: 1) writes that doublespeak

> is a language that avoids or shifts responsibility, language that is at variance with its real or purported meaning. It is a language that conceals or prevents thought; rather than extending thought, doublespeak limits it.

For instance, Lutz reports that in 1984 the U.S. State Department announced it would no longer use the word "killing" in its annual report on the status of human rights in countries around the world. Instead, it chose to employ the term "unlawful or arbitrary deprivation of life." While the State Department claimed that this was a more accurate description of the condition, the term actually functioned to direct attention away from the embarrassing situation of government-sanctioned killings in countries supported by the United States and who have been certified by the United States as respecting the human rights of its citizens (p. 3). "Radiation enhancement device" is a term that has been used by Pentagon officials to nuclear bombs. The neutron bomb was called a "cookie cutter" because it could kill people inside less than a three-quarter-mile radius without harming allied soldiers and civilians nearby.

Doublespeak occurs through the use of terms that are to a large extent technically true but which serve to function as a lie. For instance, a profit may be described as a "negative deficit;" euphemisms for firing staff may be described as "staff reduction," "non-retention," "dehiring," or "rationalizing of resources."

During the media's production of the Gulf war, there existed, in the words of Carol E. Cohn (1991: 88), a "reversal of metaphors between sentient beings and insentient things." For example, the term "air support" overlooks the devastation and loss of life during bombing raids; "collateral damage" refers to civilian deaths; "incontinent ordinances" are bombs or missiles that hit allied troops under conditions of "friendly fire"; a "party" is a battle; "bags of tools" refers to weapons; "theater of operations" to a battlefield; "surgical strike" refers to precision bombing; and "delivering a package" to dropping bombs.

Cohn (p. 88) describes a radio news briefing on the Persian Gulf as "Madison Avenue's idea of a housewife's dream: General Colin Powell talks about fighting in a "sanitary fashion." The air force launches "surgically clean strikes." Instead of bombing the Iraqi troops, U.S. forces are "flying sorties," "engaging" the enemy, "taking out" Iraqi "assets," "servicing" targets, and "softening up" the Republican Guard. Iraqi soldiers do not blow up when they are hit by bombs or missiles. Instead, their "emplacements absorb the munitions" (p. 88). Human beings become insentient things while weapons become the living actors of war. "Smart" weapons that have eyes and computer "brains" make the decision when and where to drop seven and a half tons of bombs, taking away the moral responsibility of the combatants themselves (p. 88). Margot Norris (1991: 224) has noted the Pentagon's consistent strategy of juxtaposing "excessively specific information on the deployment and destruction of weaponry, machines, and 'hard' targets with refusal to stipulate the 'soft' targets or Iraqi bodies"—a move that "has shaped both the fiction and the ideology of the 'technological utopianism' that has become the central defense narrative in President Bush's 'new world order'."

CNN's spectacularization of the Gulf War managed to position the viewer so that to be against it was to be 'biased' and to be in favor of it was to be 'objective.' Its narrative apparatus with its apparent realism, or representionality, not only restructured our feelings surrounding the historical conditions being played out but through strategies of indirection and disinformation was also able to mobilize particular economies of affect. Again, our argument is that the war could be read as one large advertisement that served as unquestionably the "best show in town." Just as sure as U.S. bombs obliterated Iraqi soldiers and civilians, the media's war obliterated the particular historical and political background of Western imperialism that served as the context for the actual fighting. In the words reminiscent of an advertisement, Richard Blystone of CNN (1/2/91) described a "Scud" missile as "a quarter-ton of concentrated hatred" while the Patriot missile was described by *USA Today* (1/22/91) as "three inches longer than a Cadillac Sedan de Ville" (Naureckas, 1991).

It is ironic if not profoundly disturbing that the substanceless unreality of the Gulf war—its hyperreality—has become the metanarrative for a renewed U.S. patriotism and the meaning of citizenship. The construction of patriotism through the production of media unreality works—has meaning—as long as the viewer does not know his or her desire is being mobilized and structured through the advertisement mode of information. According to Mark Poster (1990: 63):

> As ad after ad is viewed, the representational critical gradually loses interest, becomes lulled into a noncritical stance, is bored, and gradually receives the communication differently . . . the ad only works to the extent that it is not understood to be an ad, not understood instrumentally. Through its linguistic structure the TV ad communicates at a level other than the instrumental which is placed in brackets. Floating signifiers, which have no relation to the product, are set in play; images and words that convey desirable or undesirable states of being are portrayed in a manner that optimizes the viewer's attention without arousing critical awareness.
>
> A communication is enacted, in the TV ad, which is not found in any context of daily life. An unreal is made real, a set of meanings is communicated which is more real than reality.

THE MASS SPECTACLE AS TOTEMIC ADVERTISEMENT

Perhaps the most important point to be made about the construction of subjectivity through media as a form of advertisement is its religious function. As Sut Jhally (1990: 202) has noted in his historical tracing of the person-object relation in advertisements, advertisements now function as a form of *totemism* in which "utility, symbolization and personalization are mixed and remixed under the sign of the group." Products no longer become venerated for their utility, their value as icons, or their power as fetishes; rather, they now serve in the post-Fordist service economy as a badge of a group—*a form of shared lifestyle*. New world order patriots are now held together by lifestyle rather than particular political commitments. For example, Arnold Schwarzenegger recently purchased a special jeep (nicknamed the "Hummer") used in the Gulf war by U.S. troops for his own personal use. In New York City, manufacturers of bullet proof vests are starting *special fashion lines* for toddlers and elementary school children who might accidently absorb stray bullets from homeboy dealers in pumps, ten-dollar gold tooth caps and who carry customized AK 47 assault rifles. The guns are not lifestyle accessories—yet. But gas masks are. New York celebrity fashion designer, Andre Van Pier, has recently announced a new Spring fashion line based on the theme of "Desert Storm." It attempts to capture the "Gulf war look." Fashion accessories revealed include neon-colored gas masks slung renegade-chic over the shoulder. To add insult to injury, a major New York baseball card manufacturer has revealed a new line of Gulf war cards that are supposed to be "educational." Of course, the cards include photos of all the major U.S. war hardware and portraits of the American Generals, but the only item represented from Iraq in this 'educational' collection is a "Scud" missile.

The Gulf War was packaged for U.S. viewers in the form of the lifestyle politics of watching football spectacles. According to Ernest Larsen (1991: 5), following the Gulf War Superbowl, January, 1991, "General Schwartzkopf explain [ed] the fine points of bombing runs, with the same delivery style and the same instant replay as the network football commentators have just used."

> Further, he notes that the idiom used on television to describe the war also evoked the jingoist jocksniffery of football announcers. The emphasis on number, names, and stats, on graphics, plays, and kicking ass, and later, on "cutting it off and killing it," in Colin Powell's unstudied phrase, are all derived from the sports world, that sweaty utopia of repressed homoerotic ritual combat made up of grown-up males in uniforms whose entire livelihood is concentrated on their ability to use their fetishized bodies with the forceful precision of high-tech weapons. At one point Bush even called the war his Super Bowl. (p. 8)

TELEVISION REALITY AS THE DISCOURSE OF THE OTHER

Soon after the war ended, our students (both from our respective classrooms in Canada and the United States) began to express regret that they could no longer return to their television sets with the same mixture of commitment and enjoyment that many of them confided they reserved only for their favorite soap operas. CNN's staged desire in its coverage of the war had presented them with unambiguous co-ordinates to construct *national economies of affect* in the form of binary oppositions (patriot/traitor; good/evil; Christian/Muslim; democracy/dictatorship; liberators/enslaved). Hussein was compared to other dark-skinned leaders such as Idi Amin, Qadafi and Noriega while the only European who made this rogues gallery was Stalin (Shohat, 1991). As Shohat points out, television anchors in the U.S. followed George Bush in calling Hussein by his first name—"Sadd'm"—in order to evoke a series of associations such as Satan, Damn, and Sodom. How many television anchors have you heard refer to George Bush as George? Furthermore, it is interesting to note why Hussein was never compared to Hitler when he was armed by the U.S. and when he used chemical weapons against Iranians and Kurds. Why, for instance, did television archives reveal the brutal consequences of chemical warfare by using images from WWI or from the Iran-Iraq war while avoiding any images of destruction caused by Agent Orange or napalm during Vietnam strikes (Shohat, 1991: 137)? Shohat (1991:37) further notes that

> the Hussein-Hitler analogy prolonged the historical intertext of Israeli and American imagery linking Arabs to Nazis. This link, both metonymic and metaphoric, had been a staple of didactic Israeli films (*Hill 24 Doesn't Answer, Rebels, Against the Light*) as well as of Hollywood cinema (*Ship of Fools, Exodus, Raiders of the Lost Ark*).

The use of warring oppositions such as "good/evil" and "democracy/dictatorship" to frame associations between Hussein and Hitler served to decontextualize and dehistoricize the events surrounding the war and to effectively "symmetrize" existing relations of power and privilege in the Gulf region. For instance, by establishing chains of equivalences between the war in the Gulf and WWII, the colonial and neo-colonial legacy of European nations who "parcelled up" the inhabitants of the Ottoman empire and installed monarchies and regimes loyal to the imperial powers was successfully elided. This made it easier for typical colonial narratives to be constructed such as "the rescue of white or dark women from a dark rapist" under the metaphor, "the rape of Kuwait," which followed the "historical oversexualization of Blacks and Indians . . . [which was continued] . . . in the image of Saddam and the Arabs" (Shohat, p. 140).

The colonial narratives played out for American viewers during CNN's production of the Gulf war echoed the way in which contemporary forms of media knowledges reproduce national images of citizenship such as those modelled on the John-Wayneing of America and captured in the renumerative cliches, "Go for it!" and "Go ahead. Make my day!" Rocky Balboa's "Go for it!" (which has become the clarion call for the U.S. brand of rugged individualism) and Clint Eastwood's "Go ahead. Make my day!" adorn the discursive fountainhead of United States bravado culture. These slogans have become cultural aphorisms that reveal a great deal about the structural unconscious of the United States. Both Ronald Reagan and George Bush have referred to "Go ahead. Make my day!" during their time in office. When Clint Eastwood delivered his famous lines in the movie, *Sudden Impact* (made during the Reagan presidency), he is daring a Black man to murder a woman so that he (Dirty Harry) can kill him. As Michael Rogin (1990) has pointed out, Dirty Harry is willing to sacrifice women and people of color in the name of his own courage. Reagan had made women and Black people his targets by destroying their welfare-state tax benefits—an act he was defending when he dared his detractors to "Make my day!" Similarly, George Bush made the Black criminal and white rapist of *Sudden Impact* into the figure of Willie Horton, as he attempted for the first time to organize American politics around the ominous image of interracial rape (Rogin, 1990).

With the upcoming 1992 election campaign in mind, Bush appears to be using the issue of racial hiring quotas in order to achieve a similar effect—the fear of darker-skinned immigrants taking away jobs from better qualified white people. And he will undoubtedly use Gulf war footage to remind Americans that they are back on top as a world military power and and that future threats from dark-skinned peoples (whether Latinos, African-Americans, or native Americans inside its borders or Arabs or South Americans outside its borders) will be met with a force as swift and as deadly as that of Desert Storm.

The coverage of the Gulf war recalled the warning sounded by the 1975 Trilateral Commission that claimed that the electronic media were creating situations of surplus democracy that made the United States more difficult to govern because television was becoming too adversarial and challenging leadership practices, policy initiatives, and delegitimizing established institutions (Kellner, 1990: pp. 6-7). In the case of the Gulf war, only 1.5 percent of network sources protested the war, about the same number as the sources who were asked about how the war had affected their travel plans (Naureckas, 1991: 5). The Brookings Institute, which was the most important think tank consulted by the media during the Gulf War, was passed off as a think tank of the left. Representatives from Brookings were called upon to debate those from hard-line conservative think tanks such as the Center for Strategic and International Studies and the American Enterprise Institute. However, the Brookings Institute has been "an institution of the center-right for more than a decade" (Soley, 1991: 6). In fact, topping the list of corporate donors to Brookings were media corporations "which drew heavily on Brookings for 'liberal' opinions and sound bites" (ibid.).

It should come as little surprise that views from an authentic progressive think tank such as the Institute for Policy Studies were rarely solicited or cited. In fact, "In seven months of the conflict, IPS was cited 26 times by six major papers (6 percent of Brookings' citations); in the first month, not one IPS representative appeared on a nightly newscast" (Soley, 1991, p. 6).

THE NEW RIGHT AND THE DEFORMATION OF REALITY

> "And we've now moved what amounts to a medium-size American city completely capable of defending itself all the way over to the Middle East."
>
> —President George Bush

> Statement to the press about the U.S. military deployment in Saudi Arabia, Kennebunkport, Maine, 22 August, 1990, as cited in O.K. Werckmeister, *Citadel Culture*, p. 187.

An important, if not urgent reason for students to become media literate is the power of postmodern literacies such as film and television to encode our subjective formations with cultural memory. Since the vector-field of identity has expanded into the electromagnetic spectrum, McKenzie Wark warns that:

> the encoding of memory in postmodern culture is in the hands of ever more sophisticated cultural technologies. We no longer have roots; we have aerials. George Lukàcs spoke of a second nature, composed of the products of physical labour, over and against which living labour is formed and struggles. It would seem appropriate now to speak of a *third nature*, of an environment shot through with the products of intellectual labour, over and against which intellectual labour is formed and struggles. It is this third nature which replicates itself in us, and hence, it is no small matter who owns this 'little piece of America's soul'. For we all grew up in America, in a place called Hollywood, a place where movie stars have been replaced in the image-bank by teenage crackheads and serial killers (1991, p. 45).

The New Right has used the media effectively (and affectively) not simply to transform war into a spectacle of national unity based on the Manichean grandeur of good triumphing over evil; nor have they used the media primarily to turn generals into talk-show guests through the prodigious use of high-tech image consultants (although they have done both very successfully; see Giroux and McLaren, 1989). Even more impressively, the New Right has been able to seduce Americans through the media to retreat into cultural nostalgia and social amnesia as a way of draining attention away from escalating social problems such as rising incidents of racism in urban settings, growing numbers of homeless, and the devastation of AIDS. Part of this has to do with the media's ability to reduce the historical present to a collage of images, a symbiotic coupling of machine and body, a new cult of the simulacrum.

Kellner (1990) claims that under the control of multinational capital, the media have effectively served as ideological mouthpieces for Reagan/Bush disinformation and in so doing have helped to forge a conservative ideological hegemony—what Schiller (1989) calls the "shadowy but many-tentacled disinformation industry." Kellner writes:

> It is a historical irony that the 1980s marked the defeat of democracy by capitalism in the United States and the triumph of democracy over state communism in the Soviet bloc countries. At present, the "free" television media in the United States are probably no more adversarial and no less propagandistic than Pravada or the television stations in the Eastern European countries. Hence the very future of democracy is at stake—and development of a democratic communications system is necessary if democracy is to be realized. (p. 219)

Certainly recent events surrounding the official U.S. media censorship imposed by the military during the Gulf war has largely confirmed Kellner's pronouncement. However, the latest victory of the New Right's media disinformation/propaganda campaign has been through the invention of and concurrent attack upon what has been called the repressive 'left mandarin' regime of 'political correctness' that is supposedly sweeping North American university campuses. This so-called movement embraces every hate-provoking stereotype of every alleged 'radical' imaginable. Educators who work in the public schools and the universities are currently witnessing a well-orchestrated and singularly scandalous assault on efforts by progressive educators to make race, class, and gender issues central to the curriculum. The new left literacies that have been influenced by continental social theory, feminist theory and critical social theory in its many forms (postmodernist, post-colonialist and post-structuralist, etc.) are being characterized by New Right critics as a subversion of the political neutrality and ideological disinterestedness that they claim the enterprise of education should be all about.

MEDIA LITERACY AS COUNTER-HEGEMONIC PRACTICE

> Enlightenment, then, is finally bent on leaving nothing extant but its own implicit violence. As it proceeds to blast away each of its own prior pretexts, this explosive rationality comes ever closer, not to "truth"—which category it has long since shattered—but to the open realization of its own coercive animus, purified of *all* delusions—including, finally, rationality itself. Into the ideological vacuum which it has created so efficiently there rushes its own impulse to destroy and keep destroying . . .
>
> Crispin Miller, 1988, p. 315

Largely because of the way in which the media function to shape and merchandize morality and to construct forms of citizenship and individual and collective identity, our understanding of the meaning and importance of democracy has become impoverished in proportion to its dissolution and retreat from contemporary social life. Today's social ugliness that makes the bizarre appear normal is no longer just a surrealist fantasy, a proto-surrealist spin-off, or a Baudrillardean rehearsal for a futureless future. This scenario *is* the present historical moment, one that has arrived in a body bag—unravelled and stomped on by the logic of the fascist's steel-toed boot. Serial killer Ted Bundy has donated his multiple texts of identity to our structural unconscious and we are living them.

Current forms of collective sociality have been brought under the *nouvelle* aesthetic sign-form of Madonna's hyper-bra and Arnold Schwarzenegger's replicant super-cut biceps—part of a new politics of voyeurism and exhibitionism that celebrates the culture of commodified flesh over the emancipation of the body politic. We rehearse our lives under these signs rather than live them; we become curators and custodians of the detrius produced by the radical semiurgy that characterizes our current epoch rather than shapers of a new social vision. We have become unwanted visitors in the house of technology.

The fantasies of De Sade have become the urban equivalent of postmodern city life as affluent neighborhoods of the cyber-bourgeoise brush shoulders with the post-holocaust landscape of ravaged inner cities, creating new forms of envy and disgust. Given the current condition of *fin-de-siecle* ennui and paranoia, we have arrived at the zero-degree reality of the kind that once only graced the pages of surrealist manifestos and punk fanzines. Andre Breton's "simplest surrealist act"—firing a pistol into a crowd of strangers—is no longer just a turn-of-the-century symbolic disruption of the grudgingly mundane or a symbolic dislocation circulating in avant garde broadsheets. It is precisely in this current conjuncture that people really *are* shooting blindly into crowds: at children in hamburger establishments, at lunchtime patrons in small town diners, at employees and employers in factories and post-offices, at teachers and classmates in schools, at professor's and administrators, and at female engineering students in university seminar rooms. In the nihilistic extrapolation of the mass produced image as the emergent norm of postmodern subjectivity, we witness the eclipse of historical agency and the shrinkage of the democratic imaginary.

In the current historical juncture of democratic decline in the United States, ideals and images have become detached from their anchorage in stable and agreed-upon meaning and associations and are now beginning to assume a reality of their own. The self-referential world of the media is one that splinters, obliterates, peripheralizes, partitions and segments social space, time, knowledge, and subjectivity in order to unify, encompass, entrap, totalize and homogenize them *through the meta-form of entertainment*. What needs to be addressed is the way in which capitalism is able to secure this cultural and ideological totalization and homogenization through its ability to insinuate itself into social practices and private perceptions through various forms of media knowledges. Questions that need to be asked include: How are the subjectivities and identities of individuals and the production of media knowledges within popular culture mutually articulated? To what extent does the hyperreal correspond to practices of self and social constitution in contemporary society? Do we remain "sunk in the depressing hyperbole of the hyperreal" (Poster, 1990: 66), encysted in the monologic self-referentiality of the mode of information? Or do we establish a politics of refusal that is able to contest the tropes that govern Western colonialist narratives of supremacy and oppression? What isn't being discussed is the pressing need within pedagogical sites for creating a media literate citizenry that can disrupt, contest, and transform media apparatuses so that they no longer possess the power to infantilize the population and continue to create passive and paranoid social subjects (McLaren and Hammer, 1991; Hammer and McLaren, 1991).

In its unannounced retreat over the past decade, democracy has managed to recreate power through the spectacularization of its after-image, that is, through corporatized image management and the creation of national myths of identity, primarily through mass media techniques that give democracy an "afterglow" once it has faded from the horizon of concrete possibility. In other words, the mandarins of media have created democracy as a "necessary illusion." Herman and Chomsky (1988: xi) note:

> If . . . the powerful are able to fix the premises of discourse, to decide what the general populace is allowed to see, hear, and think about, and to "manage" public opinion by regular propaganda campaigns, the standard view of how the system works is at serious odds with reality.

A critical media literacy recognizes that we inhabit a photocentric, aural, and televisual culture in which the proliferation of photographic and electronically produced images and sounds serves as a form of media catechism—perpetual pedagogy—through which individuals ritually encode and evaluate the engagements they make in the various discursive contexts of everyday life (McLaren, 1986; Giroux and McLaren, in press; Giroux and McLaren, 1991; McLaren, 1988). It is a form of literacy that understands media representations—whether photographs, television, print, film, or another form—as not merely productive of knowledge but also of subjectivity. John B.

Thompson (1990) has sketched out some elements of the media literacy we have in mind.

Following Thompson, we suggest that a media literacy must elucidate the typical modes of appropriation of mass-mediated products (i.e., the technical media of transmission, the availability of the skills, capacities and resources required to decode the messages transmitted by particular media and the rules, conventions and practical exigencies associated with such decoding). In other words, how do particular individuals throughout the course of their everyday existence receive ritualized messages and integrate them on a daily basis (see McLaren, 1986)? Individuals do not soak up messages as passive onlookers or "inert sponges," but rather engage in an ongoing process of interpreting and incorporating such messages. A critical media literacy must therefore be attentive to the social-historical characteristics of contexts of reception and see them as *situated practices*. Here Thompson refers to the spacial and temporal features of reception (in the case of TV, for instance, we would be concerned with who watches, for how long, in what contexts); the relations of power and the distribution of resources among recipients; the social institutions within which individuals appropriate mediated knowledges; as well as the systematic asymmetries and differentials that characterize the contexts of reception.

A critical media literacy must also relate the everyday understanding of media messages to social-historical characteristics (i.e., race, class, and gender characteristics). It must analyze how mediated messages are discursively elaborated as individuals reject or incorporate them as part of their everyday social practices. And finally, a critical media literacy needs to explore how the appropriation of mediated messages creates *virtual communities* of recipients that are extended across time and space. Such a media literacy seeks to move beyond Eco's suggestion of creating a "semiological guerrilla movement" based on an anarchistic individualism in which each recipient of mediated messages interprets the transmitted multiplicity of images whichever way he or she chooses (Kearney, 1988). Rather, the critical media literacy that we envision seeks to create communities of resistance, counter-public spheres, and oppositional pedagogies that can resist dominant forms of meaning by offering new channels of communication, circuits of semiotic production, codifications of experience, and perspectives of reception which unmask the political linkage between images, their means of production and reception, and the social practices they legitimate.

However, the credibility of our critical pedagogy of media literacy is handicapped by a formidable paradox: Within certain academic and pedagogical circles, the very recognition of media as powerful hegemonic apparatuses impairs the validity of doing media studies in that those who critique television and other media apparatuses are often seen as complicitous with those very structures of domination that they seek to contest. In addition to constructing a model of media power that speaks to the legitimacy of engaging in a cultural studies approach, a critical media literacy needs to addresses sufficiently *the specificity and partial autonomy of media discourses*, that is, a model that "would analyze how the media produce identities, role models, and ideals; how they create new forms of discourse and experience; how they define situations, set agendas, and filter out oppositional ideas; and how they set limits and boundaries beyond which political discourse is not allowed" (Kellner, 1990: 18).

Of serious concern in our own work is how electronic prophets who manufacture personalities and manage personal images have been able to turn wimp Presidents into wrathful avengers and a frustrated and self-hating citizenry into phallomilitary warrior citizens who are currently being conditioned to re-direct a media-instilled hatred of "Sad'am" against a familiar enemy within its own ranks: the poor, the homeless, people of color, those who comprise the detrius of capitalism and white man's democracy, those who are already oppressed by race, gender, caste, and circumstance. After all, what is the mission of postmodern media if not the attempt to "Americanize the un-American" through particular forms of cultural assertion linked to capital and patterns of consumption but also on a grander scale to interlocking international networks of finance and surveillance.

Needed is a counter-hegemonic media literacy in which subjectivities may be lived and analyzed outside the dominant regime of official print culture—a culture that is informed by a technophobic retreat from emerging techno-aesthetic cultures of photography, film, and electronically mediated messages. Different media knowledges manage to reveal in different ways what is at stake in naming ourselves as gendered, sexual, and desiring body/subjects. Not only would a critical media literacy warn us of the dangers in constructing social practices that enforce misogynous, homophobic, and patriarchal acts of naming, it would also construct the grounds for a transformative and emancipatory politics of difference (McLaren, forthcoming). Much of this work necessarily involves not only understanding the disabling and emancipatory potential of the media knowledges that are available to us, but also the importance of struggling to overturn current arrangements of extra-communicational forms of power and the social relations that undergird—and in some instances help to overdetermine—the production of such knowledges. In this regard, a critical pedagogy of media literacy seeks to produce partial, contingent, but necessary historical truths that will provide some of the necessary conditions for the emancipation of the many public spheres that make up our social and institutional life, truths which—unlike those created and sponsored by the media—recognize their social constructedness and historicity and the institutional and social arrangements that they help to legitimate.

In his recent book *Common Culture*, Paul Willis argues that we live in an era in which high culture or official culture has lost its dominance. Official culture - the best efforts of Allan Bloom and E.D. Hirsch Jr. notwithstanding - cannot hope to colonize, dominate, or contain the everyday and the mundane aspects of life. Formal aesthetics have been replaced by a grounded aesthetics. The main seeds of cultural development are to be found in the commercial provision of cultural commodities.

According to Willis, one way to work for the dialectical development of cultural knowledge 'back to its owners' and letting them develop it. 'Let them control the conditions, production, and consumption of their own symbolic resources'.

This, however, is no easy task, and there are no guarantees, especially given that symbolic resources 'are lodged in ther own historical patterns of power and logics of production'. But if the grounded aesthetics of everyday cultural life for youth are concretely embedded in the sensuous human activities of meaning-making, there are implications for a critical approach to media literacy. Media literacy must help students 'to increase the range, complexity, elegance, self-consciousness and purposefulness of this involvement' in symbolic work. It must provide them with the symbolic resources for creative self and social formation on order that the can more critically re-enter the broader plains of common culture.

Symbolic work within informal cultural is unlike the symbolic work of school in fundamental ways.

> Where everyday symbolic work differs from what is normally thought of as 'education' is that it 'culturally produces' from its own chosen cultural resources. Psychologically, at least, the informal symbolic workers of common cultures feel they really 'own' and can therefore manipulate their resources as materials and tools—unlike the books at school which are 'owned' by the teachers . . .

For these reasons, creative symbolic work within informal culture offers important possibilities for 'oppositional, independent or alternative symbolizations of the self'. Moreover, human beings must not be regarded merely as human capital or labour power, but as 'creative *citizens*, full of their own sensuous symbolic capacities and activities and taking a hand in the construction of their own identities'. The pursuit of emancipation and equality, therefore, requires more than being made equal as workers. It calls for all to be fully developed as *cultural producers*.

Critical media literacy is essential to this struggle in several ways. We need to be literate enough to deny the injunctions by which identities are constructed through official culture—in whatever form it appears. This presupposes that we create what Judith Butler calls 'alternative domains of cultural intelligibility . . . new possibilities . . . that contest the rigid codes of hierarchical binarisms'. Within such hybrid pedagogical spaces educators can give greater attention too the everyday artefacts of popular culture and forms of knowledge that avoid the elitist tyranny of the center. Critical media literacy enables us to rearticulate the role of the social agent so that s/he can make affective alliances with forms of agency that provide new grounds of popular authority; ground to stand on from which to give voice to narratives of human freedom.

Critical media literacy helps us identify and answer the question: how do essentially arbitrarily organized cultural codes, products of historical struggle among not only regimes of signs but regimes of material production also, come to represent the 'real', the 'natural', and the 'necessary'? A critical literacy reveals that signs do not correspond to an already determined metaphysical real, nor are they transhistorically indeterminable or undecidable. Rather, their meaning-making possibilities and their meaningfulness are legitimized through the specificity of discursive and material struggles, and the political linkages between them. A critical perspective the media also enables teachers and students to understand the dangers in considering literacy to be a private or individual competency—or set of competencies—rather than a complex circulation of economic, political, and ideological practices that inform daily life; that invite or solicit students to acquiesce in their social and gendered positions within a highly stratified society and accept the agent-hood assigned to them along the axes of race/class/gender.

To this extent critical media literacy becomes the interpretation of the social present for the purpose of transforming the cultural life of paticular groups, for questioning tacit assumptions and unarticulated presuppositions of our current cultural and social formations and the subjectivities and capacities for agent-hood that they foster. Critical media literacy is directed at understanding the ongoing social struggles over the signs of culture and over the definition of social reality—over what is considered legitimate and preferred meaning at any given historical moment.

Perhaps it has never been more urgent for students to begin to understand how the process of representation and identification works. Precisely because it has the power to constitute our subjective identifications in particular ways, the media possess the power to influence political life. To become media literate in a world of postmodern literacies means that students must become historians of representation who realize that the shared systems of ideological representations we carry with us as agents of history *become* our history.

REFERENCES

Buck-Morss, Susan. (1989). *The Dialectics of Seeing: Walter Benjamin and the Arcades Project*. Cambridge, Mass.: The MIT Press.

Butler, Judith. (1991). "The Imperialist Subject." *Journal of Urban and Cultural Studies*, vol 2, no. 1, pp. 73-78.

_________ (1990). *Gender Trouble*. New York and London: Routledge.

Cohn, Carole E. (1991). "Decoding Military Doublespeak." *Ms.*, vol. 1, no. 5 (May 28), pp. 88.

Cooke, Miriam. (1991). "Phallomilitary Spectacles in the DTO." *Journal of Urban and Cultural Studies*, vol. 2, no. 1, pp. 27-40.

Ellis, Caroline, Khauun, Saeeda, and Plott, Steve. (1991). "Highway to Hell." *New Statesman and Society* (June 21), pp. 21-28.

Ewen, Stuart. (1988). *All Consuming Images*. New York: Basic Books.

Gerbner, George. (1989/90). "Media Literacy: TV vs. Reality." *Adbusters*, vol. 1, no. 2, p. 12.

Gitlin, Todd. (1986). "We Build Excitement." In Todd Gitlin (Ed.) *Watching Television*. New York: Pantheon Books.

Giroux, Henry, and McLaren, Peter. (in press). "Media Hegemony." Introduction to *Media Knowledge* by James Schwoch, Mimi White, and Susan Reilly. Albany, New York: State University of New York Press.

_________ (1991). "Leon Golub's Radical Pessimism: Toward a Pedagogy of Representation." *Exposure*, vol. 28, no. 12, pp. 18-33.

_________. "Introduction." In Henry Giroux and Peter McLaren (Eds.) *Critical Pedagogy, the State, and Cultural Struggle*. Albany, New York: State University of New York Press.

Grossberg, Larry. (1988). *It's a Sin*. Sydney, Australia: Power Publications.

Hammer, Rhonda, and McLaren, Peter (in press). "Le Paradoxe de L'Image: Connaissance Mediatique et Declin de la Qualite de La Vie." *Anthropologie et Societies*, special issue, "Pouvoir des Images."

_________ (1991). "Rethinking the Dialectic." *Educational Theory*, vol. 41, no. 1, pp. 23-46.

Hammer, Rhonda, and Wilden, Anthony. (1987). "Women in Production: The Chorus Line 1932-1980." In Anthony Wilden, *The Rules are No Game*. London and New York: Routledge and Kegan Paul, pp. 283-300.

Haraway, Donna. (1991). "On Wimps." *Journal of Urban and Cultural Studies*, vol. 2, no. 1, pp. 41-44.

Herman, Edward S. and Chomsky, Noam. (1988). *Manufacturing Consent*. New York: Pantheon Books.

Jhally, Sut. (1990). *The Codes of Advertising*. London and New York: Routledge.

Kearney, Richard. (1988). *The Wake of Imagination.* Minneapolis: University of Minnesota Press.

Kellner, Doug. (1990). *Television and the Crisis of Democracy.* Boulder and Oxford: Westview Press.

Laren, Ernest. (1991). "Gulf War TV." *Jump Cut*, no. 36, pp. 3-10.

Lutz, William. (1989). *Doublespeak.* New York: HarperCollins Publishers.

McKenzie, Wark (1991). "From Fordism to Sonyism: Perverse Readings of the New World Order." *New Formations*, No. 15, pp. 43-54.

McLaren, Peter. (forthcoming). *Radical Pedagogy: Postcolonial Politics in a Postmodern World.* London and New York: Routledge.

_________ (1986). *Schooling as a Ritual Performance: Towards a Political Economy of Educational Symbols and Gestures.* London and New York: Routledge and Kegan Paul.

_________ (in press). "Introduction." In Peter McLaren (Ed.) *Postmodernism, Postcolonialism, and Pedagogy.* Albert Park: Australia: James Nicholas Publishers, Ltd.

_________ (1988). "Critical Pedagogy and the Politics of Literacy." *The Harvard Educational Review*, vol. 58, no. 2, pp. 213-234.

_________. (1985). "Contemporary Ritual Studies: A Post-Turnerian Perspective." *Semiotic Inquiry*, vol 5, no. 1, pp. 78-85.

McLaren, Peter and Hammer, Rhonda. (1989). "Critical Pedagogy and the Postmodern Challenge: Towards a Critical Postmodernist Pedagogy of Liberation." *Educational Foundations*, vol. 3, no. 3, pp. 29-62.

Miller, Crispin Mark. (1989). *Boxed In: The Culture of TV.* Evanston, IL.: Northwestern University Press.

Naureckas, Jim. (1991). "Gulf War Courage: The Worst Censorship Was At Home." *Extra!*, vol. 4, no. 3 (May, 1991), pp. 3-10.

Norris, Margot (1991). "Military Censorship and the Body Count in the Persian Gulf War." *Cultural Critique*, No. 19, pp. 223-245.

Poster, Mark. (1990). *The Mode of Information.* Chicago: The University of Chicago Press.

Poster, Mark (1991). "War in the Mode of Information." *Cultural Critique*, No. 19, pp. 217-222.

Rogin, Michael. (1990). "'Make My Day!': Spectacle as Amnesia in Imperial Politics." *Representations*, vol. 29, pp. 99-123.

Schiller, Herbert I. (1989). *Culture, Inc.: The Corporate Takeover of Public Expression.* New York and Oxford: Oxford University Press.

Schulte-Sasse, Jochen and Schulte-Sasse, Linda (1991). "War, Otherness, and Illusionary Identifications with the State." *Cultural Critique*, No. 19, pp. 67-95.

Schwoch, James, White, Mimi, and Reilly, Susan. (in press). *Media Knowledge.* Albany, New York: State University of New York Press.

Shohat, Ella. (1991). "The Media's War." *Social Text*, vol. 9, no. 3, pp. 135-141.

Soley, Laurence. (1991). "Brookings: Stand-In for the Left." *Extra!*, vol. 4, no. 3 (May, 1991), p. 6.

Werckmeister, O.K. (1991). *Citadel Culture.* Chicago: The University of Chicago Press.

Thompson, John B. *Ideology and Modern Culture.* Stanford, California: Stanford University Press.

Wilden, Anthony. (1987). *The Rules are No Game.* London and New York: Routledge and Kegan Paul.

Willis, P. (1990). *Common Culture.* Boulder, Colorado: Westview Press.

Zizek, Slavoj. (1991). *Looking Awry: An Introduction to Jacques Lacan Through Popular Culture.* Cambridge, Mass.: The MIT Press.

Chapter VII

Geopolitics, Media and the Public Sphere

Susan Reilly

As we approach the year 2000 nations are going through the convulsions marking the end of an era dominated by the contest between attempts to operationalize two great political ideologies—capitalism and communism. Although these ideologies were viewed as antagonistic, Emmanuel Wallerstein (1991) summarizes their commonalties: 1) they shared the heritage of the Enlightenment, 2) they shared the belief that people could rationally construct a good society, 3) they shared the idea that the state should be the focus of collective decision making, 4) they shared a secular view of the future, 5) they shared the ideal of self-determination and equality of nations, 6) they shared the view that universal values could exist which every person could support. They also shared a belief that democracy was the form of government that would ensure the greatest opportunity for the exercise of citizenship. Both ideologies have failed.

The economic collapse experienced in the former Soviet Union and Eastern Europe was severe enough that the rival capitalist ideology is being embraced in desperation, regardless of the social and environmental consequences apparent in the west. As the victory of capitalism is proclaimed, what goes unmentioned, but fully understood, is that the promises of modernity offered by western industrialized nations have all too often proved false and that advanced capitalism too is a dying ideology. Communism's central failure, according to David Held (1987) is its reduction of political power to economic power and its refusal to recognize the dangers of maintaining accountability in a system of centralized political power. Capitalism's central failure, Held (1987) continues, is its insistence on viewing markets as benign and its refusal to recognize the distortions of economic power. The failure of the operationalization of both ideologies in the east and in the west has caused human suffering, environmental devastation, and wide-spread political disillusionment and cynicism. The perversions of the political process that exist in both the east and the west are evidence of the crisis faced by nations as they re-evaluate democratic forms of government in the light of these major ideological failures.

In order to explore the question of whether democracy is still possible, several changes in focus are occurring among critical theorists. First, there is a growing emphasis on culture in addition to economics, as an arena in which human agency may be exercised. And second, racism and sexism are being added to class as major sites of social contestation and identity formation, and as important constituencies in the struggle for the rights and responsibilities of citizenship. There is growing recognition that the interaction of race, sex, and class that constitute the effects of intra- and inter-national post colonialism form the basis for the real inequalities in the division of labor, access to education, distribution of power and assumptions of morality (Giroux, 1988; Wallerstein, 1991). In fact, the boundaries of nation states dissolve and the effects of post colonialism become geocultural. Now, nations of the "old world" as well as nations of the "new world" are multicultural and the struggle for citizenship involves the pressure of new groups against the resistance of old groups opposed to the extension of what used to be their rights and privileges (Barbalet, 1988). In the debate about the reconstruction of democracy, the political right decries the excesses of egalitarianism brought about by post colonialism which they feel threaten to make societies ungovernable (LaClau and Mouffe, 1990). The right fears an adversary culture where equality of opportunity becomes equality of results, and where equality between individuals becomes equality between groups. However, the desire to maintain an individualist definition of rights could solidify the hierarchical relations which presently prevent the inclusion of various races, classes, and genders in full citizenship (LaClau and Mouffe, 1990). The left argues that valorizing the individual exercise of rights and ignoring the conditions that influence groups based on race, class, and gender, reinforces the very forms of exclusion associated with the accumulation of private property and wealth which created the need for the designation of equal citizenship in the first place (Hall & Held, 1989). For this reason, LaClau and Mouffe (1990) contend, "the left should not totally reject liberal democratic ideology, but should deepen and expand it in the direction of a radical and truly plural democracy."

The traditional discourse about citizenship assumes the equality of citizens rights under the law, but as Hall & Held (1989) point out those "rights must be practically enacted and realized through actual participation in the community." Citizens' rights are both civil and social. Civil rights protect the citizen's life from unjust interference by the state and social rights insure the benefits guaranteed by the state (Barbalet, 1988). An interpretation of civil rights might be that there is no law which can prevent a person from buying property and social rights might protect that person from having their property taken from them illegally by another person; but the fact that only certain persons can afford to buy property to begin with is overlooked. In this case, as Hall & Held (1989) contend, "formal equity under the law may not translate to social practice." But if civil and social rights are not able to be practically applied, then as Hall & Held (1989) contend, liberty becomes an abstract principle without profound consequences in people's experience of everyday life.

In the older universalist conception of citizenship, differences are absorbed into one common identity, but that ignores the variety of needs, and diverse histories, discourses, and practices that constitute the modern political subject. Therefore a new conception of citizenship must come to terms with difference and allow for the complex interplay of identities, desires, and needs of the various groups participating in a society. A redefinition of democracy should allow for an expansive view of citizenship where new rights can be added to a body of rights as new social forces introduce themselves into the national community (Barbalet, 1988).

It is clear that citizens in media-centric societies like the U.S. are no longer willing to uphold their responsibilities. Curtis Gens, director of the Washington-based Committee for the Study of the American Electorate, reports that the U.S. has the lowest rate of voter participation of any democracy in the world—less than 40% (Gens, 1988). Gens suggests that this may be the result of video politics. He asserts that citizens become spectators, entertained by the political melodrama, but not involved in the democratic process that it is supposed to promote. However, as David Held (1987) states in *Models of Democracy*, people cannot escape from politics because it shapes and influences every aspect of their lives. It is at the center of the resolution or exacerbation of the problems people experience on a daily basis. Held (1987) contends that politics is about power and about the ability of social agents to utilize power to transform their environment. Although, at present, politicians are not trusted and politics is associated with hypocrisy, no politics is not an option. People must empower themselves by transforming politics and the forces that constitute it in ways that enable them to shape and control their lives. In order to do this, Held (1987) contends, citizens must not only be willing to accept the fact the political life is a central part of their existence but also agree to participate in a system of collective decision making which maximizes involvement in public affairs. Such a system must promote discussion and debate leading to competition, contestation, and separation as well as mediation, negotiation, compromise, and affiliation between diverse groups struggling to realize their needs and desires as citizens of a radical democracy.

The centrality of "the common good," maximum participation in government by the people, and rational debate about political issues are considered essential elements of democracy (Herbst, 1991). This national debate takes place in the public sphere. Jurgen Habermas (1990) defines the public sphere as a space in which citizens deliberate about their political interests and attempt to determine what actions to take to arrive at "the common good." Habermas (1990) suggests that this space should be distinct from the state in order to allow for critique of state policies and distinct from the economy in order to be free of market relations and material concerns.

The public sphere, Habermas contends, emerged at the end of feudalism when the economic independence provided by the ownership of private property allowed for the formation of independent presses, universities, and political parties where institutionalized discursive interaction was practiced and the resulting public opinion shaped the direction of the state. However, in modern liberal democracies where government functions primarily as a protector of private property, the uneven distribution of wealth caused by monopoly capitalism led to unequal access to and subsequent control of the public sphere by advantaged groups. The bourgeois public sphere suppressed the alternative and oppositional political interests of the proletariat, and both the bourgeoisie and the proletariat repressed internal interests related to race and gender. Therefore, the political interests of the counter publics which formed around issues of class, race, and gender were not included in the liberal debate concerning "the common good."

The introduction of commercial electronic media further transformed the public sphere, reducing the importance of the old public spaces where people interacted with one another, creating a mass audience that passively watched a small elite group of public figures and journalists present and consider political issues. Both the state and the economy influenced this public arena. Here the repressive mode of domination found in the bourgeois public sphere was replaced by a hegemonic one based on acquiescence to a dominant view of "the common good" (Eley, 1991). This hegemony was conveyed through a politics of representation presented as entertainment, news, and advertising presented on the electronic media. Maximum public participation in national debate about "the common good" was curtailed by a pervasive view of capitalism as good and socialism as evil and an appeal to the self-interest of the private consumer in his/her own domestic environment rather than the civil responsibility of the citizen who is part of a larger public life (Garnham, 1986).

Although Habermas' idealized public sphere was restricted to the discussion of issues relevant to certain aspects of the life of the propertied classes, the notion of a space where access to information affecting multiple public goods is available, where discussion is as free as possible of both state and economic influence, and where groups expect to represent their views on an equal basis, is a powerful view of how the media could function in a democratic society (Curran, 1991). The media, and in particular television, are central to the formation of public opinion because they not only distribute, on a national scale, the information necessary for citizens to make informed choices but also because they provide a national forum for debate. Therefore, they are logically the principle institutions of the public sphere in contemporary media-centric societies (Curran, 1991).

However, major restructuring of the media is necessary in order for them to assume the function of primary public spheres in democratic societies. It is important to note at this point, that an important debate is taking place in Western and Eastern Europe as well as in Central and South America about the efficacy of market-based media systems. For the past twenty years, commercial television has made increasingly significant in-roads into Western European societies which used to strongly support public service television as central to both the dissemination of political information and the preservation of culture. In the argument for deregulation, market competition is being associated with freedom from state censorship and seen as the way to maximize individual choice.

Changes in the broadcasting systems in the newly configured states in Eastern Europe also seem to be moving in the direction of the deregulated market-led television model in opposition to former state operated models. In Central and South America, debate is occurring about the value of commercial media as corporate entities which may stimulate the economy versus increased state expenditures on public service media which may aid in national development. In the light of the movement toward a commercial media model, a number of myths about the value of commercial media need to be examined clearly. According to the market liberal rationale, competition between commercial media businesses provides for the greatest variety of media outlets offering the highest quality programming. Further, a free market is believed to ensure entry for any worthy media enterprise with a good product to offer. People are supposed to be able to get what they want when they exercise their free choice because the surviving businesses will provide the services most desired and valued.

The idea that unrestricted competition is possible in commercial media markets is questionable. Media monopolies like the corporate owners of the three U.S. commercial networks—General Electric, Lawrence Tisch, Capitol Cities Communications—end up controlling the market by buying up smaller competitors. As a result the cost of entering the media market become prohibitively high and only the cartels can afford to take the economic risks (Keane, 1991; Curran, 1991). The high cost of establishing a media enterprise restricts access to those groups who do not have wealth or influence. Their points of view rarely reach a national audience. If they do, they are filtered through the lens of dominant ideological forces (Keane, 1991; Curran, 1991; Schwock, White, and Reilly, 1991).

Talk of the availability of multiple channels of information available through technologies like cable or satellite distribution, in the U.S. experience, becomes the endless repetition of network programming on various affiliate stations plus a handful of new channels like CNN, MTV, and the Sports Channel. Viewers with sufficient income can purchase additional entertainment programs by subscription or pay-per-view arrangements. It is clear that sheer numbers of media outlets do not ensure that people have access to the information they need to secure or defend their rights as citizens nor does it allow them to enter the debate as producers.

The claim that market competition maximizes individual choice is problematic. First, the media monopolies, concerned primarily with profits, support a constricted and homogenous selection of programs tailored to attract the largest possible audience, which maximizes advertising revenue. Since the mid-eighties when new management procedures were introduced by corporate owners, all three U.S. networks have lost significant numbers of news personnel and must operate with reduced news budgets, because news is not a money maker in the U.S. media market. Second, regarding the audience as an array of individuals, works against the development of programming that meets the needs of groups that form for a variety of reasons; for example, ethnic or racial groups, groups formed on the basis of sexual orientation, age groups (the elderly or children), political parties, religious groups, social activist groups and unions (Keane, 1991; Curran, 1991). The majority audience, composed of the individual consumers sought by advertisers, has little to do with the political collectives that need to be responded to in a pluralist democracy. Presently there is no place for these interests within the economic rules of commercial media in media-centric countries.

The necessity to hold the interest of viewers long enough for them to see the commercials creates production values which include quick cuts, short sound bites, fast-paced action and skeleton narratives. It is difficult for an audience to develop an appreciation for the complexity and nuance which characterizes cultural difference when they are conditioned to hop from one thing to the next with only the simplest connections (Keane, 1991; Schwock, White, and Reilly, 1991).

The problems mentioned above relate to the influence of economics on media corporations. According to market liberal thinking, the constraints of the market should be tolerated in order to guarantee that the media are free from state intervention. In fact, the media are supposed to serve as watchdogs overseeing the actions of the state and warning citizens about potential abuses of power. This view of the role of privately owned media was developed in reaction to the period of absolute monarchy, when the state was unrepresentative and arbitrary. Free speech and free press were a defense against the authority of feudalism (Curran, 1991). A free press was supposed to make possible the spread of rational knowledge which contained universal values (Keane, 1991). There are several basic problems with the modern operationalization of freedom of speech and of the press. Too often these "freedoms" have been construed as the right of media corporations to gather and disseminate information, in the words of the universal Declaration of Human Rights, "regardless of frontiers," in order to profit from the use of that information. Too often those in control of media corporations view themselves as the agents of rational consensus and as a result all opinions are subject to disputation except their own (Keane, 1991). It is ironic, as John Keane (1991) points out, that the language of free speech is used often to silence free speech.

Additionally, the state does interfere in the working of commercial media but this interference is not openly acknowledged. John Keane (1991) outlines a number of examples of such interference in *Media and Democracy*: 1) attempts to convince media owners, editors, and journalists to conform to government wishes about the release of certain information by means of instructions, threats, warnings, guidelines, or off-the-record phone calls. In extreme cases, outright bans and arrests have occurred after publication as, for example, in the case of the Pentagon papers in the late stages of the Vietnam War; 2) monitoring the activities or finances of members of the press or members of political organizations covered by the press, with surveillance devices, by government agencies such as the FBI, the CIA, or the IRS. This occurred extensively during the civil rights activities of the late '50s and '60s in the U.S.; 3) the use of lies or calculated secrecy to mislead the press when it is decided that certain policies or activities might be resisted or negatively construed; for example, the Reagan administration's handling of the press during the Grenada invasion; 4) the government's use of public relations campaigns, including the staging of pseudo-events, planned leaks, off-the-record briefings, arranged interviews and journalist fact finding trips organized by the Pentagon or the State Department, in order to ensure a particular slant to important new stories; 5) the formation and/or use of private organizations, such as executive clubs, paramilitary organizations, and special interest groups to provide unpublicized services to the government like information collection or financial support for clandestine activities, as was the case in the Iran/Contra affair. The public knowledge of the existence of this kind of government interference causes people to place the media and journalists in the same hypocritical category as politics and politicians.

If the media, and in particular television, are going to become revitalized public spheres in a new pluralist democracy, radical structural changes must occur. In order to create a neutral ground where the struggle for citizenship rights occurs in civil society, the media must be as independent as possible from both state and market influence. Only then can a complex articulation of vertical, horizontal, and diagonal channels of communication be possible between individuals, groups, and state and economic power structures (Curran, 1991).

John Keane (1991) and James Curran (1991) have developed models of new democratic media systems, which would allow for the contest of a plurality of opinions, experiences, histories, discourses, demands, and desires in a national arena. The main points of these models warrant consideration. Curran's model has three major features. First, the media must provide for public dialogue which includes a diversity of perspectives in both news and entertainment programs. The media should enable groups to interrogate their social experience and question dominant cultural myths about their identifies. If people could explore what it is like to be "other," then arguments opposing ideological subordination might be understood and supported by empathetic coalitions. Second, the media should invigorate civil society by assisting various organizations to operate as representatives for the views of their supporters. As agencies of representation, media could facilitate the expression of alternative viewpoints. Third, the media should facilitate democratic procedures for achieving collectively agreed upon aims, like informing the electorate about political choices. But rather than reinforcing a single national identity and promoting universal values, the media should promote collective self-reflection and encourage critique and dissent so that an informed public opinion can influence matters of state.

Curran's model includes a core public sphere consisting of competing publicly owned media organizations. Feeding this core are connections to different organizations in civil society such as a civic media sector, which would include media linked to collective organizations like political parties, subcultural media like magazines for minority groups, and organizational media like trade union newsletters; a professional media sector, where committed social service organizations would employ journalists to work on their behalf to heighten people's social consciousness; a private enterprise sector, where competition between commercial media would be encouraged but regulated, so that it would not dominate the system; and a social market sector, where new forms of programming unrepresented elsewhere would be allowed to flourish, similar to channel 4 in Britain.

Curran's model would not only provide a public forum for debate, but also would provide the network to link groups to this forum, as well as providing room for a variety of extra-political experiences and performances.

The aim of John Keane's model for public service media is the development of a publicly funded self-organizing, cosmopolitan civil society which is not dominated by commodity production or by the state. Keane's public access media would be central to the social life of such a civil society. It would break down media monopolies, lift restrictions on audience choices of programs, and promote itself as an instrument of public good enabling people to both receive and send a plurality of opinions. Media access by minority groups would be assured by regarding media organizations as common carriers and guaranteeing certain open access hours. Democratic decision making procedures would guide program development and editorial choices. These democratic procedures, such as including representatives from relevant social groups would also be applied to the organizational structures of media corporations in the selection of boards of directors and managers. Both Keane and Curran support the subsidy of small newspapers, magazines, television, and radio stations representing minority opinions, in order to strengthen the foundations of a pluralist civil society.

A view of a media system specific to the U.S. that would promote democracy is provided by Douglas Kellner (1990). Kellner identifies the 1980's as the period when the worst aspects of commercial broadcasting were intensified in the States. During this decade, the three major commercial networks merged with other corporate conglomerates and the bottom line became all important. As a result, news staffs were cut and the number of traditional documentary and public affairs programs were reduced in favor of an increased number of entertainment programs with increased advertising. Concomitantly, during this decade, the U.S. exhibited the lowest voter turnout in major elections of all the western capitalist democracies. The scarcity of information about significant social issues may well have contributed to creating an uninformed and unmotivated electorate.

At the same time that citizens were detaching from national party politics, there was tremendous growth in special interest groups, an increasing number of social action groups organized around issues of race, class, gender, and sexual orientation. The general strengthening of non-governmental organizations (NGO's) that intervened in social policy, by-passing grid locked government agencies (Serra, 1993). These groups began to utilize alternative modes of communication, including new computer technologies and direct mail to provide information to members and to organize new recruits. The media system that Kellner proposes for the States provides the means for these organizations of civil society to influence media content at both a local and the national level, thereby diversifying the number of points of view available to all citizens.

Firsts, he suggests that there be an enlarged and strengthened system of public television and radio. This would require instituting a means of guaranteed funding that would free the Corporation for Public Broadcasting (CPB) from the political strangle hold of annual appropriations from Congress and would insure sufficient funds for long term program planning. Additionally, a revised selection process for the selection of members of the CPB would be required, that would minimize political influence and maximize public input. Examples may be found in Western Europe where organizations in civil society provide representatives for public service television boards of directors.

Second, Kellner suggests an expanded system of public access television and radio. With some notable exceptions like Austin (Texas) Community Television (Kellner, 1990), public access has languished in the States since the FCC mandated that cable systems provide channels for state and local government, educational and community use. But public access provides a place for progressive intervention into a closed media system. Special interest groups, social action organizations, and NGO's could work separately or in unison to provide the resources to put together segments for weekly programs to advance common concerns and interests. This kind of programming could play a decisive role in local political life by forming broader constituencies.

Finally, Kellner suggests the development of a public satellite network that would be open to groups presently excluded from national news programming. Network news programs tend to be closed systems relying on the same government sources over and over for commentary (Kellner, 1990). If the FCC mandated a national public access satellite channel required by all cable companies, not only would good local public access programming be able to be seen nationally, but also many national NGO's could provide programming, for example, trade unions, religious organizations, the Red Cross, Amnesty International, the Sierra Club, etc.

These new visions of the media as revitalized public spheres functioning as integral parts of pluralist democracies rest on the premise that media should be instrumental in the struggle between various social forces for the rights and responsibilities of citizenship. But how will the public be prepared to take part in this public sphere? In the U.S., a colonized country populated by native peoples, colonizers, slaves, and immigrants, plurality is embraced symbolically but is extremely difficult to achieve in reality. Racism, classism, and sexism have been malignant forces for hundreds of years. European nations, now in the post colonial era, are beginning to experience the intractability of the fear of difference that the "new world" has known for some time. This realization comes about as old universalist claims about the cohesiveness of nationality are being challenged and the acceptance of difference is being recognized as essential for democracy's survival. Many people are not prepared to value difference, nor are they prepared to accept the need for confrontation and contest. These new ideas run counter to the soothing platitudes about everyone being part of the melting pot. It is frightening to recognize that some aspects of cultural difference just don't melt down or fit in. Dealing with difference presents a challenge to the vision of pluralist democracy. Before citizens can participate in a revitalized public sphere, they need to be educated about difference and its role in the process of acquiring the rights of citizenship.

Public education has gone through a transformation similar to that described by Habermas (1990) in relation to the public sphere. In the early eighteen hundreds public education was a reaction against the abuse of authority exercised by the aristocratic class for whom education was part of a tradition of noblesse oblige. The movement for universal suffrage in the States was borne out of the same liberal principles that supported democracy as the most representative form of government. The extension of the right to education to the lower classes was premised on the Miltonian notion that individuals would be able to make the right decisions as part of an electorate if they were able to read many political arguments. Like the public sphere, public education was originally a transformative site, where the existing social order based on power and privilege was to be challenged and re-made, maximizing justice and equality for all citizens. However, with the advance of monopoly capitalism, public education began to lose its place as a site of democratic political struggle and began to perform a primarily economic function as an institution responsible for training people to take their places in the corporate, industrial, and military work forces. Teachers became political professionals rather than reformers, and curriculums reinforced conflict-free, ideal cultural narratives which smoothed over social contradictions and equated the support for economic productivity, the national defense and patriotism with good citizenship. The valuing of compliance and harmony as necessary conditions for industrial production resulted in the regulation of dissent to deviant behavior (Giroux, 1988).

After the second world war, the ascension of technology, the advent of the cold war and the expansion of mass culture, in the States, interacted to solidify public education's role in establishing cultural uniformity. An educational discourse that valued competitive individualism and submerged the continuing struggle of ethnic, racial, and gender groups emerged. Culture was presented as if it were a warehouse of artifacts instead of a continually changing process (Giroux, 1988). Educators encouraged an uneasy harmony—called "getting along with one another"—that denied the constant conflicts and contradictions of people's lives. This refusal to acknowledge difference led to a form of cultural amnesia thought to be instrumental in the 70-80 percent school drop out rate for urban Puerto Rican students in the States; the 48 percent drop out rate for African Americans; and the 65 percent drop out rate for Native Americans (Giroux, 1988). Ironically, the poor performance of these students is all too frequently attributed to inherent imperfections in the social structure of the groups they represent rather than a result of an educational system that is unresponsive to their identities, histories, and discourses.

Consistent with the notion that education is valuable because it provides the technical knowledge and entrepreneurial skills necessary to compete in world industrial markets, efforts to improve education involve offering more rigorous science and mathematics programs which are associated with technological progress. These are accompanied by an emphasis on the canons of western civilization, arranged in ways that can be rendered morally neutral and measured empirically (Giroux and McLaren, 1991). People who experience this kind of public education develop a narrow vision of political life. They do not learn to value the historical struggles for social change that have transformed civilizations. Their ability to understand alternative views of social situations is limited by their belief in a single western industrial version of existence. While homage is paid to cultural diversity in U.S., there is a corresponding attempt to contain cultural difference by locating it within an established social grid (Bhabha, 1990). Hence racism, sexism, and classism remain virulent beneath a multicultural surface.

Just as the media need to be restructured in order to function as public spheres, public education must be restructured to prepare citizens to take part in a revitalized pluralist democracy. Public schools need to refocus on educating people to become citizens. People do not need to simply work in the market place, they need to transform it as they struggle to create a just society (Giroux and McLaren, 1991). A public philosophy needs to be developed that will return the goal of social transformation to public life. Instead of considering cultural difference a frightening thing, a crucial aspect of education must be teaching people to read various cultural codes, recognizing their possibilities and limits, including the ones they use to construct their own lives (Giroux, 1991). Further, people need to learn to deal with the ways in which difference is negatively constructed through representations that marginalize, subordinate, and exclude (Schwock, White, and Reilly, 1991).

In media-centric cultures a politics of representation shapes public knowledge through the media structures and the media logic of advanced capitalism. It is necessary for people to learn to resist this politics of representation by developing oppositional pedagogies of representation. The term pedagogy is used here as Freire (1985) uses it; to mean how individuals learn, how knowledge is produced, and how subject positions are constructed, in the arena of political life. Giroux (1990) suggests that pedagogy is "a technology of power, language, and practice that produces and legitimates forms of moral and political regulation that construct and offer human beings particular views of themselves in the world." Critical pedagogies that oppose the politics of representation would offer, as Giroux and McLaren (1991) suggest, new modifications of experience and new perspectives of reception which would unmask the political linkage between images, their means of production and consumption, and the ideological and social practices they legitimate.

This process would involve identifying whose interests are being served by a politics of representation, who speaks for whom, with what authority, and under what conditions. It is also important to determine what ideological principles support representations and how they are positioned ethically and morally in regard to issues of race, class, gender, and ethnicity. In this sense, developing critical pedagogies becomes a domain from which to carry on the struggle for critical citizenship in societies where media knowledge is constitutive of democracy. As Paulo Freire (1985) suggests critical pedagogy integrates culture and politics. A critical pedagogy is necessary to empower people to assume authority over their own lives by participating in the production of knowledge that shapes political action.

Giroux and McLaren (1991) describe a number of conditions for the development of critical pedagogies of representation. The subjectivity/relativity of all representations must be established by situating them historically and politically in contexts that reveal their content, structure, and ideological position. A critical pedagogy of representation must reveal how representations are read as texts in terms of the ascription of power and responsibility to various institutions and individuals within social systems. A critical pedagogy of representation must be able to articulate between similar and diverse representations that operate in political sites as well as in other sites such as art and popular culture. A critical pedagogy of representation must provide a means of ethically evaluating scenarios on the basis of whether they advance positions that promote responsibility and solidarity, or oppression and suffering, in regard to class, race, gender, and ethnicity.

Public education is a privileged site for the development of critical pedagogies in contemporary media-centric consumer cultures. It must be recognized that public education produces political subjects (Friere, 1985). Instead of providing replacements for the work force, public education should provide critical citizens who are empowered to participate fully in a democratic society. The introduction of critical pedagogy as an operational force, particularly in the curriculum development of media studies within world wide educational systems, could create new forms of knowledge by breaking down disciplinary and social boundaries and creating new spaces and relationships where knowledge is produced—counter narratives—which would challenge entrenched systems of power and privilege (Giroux, 1990).

In order for schools to be sites of cultural struggle, teachers would have to become engaged intellectuals (Gramsci) rather than public functionaries, who would provide students with the languages of critique and possibility, and could treat issues of difference and otherness in ethically and politically transformative ways (Giroux, 1990; Schwoch, White, and Reilly, 1991).

The struggle for democracy can be regarded as a utopian political project which provides a vision of the future grounded in the notion of a common good. In *The Concept of Utopia,* Ruth Levitas (1991) describes Ernst Bloch's conception of anticipatory consciousness—a not-yet consciousness—which allows human beings to entertain hope for the future. Bloch sees the world in a constant state of change, the outcome of which is never predetermined; because of this he posits many future possibilities—not-yet becomes. Levitas (1991) explains that "utopia, as the expression of the not-yet conscious, reaches forward to the real possibility of the not-yet become and therefore is the catalyst of the future through its effect on human purpose and action."

It must be recognized, however, that it is very difficult, sometimes incommensurably so, for cultures to co-exist in a democratic community. Homi Bhabha (1990) asserts that cultures articulate, not because of similarities of behaviors or attitudes or even because of empathy or morality. The common ground lies in the fact that all cultures are symbol forming, subject constituting, interpolative practices. The act of translation between cultures sets up "a third space" which displaces the histories of the cultures that produce it and creates a new structure in which to develop political initiatives (Bhabha, 1990). The inventions of language and the uses to which new discourses are put is central to people's ability to define themselves in relation to both their natural and social environment (Mgugi wa Thiong 'O, 1986). In this sense, the establishment of new discourses that allow people to think about themselves and others in new ways becomes a condition for human agency. Agency remains the central issue in revisioning democracy because people must feel so strongly about possibilities for positive change in the future, that they take action in the present. In the words of Paulo Friere (1985), "a true revolutionary project, on the other hand, to which the utopian dimension is natural, is a process in which people assume the role of subject in the precarious adventure of transforming and recreating the world."

A third space must be created in the public sphere where new discourses can be used to define subjectivity, identity, and politics in the hegemonic struggle of critical citizens toward a true pluralist democracy. People must be moved to translate hope into agency. A critical pedagogy of representation is part of the process of reawakening hope.

REFERENCES

Barbalet, J.M. (1988) *Citizenship*. Milton Keynes: Open University Press.

Bhabha, Homi. (1990) The third space. In *Identity, Community, Culture and Difference*. Jonathan Rutherford (Ed.). London: Lawrence Wishart.

Curran, James. (1991) Mass media and democracy: a reappraisal. In *Mass Media and Society*. James Curran and Michael Gurevitch (Eds.). New York: Routledge.

Curran, James. (1991) Rethinking the media as a public sphere. In *Communication and Citizenship*. Peter Dahlgren and Colin Sparks (Eds.). New York: Routledge.

Eley, Geoff. (1991) Nations, publics and political cultures: placing Habermas in the nineteenth century. In *Habermas and the Public Sphere*. Craig Calhoun (Ed.). Cambridge, MA: MIT Press.

Freire, Paulo. (1985) *The Politics of Education: Culture, Power and Liberation* . South Hadley, MA: Bergin and Garvey.

Garnham, Nicholas. (1991) The media and the public sphere. In *Communicating Politics*. Golding, P.; Murdock, G.; Schlesinger, P. (Eds.). New York, NY: Holmes and Meier.

Gens, Curtis. (1988) Is TV turning off the American voter. In *The New York Times, July* 3, , Section II, p. 34.

Giroux, Henry (1988) *Schooling and the Struggle for Public Life*. Minneapolis, MN: University of Minnesota Press.

Giroux, Henry. (1990) Rethinking the boundaries of educational discourse: modernism, post-modernism, and feminism. *College Literature*, Vol. 17, No. 2/3, 1-50.

Giroux, Henry. (1992) *Border Crossing: Cultural Workers and the Politics of Education*. New York, NY: Routledge.

Giroux, Henry and McLaren, Peter. (1992) Media Hegemony: toward a critical pedagogy of representation. Introduction to Schwoch, J.; White, M.; and Reilly, S., *Media Knowledge: Readings in Popular Culture, Pedagogy and Critical Citizenship*. Albany, NY: SUNY Press.

Habermas, Jurgen. (1989) *The Structural Transformation of the Public Sphere*. Cambridge, MA: MIT Press; orig. 1962.

Hall, Stuart and Donald Held. (1989) Citizens and Citizenship. In *New Times: the Changing Face of Politics in the 1990's*. Stuart Hall and Martin Jacques (Eds.). London: Lawrence & Wishart.

Held, David. (1987) *Models of Democracy*. Stanford, CA: Stanford University Press.

Herbst, Susan. (1991) Classical democracy, polls, and public opinion: theoretical frameworks for studying the development of public sentiment. *Communication Theory*. Volume 1, Number 3. August.

Keane, John. (1991) *The Media and Democracy*. Cambridge: Polity Press.

Kellner, Douglas. *Television and the Crises of Democracy*. Boulder, Co.: Westview Press, 1990.

LaClau, Ernesto and Chantal Mouffe. (1985) *Hegemony and Socialist Strategy: Towards a Radical Democratic Politics*. New York: Routledge, .

Levitas, Ruth. (1991) *The Concept of Utopia*. Syracuse, NY: Syracuse University Press.

Schwock, James; White, Mimi; & Reilly, Susan. (1992) *Media Knowledge: Readings in Popular Culture, Pedagogy and Critical Citizenship*. Albany, NY: SUNY Press.

Serra, Sonia. Multinationals of Solidarity: The International Civil Society and the Issue of the Killing of Street Children. Paper presented at the International Association of Mass Communication Research Conference, Dublin, Ireland, June 1993.

Thiong 'O, Mgugi Wa. (1986) *Decolonizing the Mind: The Politics of Language in African Literature.* London: Heinemann.

Wallerstein, Immanuel. (1991) *Geopolitics and Geoculture: Essays on the Changing World System.* Cambridge University Press.

Conclusion

Strategies for Media Literacy

SHIRLEY STEINBERG INTERVIEWS RHONDA HAMMER

Shirley: Can you expand upon the notion that theory and practice must be treated in a dialectical fashion within academia and discuss this in relation to the role of the critical pedagogist?

Rhonda: I think I can best begin to respond to your question by citing from Herbert Marcuse's *An Essay On Liberation:*

> What appears as extraneous "politicization" of the university by disrupting radicals is today (as it was so often in the past) the "logical," internal dynamic of education: translation of knowledge into reality, of humanistic values into humane conditions of existence. This dynamic, arrested by the pseudo-neutral features of academia, would, for example, be released by the inclusion into the curriculum of courses giving adequate treatment to the great non-conformist movements in civilization and to the critical analysis of contemporary societies. The groundwork for building the bridge between the "ought" and the "is," between theory and practice, is laid within theory itself.... Denial of the right to political activity in the university perpetuates the separation between theoretical and practical reason and reduces the effectiveness and the scope of intelligence (1969: 61- 62).

It's ironic that Marcuse's words are as apt today as they were a quarter of a century ago; especially in light of the current backlash against so-called 'politically correct' radical academics. The central "pattern which connects" the writings in this text, and, I believe, the work of critical theorists, in general, is a shared emphasis on theoretical development within the practical domain.

Shirley: This seems to be a common focus of much of the research in both critical pedagogy and resistance post-modernist thought.

Rhonda: Yes; and it is hardly surprising that much of this work is also taking place within what is loosely described as the "feminist" terrain. In particular, there are a number of critical feminist theorists who are addressing these very concerns. Indeed, the lack of any one definitive description of feminist research is testament to its' empowering transdisciplinary nature. As Maxine Green puts it in her preface to an eclectic text of readings: *Feminisms and Critical Pedagogy*:

> Most of [these writers] deliberately resist temptations of harmonious agreement, although they surely come together in a concern for authentic liberatory teaching and for the rejection of patriarchy. Demonstrating at every step that there exists no "essence" of radical feminism, they are drawn to shifting viewpoints, interruptions, the idea of multiple identities. And yet, as they make clear their refusals and resistances, they identify some of the most crucial and unsettled issues confronting teachers in search of emancipatory pedagogies today (In Luke and Gore, eds, 1992: ix).

Within this context, the necessity for the development of an emergent epistemology which is defined—earlier in this text—as a "critical semiotic meta-theoretical approach" takes on a new dimension of urgency; precisely because it is a perspective informed by critical feminisms. And as transformative scholars, we have a responsibility to address pathological relations—racism, sexism, anti-semitism, classism and homophobia—in our teaching. In other words, we re-situate the theoretical into the realm of the practical. This "translation of knowledge into reality" is often mediated by the investigation of particular concrete relations. Zillah Eisenstein elaborates on the necessity of this kind of 'collaboration' by voicing concern for "... constructing theory from reality rather than plastering one onto the other, with creating a dialectic between theory and practice rather than deriving one from the other ... (1979: 3-4)." Unfortunately, the consequences of embracing this kind of "insurgent intellectualism" that which hooks and West (1991) describe as the linkage of theory and practice, of academy and community, can be perilous, especially for the junior and/or non-tenured faculty member, as it challenges the underlying tenets of the dominant academic paradigm and thus the vested interests of the hegemonic intellectual elite. As hooks asserts, "traditional rewards are often withheld from insurgent intellectuals". (1991:74)

Shirley: How can we apply these notions to the classroom, in a manner which is affable rather than alienating to our students; to make the abstract, familiar, if you will?

Rhonda: I try to situate political, controversial issues within the students' frame of reference. In relation to the situation of women, this is, unfortunately, not too difficult; especially in light of the tragic events of Dec. 6, 1989 in Montreal, Canada. Female students, here, can hardly forget that it was only 5 years ago that Marc Lepine, armed with a high-powered semi-automatic rifle, rounded up female students at Montreal's Ecole Polytechnique and screaming, "You're all a bunch of feminists," murdered 14 of them before turning the rifle on himself. You translate from there.... Susan Faludi, in her disturbing yet convincing (and highly accessible) text documents—in dazzling detail, both quantitatively and qualitatively—the terrifying reality of the contemporary female condition; the backlash against women has reached epic proportions. The success of this vitriolic hate campaign, which has incited an escalation of violent action against women, owes much to the contribution of a number of university scholars.

Indeed, at the deep structure level it is the 'academic' who has lent credibility to the mythical landscape propagated by the many dimensions of popular culture. It would be laughable, if it wasn't so appalling, that feminism has been identified as the roots of practically all of our social ills, and the feminist as evil incarnate. Hence, feminists have become one of the major targets of right-wing conservative critics such as Allan Bloom (1987); Roger Kimball (1990); and Dinesh D'Souza (1991) as well as their supporters.

In his opening arguments in *Tenured Radicals*, Kimball indicts the womens' movement by claiming that feminism is the single biggest challenge to the canon, while D'Souza—who demonstrates, in addition to a profound ignorance about the books he criticizes, a tendency towards sloppy scholarship—(and whose previous 'claim to fame' was "an admiring biography of Jerry Falwell") states that no one dares to question feminist ideology in the "politically correct" climate on campuses. Within such a reactionary context, it is imperative to acknowledge that this backlash against progressive faculty and students who advocate educational reforms, with the intention of developing an inclusive curriculum embodying voices, histories and experiences of those historically defined as the "Other" (women, blacks, jews, indigenous peoples, ethnic minorities, gays and lesbians) is occurring at a time when racial unrest, anti-feminist sentiment and gay bashing have reached a precarious state (Scatamburlo, 1993).

It is ironic, then, that even though the "feminist" stereotype repels most women from aligning themselves formally with this "satanic cult," the paradoxical nature of the ideology equates all women—at some level—with this abhorrent label. It is, thus, within this context that Marc Lepine's actions, and his charge that feminists impoverished his existence, begins to make some sense. However, the demonization of feminists is not always as consciously violent. Nor are those academics who (perhaps unconsciously) espouse the right-wing party line the only ones deserving of our scorn and disgust. Indeed some of the worst offenders are those who pay lip-service to their commitment against the violation of women and then sneak out to attend the still fashionable New Age masculinist Robert Bly sponsored "Wild Man Gathering," where they can scapegoat women as the source of their individual and collective resentments. As are those who relate a sexist joke in class ("the problem with you feminists is that you have no sense of humour!") or those so embedded in the dominant paradigm, that they neglect to incorporate, into their courses and/or research, the scholarship of those who do not embrace the white, heterosexual, patriarchal code. The backlash against women is being upheld and reinforced by those intellectuals who refuse to address inherent bigotry in societal institutions and/or keep silent when women on our campuses are raped, abused, denigrated and humiliated; who perceive equity programs as inequity for (white, straight) men. The teaching and celebration of collaborators, like Camille Paglia—the "Madonna" of Academia—(who tells us that when a woman says "no," she often means "yes") is often transformed into an excuse for misogyny, masquerading under the guise of academic freedom. Academics have both the responsibility and the power to combat this backlash and practically apply the humanistic principles espoused by our institutional context. If education is to play a fundamentally liberatory role, issues of social inequality must be incorporated into pedagogical praxis. Indeed, we must heed Audre Lordes foreboding warning: "What does it mean when the tools of the racist patriarchy are used to examine the fruits of that same patriarchy?

It means that only the most narrow perimeters of change are possible and allowable" (In Fulton, 1993:11).[1]

Shirley: Within this context, I understand that in your teaching you emphasize the liberatory nature of "media literacy" (32-38). I know that you are an educational video producer and that you have taught, and currently teach video production at the University of Windsor. Can you discuss this process?

Rhonda: The student video projects evolve within a classroom environment predicated on the notion of "academic freedom," in the legitimate sense. It is unfortunate that contemporary attitudes towards this fundamental right has excluded one of its most seminal components: the academic rights of students in that "their freedom to learn requires an inclusive curriculum which reflects reality" (Golden, 1993:3). Faculty Associations are finally recognizing that ". . . the classroom can be an inhospitable ('chilly') place for some women, students of colour, first nation peoples and the disabled because of the curriculum content and teaching practices of some faculty members" (ibid.). This is precisely the type of atmosphere which necessitates the production of metacommunicative, counter-hegemonic projects. Moreover, the qualitative excellence of some of these student productions has been demonstrated by both their successes at competitions (over a 2 year period, programs received 4 awards) and the extensive screening times afforded them in a diversity of courses and conferences. The emancipatory nature embodied by these media liter-

---

[1] This response is a revised version of an article, co-authored by myself and Valerie Scatamburlo, a graduate student in the Dept. of Communications Studies (forthcoming: *Beyond Political Correctness: Crossing Borders, Building Bridges*, 1993) for the University of Windsor newspaper, *The Lance*, Dec. 1992.

acy projects is further exemplified when contextually examined, in that these productions developed within a highly conservative and authoritarian academic department. (As a representative metaphor, Shirley, let me relate one example. Recently, myself and another faculty member questioned the legality and mandate of a departmental committee which had failed to recognize, and include, its students members. While we were addressing the committee Chair's contravention of university senate bylaws, we were also confronting his deliberate *exclusion* of student "voice". As I emphatically articulated my opposition to his restrictive approach, I was promptly told by the head of our department to "go file a fucking grievance.") Hence, I can only fantasize about the potential for these kinds of exercises, which find their basis in the concrete relations of every-day life, within a supportive academic environment. The process by which this media literacy is practically applied is through a systematic examination of both the practical techniques, employed within the hegemonic codes of the mass media, as well as through investigation of the underlying ideological subtexts and myths. Through exercises, which include the study of a variety of media genres in a semiotic manner, as well as technical assignments the collective unconscious media literacy, we all share, becomes consciously realized. Metacommunicative praxis is then linked with counterhegemonic meaning. In other words, media are identified within an emergent epistemological framework as a multi-levelled dialectical set of relationships and codes, and thus transformed, by the students, in their video productions. Their voices are thus articulated in a multi-dimensional iconic fashion. Needless to say, a comprehensive description of their work defies digital description due, in part, to the analogic nature of these texts. As Isadora Duncan declared: "If I could tell you what it meant, there would be no point in dancing it" (In Bateson, 1972: 137).

Shirley: Regardless, could you provide us with some kind of feeling for the essence of some of these video productions, as well as some of the techniques employed by both yourself and the students?

Rhonda: Humour plays a seminal, and of course, metacommunicational role in a number of these programs. As Regina Barreca (1991) reminds us in *They Used To Call Me Snow White ... But I Drifted*, humour is often a dialectical process, provoking change. "Humor leads the way; it moves us past those inbred, ingrained resistances. . . . Sometimes just the very act of naming something, saying something out loud, admitting something about how we view our lives is enough to make us laugh. It's so absurd, we realize as soon as we see it clearly that it's funny" (182; 186). She goes on to argue that "the emperor's-new-clothes mentality" can be adapted to laugh the perpetuators "out of their sanctimonious self-assurances" (190).[2]

---

[2] For example, one of the assignments in my video course was to produce an anti-rock video or anti-commercial. One of the productions, entitled *Sum Kinda Wunnerful* edited a heavy metal band, to a polka rendition of a rock tune. She taped it in a pretty grungy local club, utilizing students—dressed in the local S&M/leather store duds—polka dancing! On first hearing her proposal, I must admit to being sceptical, but the final production is a brilliant and entertaining semiotic validation of the hierarchical reality of rock videos in that form constrains substance (not entirely unlike the hyperreality of Baudrillardian vulgar post-modern theory, I suppose). Another student, in the same course, produced a pseudo-investigative report (based loosely on the parodic genre of the Australian documentary *Cane Toads*). *The Sun Also Sets* examines both the etiology and symptoms of a rare but insidious disease, found almost exclusively on the campuses of universities and colleges: *smoochious butticus* (from the latin) victims are more commonly referred to as SUNNIES. Incorporating students, student actors, and professors the genetic, neuro-physiological, and psychological explications for this "obsessive need of certain individuals to curry favour or kiss up to their professors" is revealed. The effectiveness of the student productions metacommunicative and subversive abilities, lies in their successful employment of the dominant rule governed system of signs (the codes) of contemporary television programming (especially an understanding and, thus, translation of what John Fiske identifies as "Level one: 'REALITY' and Level two: 'REPRESENTATION' of the codes of television) (1987:5).

Indeed, this dimension of humour punctuates a 100 minute video 'montage' produced by myself and four undergraduates which tied for first place in the Zalampas Multimedia Award competition for best media production at the 1991 Annual Popular Culture Association Meeting. The students' expression of this project is, for these purposes, worth citing. Here is what they wrote:

"PCA 1990—'THE VIDEO!!!"

The popular culture of a country may be the guardian of a democracy as it is consistently testing freedom of speech.

Ray Browne, Secretary-Treasurer
Popular Culture Association

The Popular Culture Association held the annual 1990 conference in Toronto, Ontario. As a group of undergraduate students, in the Dept. of Communication Studies at the University of Windsor, our participation in the conference involved videotaping various sessions and editing the footage together with media material to present a visual exposé of panel analyses. The following year, we were invited to present the video at the Popular Culture Conference in San Antonio, Texas.

Our video montage presented highlights of various sessions from the 1990 conference including: *Doing Some Things With Do The Right Thing, Vietnam and Eugene McCarthy, From Virgin to Vampire, Married With Children, Filmmakers and Political Themes, The Three Stooges.* The introduction to the series includes interviews with Pat and Ray Browne, the co-ordinators of the conference, as well as a visual montage to Billy Joel's *We Didn't Start The Fire,* depicting academics in their scholarly pursuit of analyzing and criticizing popular culture.

The favourable responses to these tapes has proven that the combination of theory and production provides an alternative media practice that is highly instructional. The edits have been distributed to educate teachers and students about the study of popular culture and also of the possible media strategies that are available. Moreover this tape facilitates a transformation in media technology with regard to the conventional codes and the 'fair use' of media material for educational purposes.

We hope that our successful experience with the production of this videotape will inspire future research into the production of alternative media" (Roussell, L., 1991).

Shirley: I think we could gain a better understanding of this production if you could situate it within a wider framework.

Rhonda: For lack of a better explanation, I regard this montage as an academic rock video. Responses to our work has been, generally, quite positive and gratifying. Indeed, we have been delighted to have received a "thumbs up," from far more than our immediate families. Within this context, I'll cite excerpts from two such reviews:

> "I wish to formally commend you and your students for the truly outstanding video projects presented last week at the Popular Culture Association Convention in San Antonio, Texas. Unable to attend last year's convention, I am very grateful to you for documenting and actually enhancing with visual imagery some of the more interesting paper presentations from the PCA convention in Toronto. From your introduction to the series through the last video concerning filmmakers and political themes, the presentations were characterized by excellent production work, particularly the editing work. I can appreciate the thousands of hours spent in documenting tape, finding archival material, and doing the edits necessary to produce the high-quality product that you and your students achieved. Pedagogically speaking, I think your project was of great educational value to your undergraduates, who attended academic conventions, learned the skills to create video documentaries . . ." (Ron Jacobson, Dept. of Communications, The Jesuit University of New York City, April 3, 1991).

> "Just spent time looking at the tape from the Popular Culture Association. I think what you and your students have done, breathing life into conference papers, is quite extraordinary. . . . What impresses me most of all, is the potential for taking conference papers—which, despite content, can be dull going—and using them as an armature for interesting video presentation" (Stuart Ewen, Sociology, CUNY,

New York & Dept. of Communications, Hunter College, New York).

I believe that the role of critical pedagogists is, in part, to practically apply critical theory into counter-hegemonic praxis. For as Doug Kellner advises:

> The future of democracy thus depend upon the use of new technologies to promote democracy and to counter capitalist control of the state and broadcast media. Ultimately, then the struggle for a democratic communications system is a struggle for democratic society. The technologies are there, but imagination, will, and struggle will be needed to realize the democratic potential that still exists in a system organized for the hegemony of capital in an era of conservative political rule (1990:222).

BIBLIOGRAPHY

Barreca, Regina. *They Used To Call Me Snow White ... But I Drifted: Women's Strategic Use Of Humor*. New York: Penguin Books, 1991.

Bateson, Gregory. *Steps To An Ecology of Mind*. New York: Ballantine Books, 1972.

Briggs, David. *The Sun Also Sets*. Windsor: University of Windsor, 1992 (videotape).

Eisenstein, Zillah. "Introduction." In *Capitalist Patriarchy And The Case For Socialist Feminism*, pp. 1-4. Edited by Zillah R. Eisenstein. New York: Monthly Review Press, 1979.

Faludi, Susan. *Backlash: The Undeclared War Against American Women*. New York: Crown Publishers, Inc., 1991.

Fiske, John. *Television Culture*. London: Methuen, 1987.

Fulton, Keith Louise. "Audre Lorde: Sister Outsider." In *CAUT Bulletin* (March 1993): 11.

Golden, Jean. "Harassment Policies, Academic Freedom and Consensual Relationships." In *OCUFA Forum: Special Supplement* (January/February, 1993): 3.

hooks, bell and West, Cornel. *Breaking Bread: Insurgent Black Intellectual Life*. Toronto: Between The Lines.

Kellner, Doug. *Television and The Crisis of Democracy*. San Francisco: Westview Press, 1990.

Krech, Lori. *Sum Kinda Wunnerful*. Windsor: University of Windsor, 1992 (videotape).

Luke, Carmen and Gore, Jennifer, eds. *Feminisms and Critical Pedagody*. New York: Routledge, 1992.

Marcuse, Herbert. *An Essay On Liberation*. Boston: Beacon Press, 1969.

Scatamburlo, Valerie. *Beyond Political Correctness: Crossing Borders, Building Bridges*. (forthcoming, 1994).

SHIRLEY STEINBERG INTERVIEWS SUSAN REILLY

Shirley: In this book you offer a critical reading of a television news program as an example of an act of multicultural resistance. What other strategies can teachers use to help students create border identities?

Susan: Critical analyses of existing media texts are a good place to start, but eventually students need to create their own media programs. In these programs, students can advance border narratives which break the bonds of hegemonic discourse and provide oppositional readings of history and social practice. I would offer as an example a television documentary project that my students and I recently completed. In the course of doing research on the women's sufferage movement, a colleague of mine stumbled upon a reference to an African American woman pilot, Bessie Coleman, who was a contemporary of the suffragettes. Unable to find out any information about her locally, he sent to the Library of Congress for a book that contained a short essay about Bessie Coleman written by her sister. In the essay the sister says she had to try to write down Bessie Coleman's accomplishments so that the aviatrix would not be forgotten. Taken by the sister's recognition of the arbitrariness of history, I decided to ask my students to recreate Bessie Coleman's life.

Bessie Coleman was born in Texas in the 1890's. Her mother was African American, her father a Native American. She followed two of her brothers to Chicago in the early 1900's and worked as a manicurist in the White Sox Barber Shop. One of her brothers fought with a black regiment during WWI. When he returned to Chicago he told Bessie that women were learning to fly in France. Determined to fly herself and unable to receive flying lessons in the States because she was black and a woman, Bessie enlisted the aid of African American newspaper publisher Robert Abbott (The Chicago Defender), learned to speak French, went to France, and became the first African American woman to earn an international pilot's license. She returned to the States in 1921 and began to raise money for an negro aviation school, by barnstorming at states fairs and performing aerial stunts in exhibitions of flying across the country. She always dedicated her performances to the African American regiments in WWI. At the age of 33, after six years of flying, Bessie Coleman died in a tragic accident while practicing for an airshow the following day. Her dream of an aviation school was unfulfilled.

Asking students to create a video documentary about Bessie Coleman confronted them with two important tenets in the field of cultural studies. First, history is an arena where various groups in a culture struggle to assert which view of the past will be privileged in the present. Most women have not had access to the institutions of power that are traditionally given historical significance—government, the military, and commerce. Because the spheres of women's lives have not been considered essential to the destiny of the nation, they have been assumed to be observors rather than shapers of history.

In a new age when the contributions of women and minorities are being recovered and valorized, it is important to find examples of women in the past who fought for their identity as shapers of history. Their struggle connects with present day struggles and roots them in the authority of history.

And second, whiteness is an ethnicity. If that is ignored, then whites assume their cultural norms are neutral and universal. Only when whiteness is identified as an ethnicity can the binarisms associated with blackness be put into a cultural perspective and not assumed to be naturally determined. This recognition makes clear the need for an intercultural dialogue rather than the demand for adaptation to a dominant discourse.

In order to accomplish this documentary, the students, primarily white Euro-Americans, had to interview a number of African American women—relatives of Bessie Coleman, historians, writers, psychologists. To do this they had to participate in a rhetoric that allowed interest in Bessie Coleman's accomplishments to be explained and shared and then they had to be able to use that rhetoric to retell Bessie Coleman's story to both a black and white audience. Because there were so few artifacts remaining to illustrate Bessie Coleman's life—a few photographs, a pilot's license, a sister's essay—students had to define Bessie Coleman by asking the African American women they interviewed how knowledge of the aviatrix's accomplishments impacted their own lives. As the documentary neared completion, the students turned the camera on themselves. They identified their authorship and described the changes they had experienced asking questions of and listening to the women they interviewed. Finally, they talked about how Bessie Coleman, the historic figure, had affected their lives and why they felt her story needed to be told.

Shirley: If a condition for human agency is people's ability to redefine themselves in relation to their social environment, how can a teacher operationalize, in the classroom, the creation of a new discourse that allows students to function as liberatory agents?

Susan: An example of this process took place in a seminar I taught on the imagery of women in still photographs. During the course of the semester students criticized photographs found in popular culture as well as created their own photographs. At the end of the course the students planned an exhibition of their work for the general public. One of the assignments dealt with pornography. The young women in the class (it was a class crosslisted in Mass Communication and Women's Studies; only women enrolled) were asked to acquire—*Playboy, Penthouse, Hustler, Nugget, Gent,* etc. magazines, examine the photographs of women in them, and construct a visual statement liberating the photographs from their original intent as pornography. The students discussed various opinions about pornography, from Andre Dworkin to Christy Hefner. They discussed the first amendment and the merits of prohibiting pornography as a clear and present danger. Then the class agreed they had to move beyond discussion and confront the issue of domination that pornography epitomizes by creating visual messages as powerfully resistant as the pornographic photographs were subjegating.

First, the young women had to acquire the "adult" magazines. The social behavior surrounding the use of pornography was so intimidating that some women were humiliated to pick one up in a store and pay for it. But they had agreed not to ask male friends to do it for them. This dynamic began the process of confrontation and resistance. Most of the students had never looked at one of these magazines carefully before. They had seen them in the possession of fathers, brothers, and boyfriends, but they had no first hand experience concentrating on the photographs within the context of accompanying text and advertisements. The students read the magazines on their own and came to class prepared to discuss their reactions. The support of the group helped them to express their rage as they worked through their readings of the photographic messages. At first, they wanted to blame someone—the owners' of the magazines, the subscribers, the women in the photographs. But then they moved to a discussion of issues very different from the first amendment. They talked about fantasy and reality, mutilation and shame, expectation and desire. They could only construct messages of resistance if they had hope that others could be as affected as they were by them. Slowly they moved past despair to possibility and began to take action. Their visual messages took many forms from clothing the women in the photographs by painting on the images to breaking the restraints of women photographed in bondage to creating new accompanying texts that provided statistics of incidences of sexual abuse, rape, and domestic violence. These acts of changing the meanings of the photographs allowed students to experience the liberating effect of agency. The atmosphere in the classroom became celebratory. The initial power of those images to humiliate and control was gone.

SHIRLEY STEINBERG INTERVIEWS DAVID SHOLLE

Shirley: In describing your general model of media literacy, you point out that tackling the media and popular culture can intrude into student's affective experience. How can we avoid simply valorizing that experience, but at the same time avoid turning students off by critically judging their involvement in popular culture?

David: This is a real practical problem in the classroom, since media literacy is not only a matter of criticizing texts, but also a matter of examining how media practices position subjects and construct forms of identity. In the context of the media criticism course, we have found that often the problem is that students are all too willing to be critical of media texts, i.e., when looking at a program's content, they nod in agreement at the surface effects of sexism, racism, hyper-patriotism, etc. But it is always "other people" who are manipulated by the media. Too often media criticism is seen as a matter of finding the "bad" messages in the media and thus, not attending to the context of the production and consumption of the media. At best this leads to a valorization of "willful playfulness" with the media, a kind of ironic "so what" attitude toward media ideology. Instead, media literacy requires confronting the manner in which viewership is constructed by the media experience.

Concretely, this means avoiding the kind of media bashing gab sessions that often define the practice of media criticism in the university. Developing an effective media literacy practice in the classroom is context specific, but we can suggest some guidelines. First of all, teachers should avoid forcing interpretations of the text. Simply, pointing out to students the myths, discursive exclusions, etc. of the popular culture text leaves them unaffected by the analysis. Second, the media text needs to be put in *context*—the reading needs to be situated in both a theoretical and historical setting. This leads to a third crucial guideline—discussion of a particular text must evolve from a confrontation with the act of consumption.

Although it might be useful to examine media texts that are obvious examples of dominant ideology, these texts might not connect to student experiences. Standard news, household product ads, family sitcoms are all examples of programs that students will find easy to analyze (in terms of surface ideology) but unable to affectively connect to. A more fruitful, if more difficult task, would be to look at media that are currently the object of student fandom. *Ren and Stempy, MTV, 90210,* etc. are examples of programs that many students affectively relate to. We need to begin with allowing students to express their commitments, allegiances, pleasures and desires in relation to these programs. In this regard, it might be fruitful to allow a dialogue session in and around questions of why these shows matter. As students begin to articulate their feelings and thoughts about the consumption of these programs, a critical moment should arise from the readings. The teacher needs to operate as a facilitator of critical media literacy by steering the discussion to attention on the manner in which the students as *readers* are also *writers*. This discussion should lead to self-reflection and give and take between affirmation of popular culture's contribution to everyday life and its potential problems.

Next, the analysis needs to turn to the context of production. Here, we need to address the historical context of media practice, the function of the programs in a general economy of media, the place of youth as an object of media strategy, etc. In turn, the theoretical background of textual and audience study can be progressively brought in, not as intellectual abstractions, but as concrete aides in understanding the contradictions and problematics that have arisen from the open ended discussion. Now we can return to the text in a new manner, hopefully, a more self-reflexive one. Discussion can now turn back to the original points of student experience, but in a way which remaps these subject positions. In all of this, the teacher does not take the position of expert critic, but rather serves to direct the discussion to an interrogation of self-production.

Shirley: You mention the complicity of current media education with dominant cultural reproduction. Can you elaborate on the current situation in university teaching on the media?

David: The primary problem is that media education is conceived as a commodity that is purchased for its use-value in procuring employment. Further, education functions in this exchange as a means of disciplining and channeling students to take up functions in industry and commerce in a manner in which they conceptualize the media-itself as commodity. Overall, there is a consistency in media education that is characterized by a dominant professional training orientation motivated, in part, by attracting students to the field through its occupational promises.

A "professional" education in the media can be defined as one which attempts to prepare students for entry level jobs in the commercial mass media or corporate communication industries by replicating professional techniques and procedures in the classroom. In media production this involves training in equipment techniques and program formats currently employed in the industry. In media journalism it involves practice in replicating the form of broadcast copy under a structure of strict deadlines. In media management and law it involves simulations of broadcast decision-making and legal procedure, often through the use of computer programs that incorporate industry data and practices.

The ideology of professionalism is primarily rooted in certain habits of the mind. Administrators see local TV operations as the logical model of "real" media production and base their expectations of production education accordingly. Production faculty replicate the professional curriculum in which they themselves were trained. And all of this takes place within the greater context of a larger environment in which the University itself is being pulled towards both the needs and the outlook of business. The alternative is to conceive of communication as a basic, specific human activity, and to offer a curriculum that explores this specificity, that investigates how communication works to create and transmit meaning. Within this approach, production classes would become, in effect, courses in applied semiotics, criticism and analysis.

Although a majority of departments pay lipservice to the goals of liberal education, the actual practice is to systematically separate liberal and professional education and most significantly in a direction that subordinates the former to the later. What is evident in this discourse of professionalism is a pedagogy rooted in a transmission model of education and a complete divorce of pedagogical concerns from cultural politics. While maintaining the need for liberal education, this rhetoric actually empties it of any political import. It is not simply that job training is present as a goal that we question, but rather that the concerns of the market dictate the terms of pedagogical encounter. As *schooling*, professional pedagogy is normalizing and controlling. Its impetus is not toward a democratic curriculum, one that encourages active subjects who grapple with the concrete problems of social and personal life.

Professional education also leads toward a transmission model of education in its specific pedagogy. The level of detail in skills acquisition, the rigid breakdown of roles of crew structure, the constant insertion of voices of authority from "successful" broadcast industry practitioners, and time-consuming rote learning of formats and managerial models all lead to a form of *schooling* requiring the student to sit still and listen. Student voice is, indeed, silenced in this process, replaced with the ventriloquist voice of broadcast buzz words.That which lies underneath the stated goals of training in professional procedures is the practice of inducing compliance to the status quo of the media industry and the corporatist ideology that it supports.

Shirley: And the alternative? How can the concerns addressed in this book practically impact media education?

David: Well, the crisis of media education is precisely its loss of relevance to the actual life situations of the majority in the United States, to any notion of public philosophy and critical citizenship. Instead, media education, by narrowing itself to the raw world of industrial work, has marginalized itself within the university. We need to reconceive of work as not something that the market uses, but rather as that which builds a democratic society. There is no better place to start the work of transforming this society into a more radically democratic one, then in media education, given that the media are the most powerful force in setting our cultural agenda. For media education this will mean more than simply adding courses on "media and society." The traditional areas of management, production and planning cannot be left to the "professionals," while liberal arts faculty conduct seminars on media criticism. These areas need to be eradicated altogether, i.e., as separate courses in "how to labor." Instead, a pedagogy of cultural politics needs to be infused into these territories, redefining them in terms of knowledge useful not only for practicing in the industry, but useful in furthering the goals of an emancipatory democracy. It is such a political project that will actually meet the needs of students in their careers by empowering them to integrate their lives of work and leisure through inventing a new "culture of work" rooted in the goals of a radical democracy.

We suggest that this practice can begin right now—media educators *can* bring together theory and practice. Each day in class come up with a couple of examples of how an esoteric study you read or a theory you reflected on has a real bearing on something that actually concerns students. If you can't, then either you have no understanding of your students' everyday concerns or you are reading the wrong esoteric essays. For example, in an audio class a question about rap music arose. Wasn't it amateurish to rely on simply playing around with a turntable? Who would let us do this when we get jobs? Isn't this really just botching up a slip cue? The instructor had been reading an article by a cultural studies scholar on rap music as a cultural phenomenon. It struck him that the use of the turntable by rap was a postmodern inflection of the modernist movement in art where the attempt was to rethink the tools, making the familiar strange. In rap, the turntable is perceived and lived differently—no longer is it a simply a playback device designed to reproduce the sounds of commodities, rather it is *seen* as a musical instrument. Thus, rap's use of the turntable is not simply a reuse of a technology, it is a political reworking of a technology, turning a passive reproductive device into an active instrument controlled by and for the black community. Such an account then sheds light on the students' questions, asking them to consider the political implications of the technology they use and to consider how what is given as a broadcast industry tool can be used differently for alternative purposes.

This example illustrates one way in which our lives as theorists can be integrated with our lives in the classrooms; and how students lives as producers and consumers can be connected.

Shirley: Is this where the third step of media literacy— counterrepresentation— enters in?

David: Our courses should continually raise questions of social responsibility and democratic citizenship and put this questioning to the test in practical work. The proclivity to conceive of the media major as a job area should be nipped in the bud. Students should see the curriculum as fundamentally concerned with *studying* the media and this should not be disconnected from *doing* it.The "product" of our programs should not be media workers, it should be citizen-viewers, citizen-producers, citizen-media critics.

Practically, this means our students should be exposed to public access centers, community action groups, broad-based arts coalitions, alternative forms of media, educational media and other types of non-broadcast media. Again, fundamental pedagogical goals must come first—do we want to simply provide cheap labor to the broadcast industry and reproduce a media work force for the dominant media, or do we want to educate students to see the media as an important public sphere, where race, gender and class issues need to be significantly addressed? The work students do must address these issues and the kind of work we presently engage them in is often closed from any considerations of how the media may be changed, how its deficiencies may be overcome.

Shirley: This notion of the public sphere arises throughout your current project and this connects up with an important trend in contemporary media studies and cultural studies: the questioning of the current structure of the public sphere or, in fact, whether one exists or has ever existed. If we assume for the moment that democratic life will require some turn toward the retransformation of the public sphere, how can we convince students that such a notion has any significance for real life?

David: If we take the models of democratic media systems developed by Keane and Curran we can begin to envision how the media might function in a different way as far as the public sphere is concerned. Within media education we might be able to take a step beyond simply abstract reflection on this functioning. We might, in fact, turn our resources away from such self-serving adventures as university sports coverage, and local news emulation and turn them directly toward the development of a model media system. Such an experiment would function as a small scale simulation of a model such as Curran's. Students would participate in the formation of associations that function as public media organizations of varying kinds. In Curran's model these would include a private enterprise sector, a general purpose public service system, a civic sector (consisting of party and subcultural tiers), and an autonomous professional sector. Students would participate in setting up the system and thus, would experience and work through the problems inherent in forming genuinely radical democratic institutions.

Whatever the final practical arrangements for the experiment, it would have to provide for public dialogue from diverse perspectives; it would allow a space for students to interrogate the social conditions of the university and it would provide assistance to various organizations in representing their viewpoints to a wider public. The result would be a publically regulated sphere of media activity with the students acting in various positions of authority—from media producers, to organizational heads, to public representatives. This would be a direct experiment in citizenship, that at the same time would provide media students with practical hands-on experience.

We could envision, here, a minature "public sphere," where students coordinate the programming of the campus cable channel, radio station and other news outlets. Students would be responsible for airing issues of importance to diverse groups of the study body—the college political party groups, the black student caucus, the gay-lesbian alliance, the fraternity/sorority system, etc. This media public sphere would provide an arena, where student concerns, experiences, histories, discourses and desires could be aired and contested. Such a project is not merely utopian. Such a project could easily take off if it were given the amount of resources current media departments plunk into sports vans, business and advertising oriented mockups, and industry tie-ins. The question is whether we in the university have the will to attempt such an ambitious experiment in democracy.

SHIRLEY STEINBERG INTERVIEWS PETER MCLAREN

Shirley: Peter, much of your work is highly conceptual and your approach quite theoretical, not to mention controversial. You started as a teacher activist in Toronto's inner-city in the mid-seventies. Now you're internationally recognized for your work as an educational critical theorist. I know that many of your readers who are both prospective and practicing teachers, wonder how you practice critical pedagogy with your students.

Peter: Many of my pedagogical efforts are aimed at sketching out with students the contours of a politics of difference in the form of an anti-racist, anti-sexist, and anti-homophobic approach to teaching. Part of this project for me involves confronting the ugly reality of racism. Let me share a recent example. One incident at a local Ohio high school provoked a strong response from some of my students, the overwhelming majority of whom are white Anglos from upper-middle class and affluent families. Two white high school students wore their grandparents Klu Klux Klan robes to a Halloween dance and harassed some black students. The white students were temporarily suspended and this provoked the Klan to march through the center of town to protest the 'violation' of the rights of the students who were suspended. Some of my students felt that while wearing the Klu Klux Klan robes was admittedly going too far, white students should be allowed to at least wear confederate flag t-shirts to promote white solidarity. After all, they argued, black students were permitted to show their racial solidarity by wearing African pendants. This wasn't a majority view among my students, to be sure, but it did signal the enormous challenge to be faced. Students not only asserted that the wearing of African medallions by black students was the equivalent of wearing a confederate t-shirt, but they believed that the racial epithet "honkey," was the equivalent of "nigger." So I had the class look at some work by Gregory Bateson and Tony Wilden on logical typing and dependent hierarchies and for some students this was a breakthrough. They came to realize that the term "nigger" was uttered from a structural position of power in which being white constrained what it meant to be black. We're not talking about warring oppositions but dependent hierarchies. So "honkey" when uttered from a dependent position of powerlessness can never be considered equivalent to "nigger." For the same reason, an African pendant can't be compared to the confederate flag. There are also historical and cultural reasons why these comparisions are inaccurate. This example became a point of departure for me to ask students to interrogate their own assumptions about race. And this meant confronting some of the racist practices we found on campus, such as fraternity parties with blackface performances and the auctioning of 'dates' by organizations (sometimes by using professional auctioneers).

Later we began to explore historically the self-congratulatory European notion that Africa was a continent of savagery and barbarism—an uncultivated continent without a history, a continent populated by the most lowly of creatures deprived of the saving grace of the 'glory' of Western civilization. Most of my students have never studied—even briefly—the history of imperialism, of colonialism. So we try to examine the historical process of colonization as it both reflects and is constitutive of racist practices and corporate interests. We examine how the Europeans tried to bequeath the gift of history to what they saw through their imperialist eyes as a history-less continent. Students frequently profess shock in learning how European theories of evolution supported white supremacist ideologies and forms colonization by equating Africans with the earliest stages of human development and likening them to beasts—reflecting Aristotle's Great Chain of Being or Gibbon's *Decline and Fall of the Roman Empire* where miscegenation was reported as the cause of the decline of civilization.

Racism is both the result and major propellant of economic expansionism and imperialist adventurism. We explore how racism was linked to U.S. expansionism and Manifest Destiny, imperial largesse, class and ethnic stratification, social Darwinism and how philology, ideologies about class, and the amalgamation of nationalism and racist discourses culminated in Nazism and the ethnic cleansing practices that are occurring among the Serbs today in what once was Yugoslavia. I refer the students to the case of Josef Moller—a black ten year-old boy who was sent for exhibition at an Antwerp Zoo where he was 'permitted' to move about uncaged. In my essay on "White Terror" I mentioned the famous case of Ota Benga, the 'pygmy' exhibited at the Monkey House in the Bronx Zoo, an "African homunculus" described by Anglo science as the "missing link," and encouraged by his keepers to charge the bars of his cage, his mouth open and his teeth bared. I try to link these historical exhibitions to student practices I've heard about on campus. Rarely have my students been challenged to trace racist discourses genealogically. So they are invited to examine, for instance, the moral economy of Christianity structured around the allegory of African morality as sinister and evil. We examine contemporary cultural forms such as music, film, and video. One student remarked that some people find African music influences with its drum rhythms as sinister. This brings to mind a comment made by Mickey Hart, drummer for the rock group *Grateful Dead*, that white people have a problem with rhythm, feeling it to be uncivilized. White people do associate drumming with pagan rites, with the 'dark continent' of Africa and the erotic frenzy and the forces of evil. Students are then confronted with the terror of democracy: We will let these "fallen creatures" become citizens as long as they remain weak and docile. Now when we examine the non-Western indigenous cultures of Latin America, for instance, it's important not to lapse either into an essentialized nativism which posits non-Western indigenous cultures as inviolably homogeneous nor views the West as all of one piece: namely, as an example of totalizing imperialism. Not all occidental influences on non-Western cultures are imperialistic or hegemonic. Of course, the question is raised: How do we identify ourselves as white, as black, as Latino? How do we problematize the struggle for the construction or 'practice' of the self? How do we view identity and maintain the boundaries of self and other? We move into discussions of status structuration in terms of how certain groups are collectively discriminated against in relation to their 'otherness.' We look at the process of subjectification in relation to historically developed patterns of capital accumulation and relations of production and the way institutions and agencies regulate differential access to goods and resources and status. This leads to another critical question: How do we theorize identity if the cultural relations on which identities are inscribed are seen not as static and fixed but as emplastic, as bricolage, as forming new wholes out of discordant and cast-off images?

Shirley: How do students react to these theoretical discussions? Do they see them as relevant to their work as future teachers?

Peter: Not initially, which is why I begin my classes with the movie, *Roger and Me,* followed by a Bill Moyer interview with Myles Horton, the great Appalachian educator from Tennessee. Before you can understand how education works you need to understand education's marriage with corporate America. Until my recent move to Los Angeles, my students were generally from the upper middle-class and were invariably white and largely female. They were from rural Ohio—mostly small towns. Some were from

Dayton, Cincinnati, Cleveland, or Toledo, or outside of Ohio. A few were from other countries. The graduate students were teachers or principals or they worked for Boards of Education in some capacity. Most of them resisted theory and looked to experience as their final court of appeal. As if somehow experience magically speaks for itself. As if experiences are self-observances, are auto-didactic, something that gives us an accurate notion of the world. Joan Scott, myself, and others have argued that knowledge is not gained through the unmediated apprehension of a world of transparent objects. As if somehow experiences precede interpretation or rhetoric. Interpretation, in fact, occurs at the very moment of perception. The problem is that teachers really see theory as the enemy of experience. So I try a little epistemological disrobing by way of critical theory. When I'm successful, and there is certainly no guarantee that I will be, eventually students confront the challenge of viewing experience as both a construction—an ideological effect—and as constitutive of reality. If we face the challenge of deconstruction—that experiences have always already occurred because pure presence doesn't exist—then we have to understand experiences as never transparent or self-present but always occurring within a textual economy. Myles Horton makes the insightful statement: "You only learn from experiences that you learn from." So experience can be understood as having always already occurred yet paradoxically having still to be produced. What are the historical processes that produce subjects through discourse? This is really the issue that challenges us. Having experiences are important—it's different than reading about experiences—but I think that having certain experiences does not guarantee a particular politics. What's important are the languages we use to understand our experiences—to help us transform them. Language is not fixed and can represent the same social relation in different ways. It can construct different meanings. By this I mean simply that language can both constrain and enable understanding. We need to struggle over meanings that formulate our conditions—as men, as women, as blacks, whites, and Latinos.

Students really see little reason for discussing critical social theory, except perhaps in the most general way in terms of spending one or two classes discussing the causes of poverty or class and racial stratification. Initially, they are quite threatened by the class readings, which include Cornel West, Henry Louis Gates, Anthony Appiah, bell hooks, Foucault, Derrida, Barthes, Freire, Giroux, Emily Hicks, Kincheloe, Goldberg, Spivak, and others. Students in colleges of education are used to classes where they primarily use readings as an excuse to "talk shop" and share techniques and lesson ideas for making generic courses in reading, history, science, and math more interesting to students. Usually they link good teaching with student motivation and enjoyment is primarily viewed in psychological terms and related to issues of happiness, enthusiasm and practical relevance.

Shirley: From your student's perspective, is the goal of the teacher to make the students happy?

Peter: In part, yes. But only in part, and this is a contingent statement. I would say most of my student teachers and graduate students (who are usually experienced teachers) define their primary mission in very broad sense—to meet the needs of the students in a rapidly changing technological world. They want students to learn survival skills to help them get jobs and they want to make this as enjoyable for students as possible. That's usually what I hear. You know, they want to make their students "feel good about themselves." When I introduce the notion that this mission that they have set out for themselves is really about "adapting" students to the social order—a very racist, homopholic and sexist social order, they begin to feel uncomfortable. When I suggest that teaching should be about transforming the injustices of the social order rather than adapting students to that order, many of them feel absolutely threatened. Teachers frequently feel that my position is a "biased" one and that teachers have an obligation to be neutral and objective and to just present the facts and let the students make up their own mind about what to do with them. Their operative assumption is that teachers should be like classical scientists who reveal fixed truths and immutable specific rules. Western conceptions of truth and goodness prevail with most of them. Of course, the theoretical readings begin to challenge the notion that teachers can or should be neutral and usually the class gets more interesting from that point onwards. The toughest part for me is to translate along with the students high theory into more mundane and quotidian pedagogical situations that have some relevance to and urgency for the students. I need to work from the students own experiences here—their own funds of knowledge. I need to make connections with how students not only construct knowledge but actively invest in it. In class, we develop our language mostly from analyzing music videos and popular films. We examine youth resistance movements, style, dance, music culture—we really let everything into the discussion. Once, two of my foreign students—one from Dublin, Ireland and one from Argentina took down the British flag hanging in the Centre for Education and Cultural Studies—it was a sign things were working. We go on to explore questions such as: Should teachers speak for the oppressed? How does one justify one's authority as a teacher? How are racist and sexist discourses unwittingly inscribed in our classroom, institution, and social practices as students, teachers, and cultural workers? What is the role of schooling in reproducing social relations of domination? How can schools become liberatory sites for radical democratic social and cultural practices? What is the role of teachers as researchers? As social critics? These questions take us into action research, critical pedagogy and Western imperialist practices specific to Latin America, Africa, and Asia. My goal over the last few years has been to develop the contours of a pedagogy of liberation that takes as its central organizing principles the ideas of critical multiculturalism and the struggle for a radical democracy. Usually my student teachers are more open than my experienced teachers in the graduate program. Let me focus more specifically on the retreat from theory I see in my classroom. It's a different kind of retreat than the epistemological relativism we're witnessing from the postmodern pragmatists lately: namely, that all decisions and judgments are based on a prior consensus among interpretive communities so every opinion is viewed as just another rhetorical slant on the world. This retreat from theory I'm talking about is different. It's more a form of ontological realism than epistemological relativism. It presumes that experience somehow speaks for itself and is untainted by ideology. If you experience it, it's the truth. It assigns truth to the "feeling" that certain things make sense—a kind of revelation or intuitive insight or *parousiá*. Donaldo Macedo talks about an anti-method pedagogy as a way to counter the "benevolent oppression" of bourgeoise radical educators whose method requires you to identify yourself and share your experiences in weepy testimonials. The sharing of experience is given the most credit—not the analysis offered by the individual. Macedo talks about how pedagogical comfort zones are created in a group therapy type of atmosphere where through a form of public reconciliation, the oppressed are made to feel good about their own sense of victimization by means of an uncritical appeal to the sharing of experiences. This allows oppressors to buffer their feelings of class guilt. Macedo calls these psuedo-critical educators "literacy and poverty pimps" because they fall victim to their own middle-class narcissism that actually consolidates their own privilege under the guise of empowering the oppressed. An anti-method pedagogy refuses to rigidify models and methodological paradigms such as these. It refuses to base its approach on cognitivism or emotionality and instead situates knowledge within the logic of capital and the project of emancipation.

As educators, we need to understand the ethical, political, and epistemological presuppositions that inform our understanding of our experiences. How do we adjudicate our experiences without resorting to transcendental narratives, without totalizing them? How do we justify our actions? How do we escape a judgmental or ethical relativism once we've accepted the epistemic relativist position that all beliefs and values are historically conditioned social constructions? These are issues teachers need to explore in developing the project that undergirds their pedagogies. For instance, how do we justify our mission as educators? Why don't we choose nihilism? What are the discursively available reasons for our actions? What forms of interest are at work in the academy, in the larger culture, to constrain such discursive availability? Are all truth claims just cultural and historical fictions? Are we, as social agents, simply ventriloquists who rehearse lives that are nothing more than the products of consensus opinion and agreed-upon communal practices? Does the language of theory possess the interent power of tropologically displacing its own preferred ideological appeal, its own suasive ideology, or its tacit foreknowledge? Is critical theory just a magnificent con game?

Shirley: What are the features of critical pedagogy that you encourage your students to develop?

Peter: Once they work through the theory-experience debate and I hope reject the idea of insight as a moment of ludic abandon, I invite them to develop a critical pedagogy that encourages reflection on their own historical formation, one that encourages students to detect the dissonance between who they are and what they want to become. We need to become historically self-conscious—and that means moving outside of our own self interest and becoming conscious of our collective roles as citizens—as a populace, as a people. We need to compel our actions to come to terms with our ethical ideals. I guess what I'm talking about here is developing a new language of analysis, one that will lead to a reformulation of agreed-upon codes used to organize everyday reality and the normalizing discourses that transform the pellucidly ideological into commonsense knowledge. From this follows the crucial question that needs to be raised: How has the monologic authority of mainstream epistemologies laundered the contextual specificity of the voices of the oppressed, silencing their marginal styles of expression, their social and cultural embeddedness or situatedness of expression, of enunciation? What vocabularies of interpretation are we going to choose to make sense of texts that are already familiar to us? But we need to do more than exaggerate the performative gestures of received authority through the ludic playfulness of irony. This new language needs to foreground the contradictions within the signifying practices of students and attempt to make explicit their alternating modes of identification. This is no easy task. I want to be clear, Shirley, that I'm not talking about trying to achieve a definitive language or searching for a universalized meaning—a soporifics of agreement, harmony, and certainty. I am talking about inviting students to become critical rhetors, to live a life that is critically examined and passionately engaged. I am talking about a language that respects the specificity of knowledge—that deals with differences without turning them into oppositions. I'm talking about entering into a voluntary contract with difference through the construction of a democratic pedagogy, one in which norms are always as provisional as our relations to our convictions, one that is contingent and struggled against even as it becomes established, a pedagogy in which differences are always conversable so they may be productive rather than destructive of human dignity and social justice.